Preparing for the Regents Comprehensive Examination in English

STEVEN L. STERN

Now with two Regents exams!

AMSCO SCHOOL PUBLICATIONS, INC.
315 HUDSON STREET, NEW YORK, NY 10013

This book is dedicated to my wife Barbara with love, admiration, and gratitude.

Cover Design: Mel Haber
Text Design, Composition, and Artwork: Northeastern Graphic Services, Inc.

When ordering this book, please specify: *either* **R 681 W** *or*
PREPARING FOR THE REGENTS COMPREHENSIVE
EXAMINATION IN ENGLISH

ISBN: 978-1-56765-056-3

NYC Item 56765-056-1

PRINTED IN THE UNITED STATES OF AMERICA

14   09 08 07

Please visit our Web site at: *www.amscopub.com*

ABOUT THE AUTHOR

Steven L. Stern has 30 years of experience as a writer and textbook editor, developing a wide range of books, educational products, and informational materials for children and adults. He has written three other high school test-preparation books and is also the author of a novel as well as numerous articles and short stories. He has also worked as an English teacher, a lexicographer, and a writing consultant. Mr. Stern grew up in New York City.

ABOUT THE CONSULTANTS

Dr. Franklin C. Cacciutto is the English Department Chair at East Meadow High School and an Adjunct Assistant Professor of English at York College of the City University of New York. He has taught English in the New York City public schools and in Connecticut. He is certified by the New York State Department of Education in the training of teachers for the rubric-rating of the new Regents and has been involved in teacher training at Brown, Wesleyan, and Yale.

A former journalist and published author, **Robert Eidelberg** served for 19 years as the chair of the English Department of William Cullen Bryant High School in New York City and a total of 32 years as a secondary school English teacher in the New York City public school system. Since retiring, Mr. Eidelberg has taught writing at Audrey Cohen College and the City University of New York, where he has also supervised student teachers in English education.

For the past 20 years, **Kathleen Kristine Forde** has served as teacher and as chairperson of the English departments at Irvington High School and Middle School in Irvington, New York. Her other positions include teaching in East Africa.

Hannah S. Hess, a published author, has been an English teacher since 1957 and an Assistant Principal of the Humanities Department at Chelsea High School in Manhattan since 1984.

Dr. William J. Hunter has been an English teacher for 35 years. He has also served as the Supervisor of English at John Jay High School in New York City for the past 18 years, where he is responsible for instruction and curriculum for staff numbering as high as 35 teachers and librarians. He's written articles and participated in panels, discussing such topics as "Censorship" and "The Problems of New Supervisors."

Barbara Rothenberg, formerly an Assistant Principal of English at the High School of Art and Design in New York City, is now working in the public and private sectors as an educational consultant.

ACKNOWLEDGMENTS

BOA Editions, Ltd. "Shoulders" from RED SUITCASE by Naomi Shihab Nye. Copyright © 1994 Naomi Shihab Nye. Reprinted with the permission of BOA Editions, Ltd., Rochester, NY 14604. (page 175)

Commonweal. "Hoop Dreams" by Timothy Schilling (6/5/98). © 1998 Commonweal Foundation, reprinted with permission. For Subscriptions, call toll-free: 1-888-495-6755. (page 195)

Co-op America Quarterly. "The Green Consumer" from the Summer 1998 issue and the article "Tree Free Papers are Taking Root" by Joel Makower used by permission of author and publisher. (page 77)

Rodger Doyle. "By the Numbers" appeared originally in SCIENTIFIC AMERICAN, June 1998. © Rodger Doyle 1998. Used by permission of the author. (page 28)

Forbes. Chart of "The World's Largest Multinational Corporations" from the July 17, 1995 issue. © FORBES Inc., 1995. Reprinted by permission of FORBES Magazine. (page 108)

Graywolf Press. "Elegy" copyright 1987 by James Houston. Reprinted from THE MEN IN MY LIFE AND MORE OR LESS TRUE RECOLLECTIONS with the permission of Graywolf Press, Saint Paul, Minnesota. (page 239)

ICM. "Baby on the Beach" by Alix Kates Shulman. Copyright © 1990 Alix Kates Shulman. Reprinted by permission of International Creative Management, Inc. (page 176)

Information Plus. "Safety on the Road" comes from TRANSPORTATION— AMERICA'S LIFELINE, 1997 edition. Used with the permission of the publisher. (page 162)

National Safety Council. Chart entitled "Improper Driving Reported in Accidents, 1995" from ACCIDENT FACTS, 1996 Edition, National Safety Council, Itasca, Ill. (page 163)

Newsweek. "My Turn: My Own Son Didn't Listen" by Carolyn Hanig from NEWSWEEK, November 10, 1997. © 1997 NEWSWEEK, Inc. All rights reserved. Reprinted by permission. (page 48)

Newsweek. Chart entitled "Encounter of the Not-So-Close Kind" from the March 23, 1998 issue. © 1998 NEWSWEEK, Inc. All rights reserved. Reprinted by permission. "When the Sky Falls" a diagram by Christopher Blumrich from the March 24, 1997 issue. © 1997 NEWSWEEK, Inc. All rights reserved. Reprinted by permission. (page 89)

Prevention Magazine. Chart entitled "Driving at or Below the Speed Limit" from the article "Auto Safety in America," 1996. Copyright 1996 Rodale Press, Inc. All rights reserved. Reprinted by permission of PREVENTION Magazine. (page 162)

Random House, Inc. "Dreams" from COLLECTED POEMS by Langston Hughes. Copyright © 1994 by the Estate of Langston Hughes. Reprinted by permission of Alfred A. Knopf Inc. (page 194)

Time Life Syndication. "Whew!" from the March 23, 1998 issue of TIME. © 1998 TIME INC. Reprinted by permission. (page 85)

CONTENTS

Chapter 1
The New York Regents Comprehensive Examination in English   1

    1 PREPARATION: YOUR KEY TO SUCCESS   1
    AN OVERVIEW OF THE REGENTS ENGLISH EXAM   1

    2 USING THIS BOOK   3

    3 REGENTS SCORING CRITERIA FOR WRITTEN RESPONSES   5

    4 ABOUT THE PROCESS OF WRITING   8

    5 CHAPTER REVIEW   10

Chapter 2: Session One, Part A of the Regents Exam
Listening and Writing for Information and Understanding   13

    1 UNDERSTANDING THE SESSION ONE, PART A TASKS   13

    2 EFFECTIVE LISTENING AND NOTE-TAKING   20
        Skill Builder 1: Recognizing Key Ideas and Information   30
        Skill Builder 2: Making Inferences and Drawing Conclusions   39

    3 ANSWERING THE MULTIPLE-CHOICE QUESTIONS FOR PART A   46
    TRY THIS   47

4 | PLANNING AND WRITING YOUR PART A RESPONSE   54

     The Basics: Quotation Marks   67

5 | CHAPTER REVIEW   73

     PRACTICE FOR PART A   75

Chapter 3: Session One, Part B of the Regents Exam
Reading and Writing for Information and Understanding   83

1 | UNDERSTANDING THE SESSION ONE, PART B TASKS   83

2 | EFFECTIVE READING AND NOTE-TAKING FOR PART B   94

3 | OBTAINING INFORMATION FROM VISUAL MATERIALS   99

     Skill Builder 3: Using Context Clues to Determine Meaning   115

     Skill Builder 4: Distinguishing Between Facts
         and Opinions   123

4 | ANSWERING THE MULTIPLE-CHOICE QUESTIONS FOR PART B   131

     TRY THIS   132

5 | PLANNING AND WRITING YOUR PART B RESPONSE   139

     The Basics: Methods of Organization   148

6 | CHAPTER REVIEW   160

     PRACTICE FOR PART B   161

Chapter 4: Session Two, Part A of the Regents Exam
Reading and Writing for Literary Response   171

1 | UNDERSTANDING THE SESSION TWO, PART A TASKS   171

2 | EFFECTIVE READING AND NOTE-TAKING FOR PART A   184

     The Basics: Literary Elements   189

     The Basics: Literary Techniques   190

     Skill Builder 5: Understanding Author's Purpose and
         Point of View   199

3 | ANSWERING THE MULTIPLE-CHOICE QUESTIONS FOR PART A   205

     TRY THIS   206

4 | PLANNING AND WRITING YOUR PART A ESSAY   214

     The Basics: Essay Structure   223

5   CHAPTER REVIEW   237

PRACTICE FOR PART A   238

Chapter 5: Session Two, Part B of the Regents Exam
Reading and Writing for Critical Analysis   247

1   UNDERSTANDING THE SESSION TWO, PART B TASKS   247

2   PLANNING AND WRITING YOUR PART B ESSAY   258

3   CHAPTER REVIEW   279

PRACTICE FOR PART B   281

Regents Exam   287

SESSION ONE, PART A

SESSION ONE, PART B

SESSION TWO, PART A

SESSION TWO, PART B

Regents Exam

SESSION ONE, PART A

SESSION ONE, PART B

SESSION TWO, PART A

SESSION TWO, PART B

Index

CHAPTER 1

The New York Regents Comprehensive Examination in English

1

PREPARATION: YOUR KEY TO SUCCESS

How much do you know about the Regents Comprehensive Examination in English? Perhaps you've heard that it's a long test or that it requires a considerable amount of writing. Maybe you've heard that it's harder than the old Regents exam.

No matter what you may have heard, taking the Regents exam is like meeting any challenge: *the better prepared you are, the better you will do.*

Preparing for the Regents Comprehensive Examination in English will help you get ready for the Regents exam by showing you exactly what to expect, sharpening the skills you will need, and giving you ample opportunity to practice those skills.

AN OVERVIEW OF THE REGENTS ENGLISH EXAM

The Regents Comprehensive Examination in English tests your reading, writing, listening, and thinking abilities. The exam consists of four parts, which must be completed during two three-hour sessions.

1

The chart below presents an overview of the tasks you'll be asked to do for each part of the Regents exam. To understand the chart, you should first be familiar with two key terms:

prompt: *A prompt consists of directions and information that explain specifically what you have to do for part of a test.* Each part of the Regents exam has its own prompt.

extended written response: *An extended written response is an essay, article, or other multiple-paragraph composition that you write in response to a test prompt.* Each part of the Regents exam requires you to write a separate extended response.

OVERVIEW: THE NEW YORK REGENTS COMPREHENSIVE EXAMINATION IN ENGLISH

Session One, Part A:
Listening and Writing for Information and Understanding

Your tasks:
- Listen as your teacher reads a selection aloud twice.
- Answer multiple-choice questions about the oral selection.
- Write an extended response based on the oral selection.

Session One, Part B:
Reading and Writing for Information and Understanding

Your tasks:
- Read a selection and examine related visual materials.
- Answer multiple-choice questions about the selection and the visual materials.
- Write an extended response based on the selection and the visual materials.

Session Two, Part A:
Reading and Writing for Literary Response

Your tasks:
- Read two literary selections.
- Answer multiple-choice questions about the selections.
- Write an essay about the two selections.

Session Two, Part B:
Reading and Writing for Critical Analysis

Your tasks:
- Read and interpret a statement or quotation.
- Write a critical essay discussing two previously read literary works.

As you can see from the chart, the four parts of the exam are similar in some ways, but different in others. Chapters 2–5 of this book will help you understand the similarities and differences between parts.

Notice also that three of the four parts of the Regents English exam include multiple-choice questions. These questions test your understanding of the selections, and they help you zero in on important ideas and information in the selections—ideas and information that you can refer to when you write your extended responses.

Q&A

What skills will I need for the Regents exam?

In addition to reading, writing, and listening skills, the Regents exam calls on your critical thinking abilities and your note-taking skills. Furthermore, to do your best with the extended responses, you'll need to apply the basic steps of the writing process: planning and prewriting, drafting and revising, editing, and proofreading.

2

USING THIS BOOK

As the title makes clear, this book is designed to prepare you for the Regents exam. In addition, it will help you develop reading, writing, and thinking skills that will serve you well both in and out of the classroom, now and in the future.

Content and Organization

The book is organized into five chapters, and each chapter is divided into numbered sections. This first chapter provides an overview of the Regents exam, describes the content and features of this book, and briefly discusses the writing process. Chapter 1 also explains how your written responses will be evaluated and scored.

Chapters 2–5 focus on the four parts of the exam. For easy reference, these chapters have a similar structure and use similar headings. Each chapter includes the following:

- An in-depth look at the prompts for each part of the exam and the tasks associated with them.
- Specific how-to strategies for carrying out the required tasks.

- Opportunities to apply, develop, and practice the reading, writing, and critical thinking skills needed to accomplish the tasks.

- A close look at the *criteria,* or standards, that readers will use to evaluate and score your writing for each part of the exam.

- Specific guidelines for planning and writing the extended responses for each part of the exam.

Special Features

The Regents exam tests a broad range of skills and knowledge. To cover the content of the exam in a way that is both comprehensive and easy to understand, this book contains a variety of helpful lists, charts, and illustrations. In addition, you will find the following text features:

- *A Quick Look,* which appears at the beginning of Chapters 2–5, presents a brief overview of each part of the Regents exam. *Q & A* boxes appear throughout the book, giving answers to frequently asked questions. *TIP* boxes also appear throughout the book, providing useful tips for doing your best on the exam.

- **Activities**. Various activities throughout the book provide practice and reinforcement of what you've learned. Most activities are intended for independent work. A few involve working with a partner or a small group of students.

  In addition, as you're reading, you'll sometimes see this symbol: **?** The symbol calls your attention to a short question about something you've read.

- *Try This* and *Thinking It Through*. These linked sections first give you an opportunity to answer questions and then lead you step-by-step through the thought processes involved in arriving at the correct answers.

- **Writing models**. For each part of the Regents exam, a detailed sample plan and an extended written response based on that plan illustrate how to respond effectively to a test prompt.

- *Skill Builder* lessons. These focused "mini-lessons" are designed to review important reading and thinking skills that you've learned in school—skills that will help you do well on the Regents.

- *The Basics* boxes. These boxes summarize basic information in an easy-to-review format. For example, one *Basics* box summarizes the correct use of quotation marks, while another focuses on literary elements.

- *Chapter Review*. Each chapter ends with a short summary of key points covered.

● **Actual Regents Exams.** The book contains two actual Regents exams. There is also a practice exam separated into four parts, with each part appearing at the end of its corresponding chapter.

Cumulative Learning

Although the four parts of the Regents exam are separate and distinct from one another, they do share certain basic elements. For example, all four parts call on your ability to understand key ideas in the selections and demonstrate your understanding in well-organized, clearly written responses.

Because of this shared common ground, you'll find that the knowledge you gain through this book is *cumulative*. In other words, each chapter builds on the chapter that came before. Much of what you learn regarding one part of the exam will also help you with other parts.

? *Fill in the blanks:* The Regents English exam consists of _____ separate parts. Each part has a writing task, but only _____ parts have multiple-choice questions.

3

REGENTS SCORING CRITERIA FOR WRITTEN RESPONSES

Scoring an extended written response is more complex than grading a multiple-choice test. Specially trained teachers will evaluate your writing on the Regents exam according to pre-established criteria, or standards. Specifically, there are five criteria:

MEANING: the extent to which your written responses show your sound understanding, interpretation, and analysis of the task and text(s)

DEVELOPMENT: the extent to which you develop ideas using specific and relevant evidence from the text(s)

ORGANIZATION: the extent to which your responses show direction, shape, and coherence

LANGUAGE USE: the extent to which your responses show your awareness of audience and purpose through effective use of words, sentence structure, and sentence variety

CONVENTIONS: the extent to which your responses demonstrate conventional spelling, punctuation, paragraphing, capitalization, grammar, and usage

Readers will use these same basic criteria to evaluate your writing for all four parts of the Regents exam. However, there are differences in how the criteria are *applied* from part to part. In Chapters 2–5, you will learn how the criteria are specifically applied to each part of the exam.

Holistic Scoring: Evaluating the Whole

When readers score your written responses, they will apply the five criteria *holistically*. That is, the criteria will all be applied together, simultaneously. In other words, your written work will be viewed as a *whole*. Readers will form an impression by considering all five criteria at the same time, weighing them equally, and arriving at a single score.

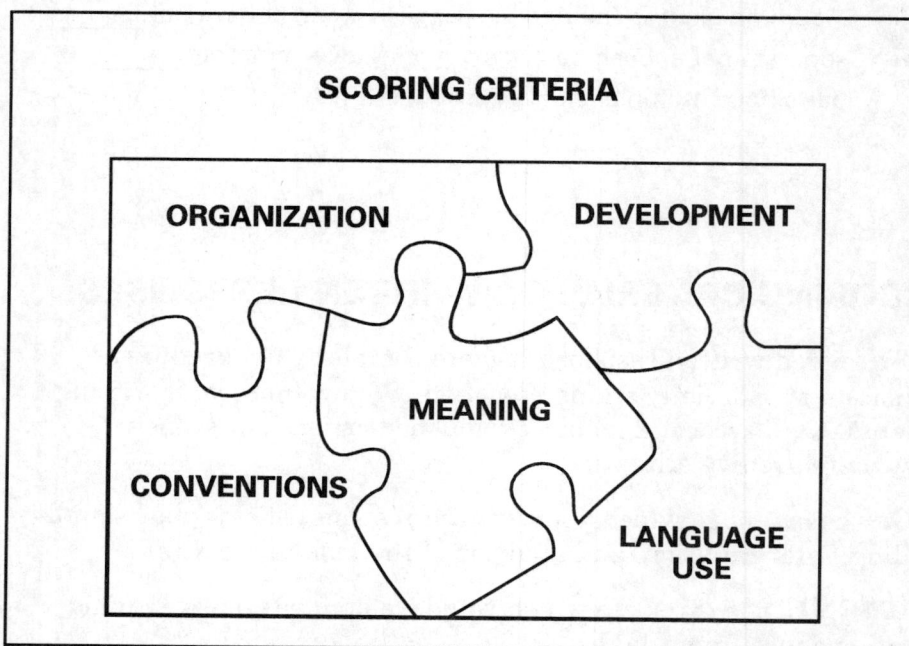

SCORING CRITERIA

ORGANIZATION   DEVELOPMENT

MEANING

CONVENTIONS

LANGUAGE USE

On the Regents exam you don't earn points for doing one thing or lose points for doing something else. There are no preset point values for different writing elements. Instead, readers will consider the overall effectiveness of your written responses.

Based on this *holistic scoring* approach, each piece of writing is graded on a six-point scale, with 6 being the top score. The writing that you do for each part is scored separately.

(You may be interested to know that for each part of the exam, readers will refer to a detailed scoring *rubric* when evaluating your writing. This rubric is a set of descriptive guidelines that helps readers determine the appropriate score.)

Q&A

Why does the Regents exam use "holistic" scoring to evaluate the written responses?

Content, organization, and other aspects of writing must all work together in order for a writer to communicate effectively. Holistic scoring emphasizes the combination and blending of these elements—that is, the writer's *whole* piece of writing, rather than individual elements.

Activity A: Reviewing Key Terms

In your own words, define each of the following terms. Write complete sentences.

1. *prompt:*

   _____

   _____

   _____

2. *extended written response:*

   _____

   _____

   _____

3. scoring *criteria:*

   _____

   _____

   _____

4. *holistic scoring* approach:

   _____

   _____

   _____

4

ABOUT THE PROCESS OF WRITING

As you've probably discussed in class, writing is not just a task, but a *process* made up of several steps. When you take the Regents English exam, you can use this process to plan and write your extended responses.

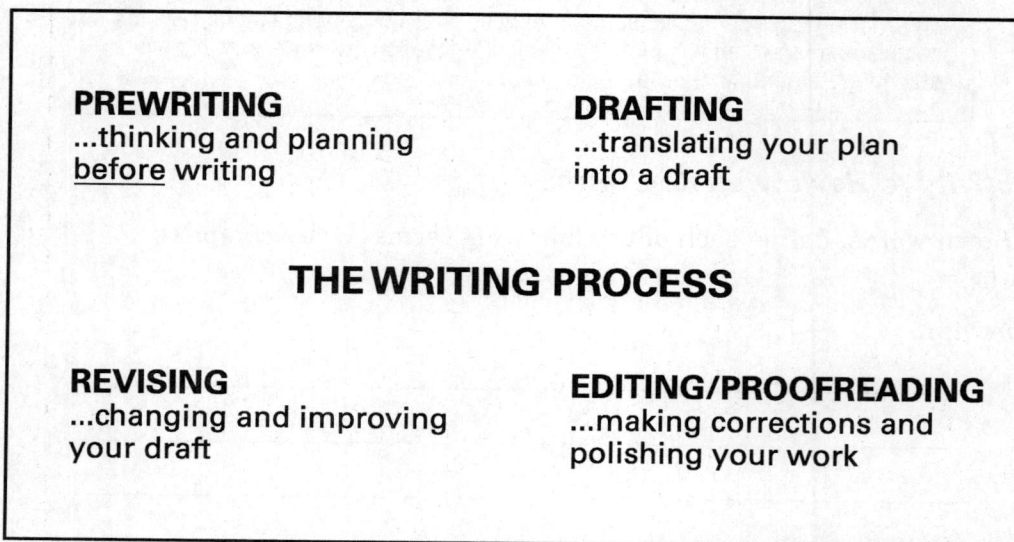

PREWRITING
...thinking and planning
<u>before</u> writing

DRAFTING
...translating your plan
into a draft

THE WRITING PROCESS

REVISING
...changing and improving
your draft

EDITING/PROOFREADING
...making corrections and
polishing your work

The writing process consists of four basic steps: prewriting, drafting, revising, and editing/proofreading. Here's an overview of how you would apply these steps. Keep in mind, of course, that you have to budget your overall time so that you can complete your writing task within the available time.

- *Prewriting:* This first step involves careful thinking and planning. You need to plan both the content and the organization of your response.

- *Drafting:* Once you have a working plan or outline, you're ready to start writing. You'll probably modify and expand your plan as you go along.

- *Revising:* After getting your ideas down on paper, you'll want to reread and think about what you've written. You can rearrange ideas, add or take out details, change wording, and make other adjustments to improve your work.

● *Editing/Proofreading:* This final step is your opportunity to polish your paper. You can fix errors in grammar and punctuation, check spelling, fine-tune language, and make any other changes that you think will add to the clarity and quality of your writing.

? *Complete the sentence:* The four steps of the writing process are

_____

Making the Process Work for You

As a writer, you have great flexibility in how you carry out the steps of the writing process. You may devise a working plan, start writing your first draft, and then decide to go back and change your plan before continuing. Or, you may write a first draft and then, depending on how much time you have, a second or third draft. You may decide that your draft needs major revision or just light editing.

The point is that there is no one "correct" way to use the writing process. Different people carry out the steps in different ways. You have to make the process work for *you.* Furthermore, you won't always carry out the process in the same way. Some writing tasks are easier than others. This is true for any writing you do in school or outside of school.

On the Regents exam, you may approach the writing process one way for Part A and a different way for Part B. That's fine. The process is adaptable. You can adjust or expand its steps to meet both the demands of the task and your needs as a writer.

Q&A

Generally speaking, how much time should I devote to each step of the writing process?

Every writer must answer this question for himself or herself. Some students find that planning their response in great detail lets them do the actual writing relatively quickly. Other students feel more comfortable preparing just a brief outline, dashing off a first draft, and then doing extensive revision and rewriting. As a writer, you need to discover the method that works best for you.

However, here are two suggestions for everyone: (1) Do at least some basic planning (prewriting) before you begin to write, and (2) always leave enough time to reread your finished paper from start to finish and make necessary changes and corrections.

Activity B: Using the Writing Process

Answer the following questions about the writing process.

1. How can approaching writing as a process help you do your best when you write an extended response?

   _____

   _____

   _____

2. Explain this statement: "This process is adaptable. You can adjust or expand its steps to meet both the demands of the task and your needs as a writer."

   _____

   _____

   _____

Help Yourself

TIP

You probably have a good sense of your strengths and weaknesses as a writer. Maybe you're able to organize your ideas well, but your grammar could be better. Or, perhaps you have a terrific vocabulary, but you're a poor speller.

Devote time and effort to improving in those areas that need improvement. For example, look back at your papers and identify words you often spell incorrectly. Learn the correct spellings. Keep a running list of words that give you trouble and review the list often. Or, if you have trouble with run-on sentences, subject-verb agreement, or the like, ask your teacher for help.

---

5 | CHAPTER REVIEW

Look back at the various lists, boldfaced items, boxes, and charts to quickly review many of the important ideas presented. Here are a few key points to get your review started:

● The New York Regents Comprehensive Examination in English is a test of your reading, writing, listening, and thinking abilities. The exam consists of four parts. Each part has its own prompt and requires you to write a separate extended response.

- The multiple-choice questions on the Regents exam test your understanding of the selections. In addition, they help you focus on important ideas and information that you can use when you write your extended responses.

- Readers will evaluate your written responses holistically on the basis of five criteria: meaning, development, organization, language use, and conventions.

- The writing process, which consists of four steps (prewriting, drafting, revising, and editing/proofreading), can help you plan and write your extended responses.

CHAPTER 2

Listening and Writing for Information and Understanding

1

UNDERSTANDING THE SESSION ONE, PART A TASKS

For Session One, Part A of the Regents Comprehensive Examination in English, your teacher will read aloud an informational selection. You'll listen to the selection twice and take notes on what you hear. You will not see the selection in print.

Next, you'll answer six multiple-choice questions, focusing on important ideas in the selection. Finally, you'll write an extended response—such as an article or essay—based on your understanding and analysis of the selection that you heard.

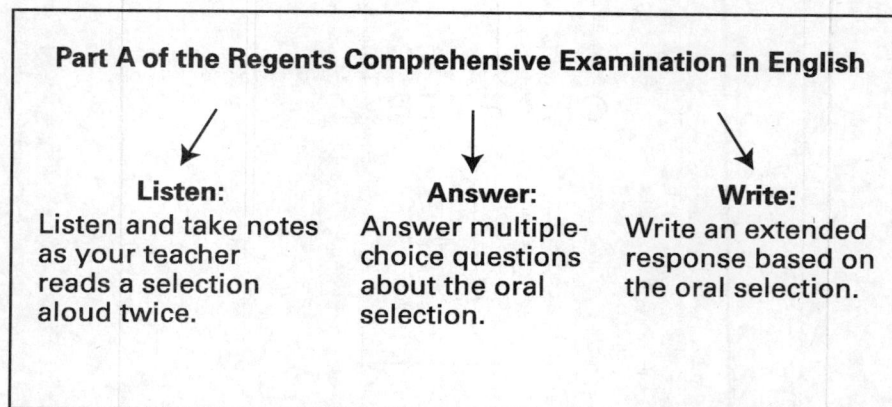

Part A of the Regents Comprehensive Examination in English

Listen:
Listen and take notes as your teacher reads a selection aloud twice.

Answer:
Answer multiple-choice questions about the oral selection.

Write:
Write an extended response based on the oral selection.

※ A QUICK LOOK ※

What is Part A testing me on?
Part A tests your ability to listen to, understand, analyze, and respond to information presented orally.

How is Part A similar to other parts of the exam?
Part A, like most other parts, requires you to answer multiple-choice questions and then write an extended response.

How does Part A differ from other parts of the exam?
Part A is the only part of the test that requires you to listen and respond to an oral presentation.

Examining the Session One, Part A Prompt

To understand the tasks that make up the first part of the Regents exam, look at the typical Part A prompt that follows. It consists of five elements:

- Overview
- The Situation
- Your Task
- Guidelines
- Multiple-choice questions about the oral selection

14

NOTE: *For now, just look over the prompt to get a feel for it. You will see more of it later in the chapter.*

Multiple-Choice Questions

Directions (1–6): Use your notes to answer the following questions about the _____ on you _____ wish.

_____ ed in

_____ at belt

PART A

Overview: For this part of the test, you will listen to a speech about the importance of seat belts, answer some multiple-choice questions, and write a response based on the situation described below. You will hear the talk twice. You may take notes anytime you wish during the readings.

> **The Situation:** You work as a volunteer for Safety First, a citizens' group for public safety. The group is launching a national campaign to reduce automobile-related injuries and fatalities. The director of Safety First has asked you to write an article for the *Safety First Newsletter* explaining the need to increase seat-belt use and suggesting how. This newsletter is read by high school students and their parents as well as state lawmakers across the nation. In preparation for writing your article, listen to a speech given by nurse Carolyn Hanig. Then use relevant information from this speech to write your article.

_____ a
_____ lt.
_____ lt like

Your Task: Write an article for the *Safety First Newsletter* using relevant information from the speech to explain the need to increase seat-belt use and suggesting how.

_____ ent

Guidelines:
  Be sure to
  • Tell your audience what they need to know about the importance of wearing seat belts and how to increase belt use
  • Use specific, accurate, and relevant information from the speech to support your discussion
  • Use a tone and level of language appropriate for a newsletter read by students, parents, and lawmakers
  • Organize your ideas in a logical and coherent manner
  • Indicate any words taken directly from the speech by using quotation marks or referring to the speaker

Each of the five elements of the prompt has a particular purpose:

- The *Overview* summarizes what you'll have to do for Part A.
- *The Situation, Your Task,* and *Guidelines* describe the extended response you will write, which will be based on a real-life situation that requires both listening and writing skills.
- The *multiple-choice questions,* seen later in the chapter, will focus on key points of the oral presentation.

Let's take a closer look at these elements.

The first part of the prompt gives you an overview. This prompt, for example, tells you that you're going to do three things: (1) hear a speech about seat belts, (2) answer questions about the speech, and (3) write a response to a given situation.

> **Overview:** For this part of the test, you will listen to a speech about the importance of seat belts, answer some multiple-choice questions, and write a response based on the situation described below. You will hear the talk twice. You may take notes anytime you wish during the readings.

This part of the prompt also suggests that you take notes. *You should take good notes as you listen.* You'll be able to refer to your notes both when you answer the multiple-choice questions and when you write your response.

The prompt then goes on to describe the specific situation and explain your writing task:

> **The Situation:** You work as a volunteer for Safety First, a citizens' group for public safety. The group is launching a national campaign to reduce automobile-related injuries and fatalities. The director of Safety First has asked you to write an article for the *Safety First Newsletter* explaining the need to increase seat-belt use and suggesting how. This newsletter is read by high school students and their parents as well as state lawmakers across the nation. In preparation for writing your article, listen to a speech given by nurse Carolyn Hanig. Then use relevant information from this speech to write your article.
>
> **Your Task:** Write an article for the *Safety First Newsletter* using relevant information from the speech to explain the need to increase seat-belt use and suggesting how.

This part of the prompt is particularly important because it *clearly identifies your intended audience.* In this case your audience consists of "high school students . . . parents . . . state lawmakers across the nation."

? *Be specific in your answer:* Why should you take good notes as you listen to the selection that your teacher reads?

_____

_____

_____

Q&A

Why does the teacher read the Part A selection aloud twice?
Hearing the selection twice lets you take more complete and accurate notes than you could if you heard it just once. Hearing it twice also helps you better understand key points.

Next, the prompt gives you a list of specific writing guidelines. These guidelines relate to the five criteria (meaning, development, organization, language use, and conventions) that readers will use to evaluate your written response.

Guidelines:

Be sure to

- Tell your audience what they need to know about the importance of wearing seat belts and how to increase belt use
- Use specific, accurate, and relevant information from the speech to support your discussion
- Use a tone and level of language appropriate for a newsletter read by students, parents, and lawmakers
- Organize your ideas in a logical and coherent manner
- Indicate any words taken directly from the talk by using quotation marks or referring to the speaker
- Follow the conventions of standard written English

Note that the first item on this list helps clarify not just your writing task but also your writing *purpose.* In this case, your purpose is to inform your

17

audience why seat-belt use is important and to suggest how to get people to wear seat belts.

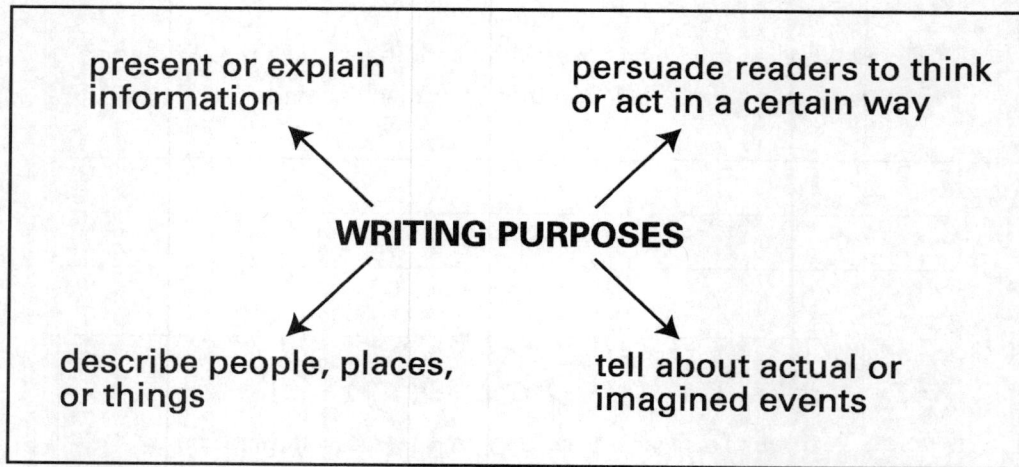

```
        present or explain                 persuade readers to think
        information                        or act in a certain way
                        ↖              ↗

                        WRITING PURPOSES

                        ↙              ↘
        describe people, places,           tell about actual or
        or things                          imagined events
```

The other listed *Guidelines* will help you develop your response. You'll read more about these guidelines later in this chapter.

The last section of Part A consists of six multiple-choice questions. This section has its own directions, which remind you to refer back to your notes:

Directions (1–6): Use your notes to answer the following questions about the passage read to you. The questions may help you think about ideas and information you might use in your writing. You may return to these questions anytime you wish.

The directions also suggest that "ideas and information" covered by the questions may be useful when you write your extended response. In other words, key points important enough to be addressed by the multiple-choice questions may also be important enough to include in your written response.

After the multiple-choice questions, the prompt reminds you to "review **The Situation** and read **Your Task** and the **Guidelines**" before writing your response.

Activity A: Examining a Session One, Part A Prompt

A portion of a Part A prompt appears below. Read the prompt, and answer the questions that follow.

Overview: For this part of the test, you will listen to a speech about space exploration, answer some multiple-choice questions, and write a response based on the situation described below. You will hear the speech twice. You may take notes anytime you wish during the readings.

The Situation: As part of your part-time job at a local science museum, you help visiting high school students understand the exhibits. Your supervisor has asked you to write the text for a printed handout to be distributed to high school visitors to help them better understand and appreciate the museum's new *Space Tomorrow* exhibit. In preparation for writing the handout, listen to a recording of a speech given by a Nobel Prize-winning astronomer about recent developments in space exploration. Then use relevant information from this speech to write your article.

Your Task: Write the text for a printed handout to be given to high school students using relevant information from the speech to help them understand and appreciate the museum's new *Space Tomorrow* exhibit.

Guidelines:

Be sure to

- Tell your audience what they need to know to help them understand the new exhibit and appreciate the significance of space exploration to our planet's future
- Use specific, accurate, and relevant information from the speech to . . .

1. What is your source of information for both the multiple-choice questions and the written response?

_____

_____

2. What three tasks does the **Overview** explain that you will have to do?

_____

_____

3. What is your specific writing task?

_____

_____

4. For what audience will you be writing?

_____

_____

5. What is your writing purpose?

_____

_____

6. How can taking notes as you listen to the speech help you?

_____

_____

2

EFFECTIVE LISTENING AND NOTE-TAKING

Hearing and listening are not the same. Part A of the Regents exam requires you to do more than just hear what the teacher is reading. You have to *actively listen*.

Strategies for Active Listening

Active listening means concentrating on what you hear and processing the information. Here are some strategies to help you listen effectively:

▶ **Keep in mind *why* you're listening.** Before your teacher reads the selection, you'll have an opportunity to read the **Overview** and **The Situation** parts of the prompt. These will give you a clear idea of why you're listening.

Remember, you're listening in order to get the specific information you need to answer the multiple-choice questions and to write the extended response.

As a helpful reference for yourself, jot down your specific writing task, your audience, and your writing purpose like this:

TASK: write text for a printed handout

AUDIENCE: high school students

PURPOSE: provide information to help readers understand space exhibit and appreciate significance of space exploration to Earth's future

▶ **Make a conscious effort.** Focus on the text your teacher reads. Don't let your mind wander. Listen for key words and phrases, main ideas, and important facts and details.

▶ ***Think about* the ideas you hear.** Analyze them. Silently repeat key points to yourself. Try to distinguish between what's important and what's not.

▶ **Listen for signals.** Pay attention to words and phrases that speakers use to focus attention on important points. Here are some examples:

therefore	*most important of all*
the reasons that	*the biggest problem*
my point is	*as a result*

Also listen for places where the speaker speaks more loudly or emphasizes or repeats certain words or ideas. Listen, too, for questions that the speaker poses and then answers.

▶ **Take notes.** Note-taking is essential. The next section of this chapter contains strategies for taking notes while listening.

▶ **Get your questions answered.** During the first reading, jot down questions and uncertainties. During the second reading, try to resolve them. For example, if you're not sure whether you heard "50 percent" or "70 percent" during the first reading, jot down "50 percent?" The "?" will alert you to listen for the correct number during the second reading.

Practice Active Listening

TIP

Good listening skills will help you throughout your life, not just during the Regents exam. Like other skills, you need to practice your listening skills to develop them.

Apply active listening strategies in your daily life: when listening to teachers and other public speakers, during conversations, when listening to radio and television talk shows and news programs. Learning to listen actively will help you absorb information and remember it.

Activity B: Identifying Task, Audience, and Purpose

Carefully review the prompt that appears on page 15. Identify the specific writing task, audience, and writing purpose. (You may want to look back at the example on page 21.)

*TASK:*_____

_____

*AUDIENCE:*_____

_____

*PURPOSE:*_____

_____

Strategies for Taking Notes

Active listening and effective note-taking are closely related skills. Taking notes helps you gather important information from oral as well as printed sources.

Whether you're taking notes based on a lecture or a magazine article, the basic principles of note-taking are the same. However, when you're *listening* to a speaker, you have to take notes more quickly than when you're *reading* printed information. After all, words on a printed page remain in place, but a speaker's words continue to flow while you're writing. In fact, speakers typically talk four or five times faster than most listeners can write.

Here are some strategies for taking notes as you listen.

> ► **Write only what's important.** Time is limited, and you can't write down everything a speaker says—nor should you try. Instead, write what's important: key words and phrases, main ideas, important facts and details. Keep in mind your purpose for listening to help you decide what is and isn't important.

> ► **Be concise.** Make your notes as brief and simple as you can without losing meaning. Write words and phrases rather than whole sentences.

> ► **Organize your ideas.** Try to keep your notes organized in a simple outline form. Doing so can be a challenge while listening to a speaker, but here are three tips that will help:

> ◊ Write main ideas at the left margin and indent supporting information beneath them. Begin each supporting detail with a dash or a number.

22

◊ Leave at least one or two lines of blank space before beginning a new main idea.

◊ Leave wide margins on either side of your notes. This will give you extra space to add or expand information. If necessary, you can write words in the margin and draw arrows to show placement.

? *Answer in your own words:* Why is it smart to leave extra room when you're taking notes?

_____

_____

▶ **Call attention to key points.** Highlight ideas, words, phrases, and numbers of special importance. You can do this by underlining or circling them, printing them in capital letters, or using another method of your choice.

▶ **Use shortcuts.** Shorten words, and use abbreviations and symbols rather than whole words whenever you can. Here are some examples:

+	and	e.g.	for example
B4	before	$	money
info	information	%	percent
w/	with	w/o	without

Also, write numerals, rather than spell out numbers.

▶ **Identify quotations.** Enclose a speaker's exact words in quotation marks.

▶ **Stay tuned in.** If you miss an important fact during the first reading, don't panic. Just leave a blank space on your paper and continue to listen carefully. You can fill in the missed fact during the second reading.

▶ **Fill in the blanks.** Review your notes after the first reading. Mark any places where your notes are confusing or incomplete. During the second reading, clarify and expand your notes as needed.

Clear notes:
easy to read and understand

Concise notes:
brief and to the point

**Three C's of
Effective Note-Taking**

Complete notes:
include the most important
ideas and information

Here's an excerpt from one student's notes taken during Part A of the Regents exam. Which of the above note-taking strategies can you identify in this example?

Computers devel in 1st ½ of 20th century

—could solve complicated probs

—could be programmed

—could store info in memory

1st true computer = "differential analyzer"

—built by Amer scientist about 1930

—1st <u>analog</u> computer:

—analog comp calculates by <u>measuring</u>

—ran on electricity

—many parts—"monster so huge, it filled an entire room!"

—weighed <u>tons</u>

"Mark I" computer

—built 1943

—1st <u>digital</u> comp:

—digital comp calculates by <u>counting</u>

—750,000 parts

—Jeremy Bernstein (physicist) said Mark I sounded "like a roomful of

ladies knitting."

Activity C: Listening and Taking Notes (Selection 1)

NOTE: For Activity C, you will need your teacher or a student to read Selection 1 aloud.

This activity will give you practice in listening and taking notes. An informational selection (Selection 1) follows. *Do not read the selection yet.* Your teacher (or another student) will read it aloud twice. You will listen for main ideas and important facts and details.

Directions to READER:

1. Read Selection 1 aloud.

2. Allow listeners a few minutes to look over their notes.

3. Read Selection 1 a second time.

4. Give listeners time to clarify and expand their notes as needed.

5. Next, give listeners enough time to read the actual selection, compare their notes against the text, and answer the *How Did You Do?* questions that follow the selection.

Directions to LISTENERS:

1. Listen *actively* and take notes as the reader reads Selection 1. Use the strategies you've learned for effective listening and note-taking.

2. After the first reading, review your notes.

3. After the second reading, clarify and expand your notes as necessary.

4. Now, read the actual selection yourself. Then compare your notes against the text, and answer the *How Did You Do?* questions that follow the selection.

Choosing Your Career

If you stop to think about it, almost half of your waking hours will be spent going to, returning from, or working at a job. That being the case, you will want to spend that time doing something you find satisfying. Moreover, the kind of occupation you will have will determine how much you will earn. That, in turn, will determine the kind of lifestyle you and your family can lead.

The job you want may or may not be there when you want it. Or, it may be available but not close to your hometown. Then, too, it is easier to find work when the economy of the country as a whole is doing well than when business conditions are poor. Given all of these factors, here are some ideas as to how you should go about choosing your career.

First and foremost, you should know what you want most out of your career. Is it money? Prestige? Helping people? Would you rather work with your hands or your head? Do you prefer working outdoors? Indoors? With people? Alone? What are your hobbies and other interests? Can they be transformed into an occupation?

Once you have put together your thoughts on these and other concerns, you should talk to your school guidance counselor. If one is available, you should also talk to a job counselor at a local counseling service. These trained specialists can help you to learn more about the careers that interest you.

Counselors can also help you match your abilities with possible careers. Knowing what your abilities are, though, is quite tricky. On the one hand, some people seem to be born with certain talents. On the other hand, a lot of what we call talent is really the result of hard work. A great athlete or musician must spend many hours learning and developing the skills that make that individual outstanding. So talent and skill (which together make up one's abilities) go together with effort. If you think you have a special talent, it is important that you develop it through education, training, and lots of hard work.

The amount of education and training you will need depends on the career you choose. Your first objective, though, is to finish high school. Then, you might continue with your education, go directly to work, or perhaps, join one of the branches of the armed forces.

If you decide to continue your education, you might attend a two-year junior or community college, both of which offer programs leading to an associate's degree. You may want to go to a four-year college and receive a bachelor's degree or to a trade or technical school to learn specific job skills.

Choosing the armed forces can open up other career choices to you. You might make the service a lifetime career or enter a training program in a specialty that you can follow in civilian life.

Entering the world of work will open up many other possibilities to you. Your first job need not be your final one. It might be merely a step up on a career ladder. In this first job, you might receive *on-the-job training* (learning a job by doing it). Or you may advance your skills by attending evening classes in subjects related to your field of interest. Remember, whatever your first job, it need not last forever. You may leave one job for another if you think the second one offers you greater opportunities. You might work for a while, then return to school or join the armed forces. After completing your education or your hitch with the armed forces, you might return to the world of work, hopefully in your chosen career field.

There are many sources of information about careers. We have already suggested a school guidance counselor. Your teachers at school may help you too, particularly teachers in your field of interest. Do not forget those close at hand—your relatives, friends, and neighbors. Ask these people questions and listen to what they have to say. Pay particular attention to people who are already working in a field in which you are interested.

Private employment agencies and state employment offices provide good information about available job openings. Your state employment office may even offer free job counseling.

Finally, do a lot of reading. There are many books and magazines related to any number of careers. Become familiar with careers that interest you. Study the *Occupational Outlook Handbook.* This biannual U.S. government publication describes some 250 occupations. For each one, it tells the nature of the work, working conditions, requirements for the job, number of jobs, job locations, typical salaries, and the *job outlook,* or chances of finding work in that occupation. Much information is also available to you elsewhere—on videos, CD-ROMs, and the Internet and in books and magazines—concerning schools, colleges, job opportunities, and other career concerns. Choosing a career is not easy. It takes much time and effort, but your time and effort will be well spent.

Selection 1: How Did You Do?

1. What important ideas, facts, or details did you forget to include in your notes?

   _____

   _____

2. How could you have made your notes more concise?

   _____

   _____

3. How could you have improved the organization of your notes?

   _____

   _____

4. How could you have made your notes clearer and easier to understand?

   _____

   _____

Activity D: Listening and Taking Notes (Selection 2)

NOTE: For Activity D, you will need your teacher or a student to read Selection 2 aloud.

For this activity, follow the same directions that you used for *Activity C* on page 25.

U.S. Wetlands

Swamps, marshes, bogs and similar watery tracts have long been thought of as dismal, unhealthy places that should be removed in the name of progress. In recent years, however, this view has changed radically as scientists realized that wetlands perform many vital functions. They protect shorelines and remove pesticides and other pollutants from surface waters. They provide a refuge for one half of the fish, one third of the bird and one sixth of the mammal species on the U.S. threatened and endangered lists. By acting as reservoirs for rainfall and runoff, they help to extend stream flow during droughts and to prevent floods. The loss of wetlands contributed to the great floods of 1993 on the upper Mississippi and Missouri rivers, the worst in modern U.S. history.

Wetlands take many forms, including salt marshes, forested swamps, floodplains, peat bogs and prairie potholes (the depressions left after the retreat of the last glacier).

Over the past two centuries, improvements in technology accelerated the conversion of wetlands to cropland. For example, the hand-dug drainage ditch of colonial times was succeeded in the 19th century by the steam-powered dredge. New implements such as steel plows and cultivators made possible the development of land previously thought unfit for farming, putting more wetlands at risk. The immense appetite for new farmland was aided by the federal government, which in a series of Swamp Land Acts beginning in 1849 turned over almost 65 million acres of wetlands to the states for reclamation and development.

The cumulative effect has been a 53 percent decline of wetlands in what is now the lower 48 states, from 221 million acres in the 1780s to 104 million in the 1990s. Alaska, which had an estimated 170 million acres of wetlands in the 1780s, has virtually the same amount now. The agricultural states of Ohio, Indiana, Iowa and California suffered the greatest percentage decline, but the most substantial loss in acreage was in Florida, Louisiana and Texas.

Although most of the wetlands gave way to agriculture in earlier years, recently an increasing proportion of the losses has resulted from industrial and housing development. As population grew in the 18th and 19th centuries, the size of wetland conversions increased. In one of the most spectacular cases, the Black Swamp in northwest Ohio—which was almost the size of Connecticut—disappeared between 1859 and 1885. The swamp, it seems, was considered a barrier to travel and settlement and contained a variety of commercially valuable trees. Today the area is mostly farmland.

Federal efforts to restore wetlands have expanded since 1987, but even so, wetland acreage has continued to shrink, although the rate has slowed. This outcome is not surprising, as restoration is a slow, complex process. In February President Bill Clinton announced a clean-water action plan that includes a strategy for increasing wetlands by 100,000 acres a year beginning in 2005. If the plan is successful, wetland acreage will have increased for the first time since record keeping began more than 200 years ago.

—Rodger Doyle

Selection 2: How Did You Do?

1. What important ideas, facts, or details did you forget to include in your notes?

_____

_____

2. How could you have made your notes more concise?

_____

_____

3. How could you have improved the organization of your notes?

_____

_____

4. How could you have made your notes clearer and easier to understand?

_____

_____

5. Overall, how can you improve your listening and note-taking skills?

_____

_____

Work on Your Note-Taking Skills

TIP

Practice taking notes, and look for ways to improve your note-taking skills. For example, review notes that you take in class. Are they clear and complete? Are there abbreviations or symbols you might have used in place of certain words? Could you have organized your notes better?

RECOGNIZING KEY IDEAS AND INFORMATION

SKILL FOCUS: All four parts of the Regents exam call on your ability to recognize important ideas and information and then use that information when you write an extended response. This Skill Builder focuses on developing your ability to recognize key ideas and information in informational selections that you read or hear.

The oral selection of Part A of the Regents exam and the printed selection of Part B both present information. To understand informational selections—oral *and* printed—you'll find it helpful to think about how writers organize their material.

Short informational selections may consist of only a few paragraphs. Longer selections often have ten or more paragraphs. Each paragraph of a selection usually has a *main idea,* and all the main ideas relate to the selection's *central point.*

CONCEPTS TO UNDERSTAND

- The **central point** of a selection is the principal point, or main focus, that the writer wants to communicate. In short selections, such as five-paragraph essays, the writer typically states the central point in the first paragraph. In longer selections, the central point may appear later. The central point is sometimes called the central idea, the controlling idea, or the *thesis.*

- The **main idea** of a paragraph is what the whole paragraph is about. A paragraph's main idea may be directly stated, or it may be implied.

  If the main idea of a paragraph is directly stated, it's usually expressed in a *topic sentence.* The topic sentence is often the first sentence in the paragraph. However, not all paragraphs have topic sentences.

- Writers develop and support their ideas with supporting information, such as facts, details, examples, reasons, statistics, and quotations. The supporting information in a paragraph tells more about the main idea.

The diagram below shows how a selection's central point, main ideas, and supporting information are interconnected.

PARAGRAPH
Main Idea
Supporting information

PARAGRAPH
Main Idea
Supporting information

CENTRAL POINT OF SELECTION

PARAGRAPH
Main Idea
Supporting information

PARAGRAPH
Main Idea
Supporting information

PARAGRAPH
Main Idea
Supporting information

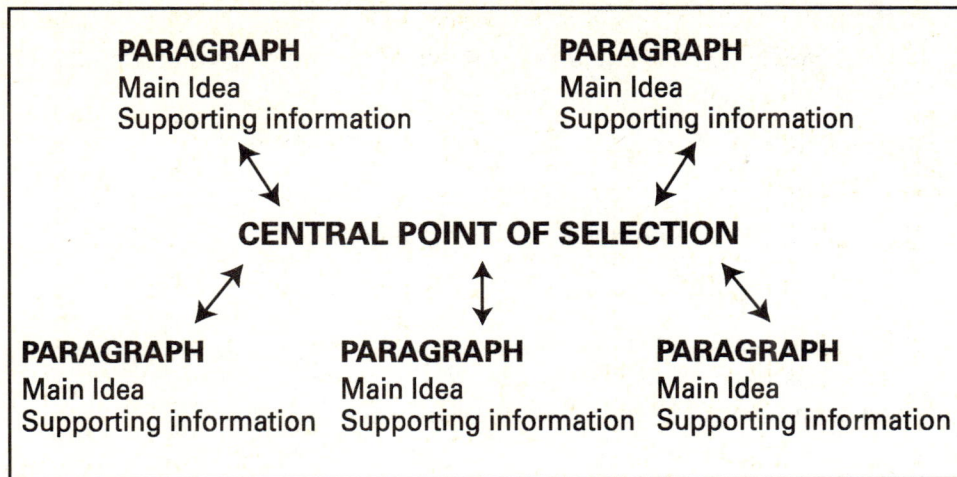

Let's see how the diagram might apply to an actual example, a selection entitled "On Hypnosis":

CENTRAL POINT OF SELECTION:

People have many mistaken ideas about hypnosis.

PARAGRAPH
Main Idea:

Most people don't understand what hypnosis is or how it works. This lack of understanding leads to many misconceptions.

Supporting Information:

The writer introduces several examples of mistaken ideas and states that the following paragraphs will examine these ideas.

PARAGRAPH
Main Idea:

Hypnotists do *not* have special psychic abilities.

Supporting Information:

The writer explains that hypnosis works by putting the subject into a state of mind in which he or she will accept the hypnotist's suggestions.

PARAGRAPH
Main Idea:

It is *not* true that only unintelligent people make good subjects for hypnosis.

Supporting Information:

The writer explains that intelligent people generally make better subjects than unintelligent people.

PARAGRAPH
Main Idea:

Hypnotized people do *not* lose consciousness.

Supporting Information:

The writer makes clear that even though hypnotized people are entirely focused on the hypnotist, they are still aware of their surroundings and know what is happening.

PARAGRAPH
Main Idea:

It is *not* true that a good hypnotist can make a person do anything.

Supporting Information:

The writer gives examples of hypnotized people refusing to carry out actions that would hurt themselves or other people. The writer also describes how subjects generally won't do anything that goes against their moral beliefs.

? *Complete the sentences:* The central point of a selection is the

_____

_____. The central point is sometimes called the

_____, the_____, or the_____.

READING AND LISTENING STRATEGIES

Use the strategies below to zero in on a selection's central point, main ideas, and supporting information. All of the strategies that follow can improve your *reading* skills by helping you identify key ideas and information. In addition, you can apply most of these same strategies when *listening* to a speech or other informational selection, as you do for Part A of the Regents exam.

Strategies for Identifying the Central Point of a Selection

▶ **Think about the title of the selection.** The title will suggest what the selection is about. When reading a printed selection, also look for headings or subtitles within the text. They may help you identify main ideas relating to the central point.

▶ **Get a feel for the entire selection, not just a part of it.** Pay special attention to the first and last paragraphs, which often summarize the central point.

For printed selections, read the text more than once to help you understand it. Pause as you read. Break a long selection into parts to make the content easier to grasp. Summarize in your mind what you read in each part.

▶ **Weigh the main ideas.** If the writer develops several main ideas, weigh them all. Think about how they are related and what underlying idea connects them.

▶ **Look for the big picture.** Ask yourself: *What is the point of this selection? What is the author's purpose in writing it?* The answers to these questions will help you identify the central point.

Strategies for Finding the Stated Main Idea of a Paragraph

▶ **Bring the paragraph into focus.** Ask yourself: *What is the whole paragraph about? What is the most important point the writer makes?*

▶ **Look for a topic sentence.** The topic sentence (if the paragraph has one) states the main idea. It's often the first sentence in a paragraph, but it may also appear in the middle or at the end of a paragraph.

▶ **Be alert for signals.** Writers use certain phrases to call attention to main ideas. Here are some examples:

the single most important	*the main reason that*
the greatest problem	*most of all*
the chief result	*above all*

Strategies for Identifying Supporting Information

▶ **First identify the main idea.** Once you've identified a paragraph's main idea, you can look for the facts, details, and other information in the paragraph that support or develop that idea.

▶ **Ask yourself the "5 W's + H."** Journalists try to answer six questions, sometimes referred to as the "5 W's + H":

Who?	*When?*
What?	*Why?*
Where?	*How?*

Ask yourself these same questions to identify important supporting information. Of course, not every paragraph will contain enough information to answer all six questions. However, the *questions you can answer* will highlight a paragraph's significant points.

TRY THIS

Read the following selection and answer the questions. After you have finished, read the *Thinking It Through* section that follows to see how one student answered the questions.

Brave Hearts in Hawaii

Certainly the inhabitants of the main island of Hawaii must be among the bravest people in the world. These islanders live about 30 kilometers from the most active volcano on Earth. This volcano, named Loihi (meaning "long one" in Hawaiian) is so active that it produced nearly 1,500 earthquakes in just one week! Even though the volcano is more than three kilometers high and about 40 kilometers long, local Hawaiians cannot see it. This is because Loihi rises from the ocean floor with its peak about one kilometer below the ocean surface. Marine scientists predict that Loihi will be the next Hawaiian island to emerge from the ocean, about 50,000 to 100,000 years from now.

Loihi has been erupting continuously for nearly 15 years. Most of the earthquakes it produces are relatively weak. However, they seem to be increasing in magnitude and frequency, causing local authorities to be concerned for the safety of the islanders. Some recent quakes have been recorded at magnitudes between 4 and 5 on the Richter scale. (Either the Richter or magnitude scale is used to measure earthquake intensity.) Seismologists, scientists who study earthquakes, fear that an underwater earthquake with a magnitude of 6.8 might produce a huge wave that would reach the big island in just 15 minutes—not enough time for people along the coast to prepare for emergency evacuation to higher ground.

Several federal agencies are monitoring the volcano's activity. Local officials have decided to set up an early warning system that will give island residents more time to evacuate in the event of a serious earthquake. The Hawaiian Undersea Research Laboratory at the University of Hawaii has plans to place a cable that would connect Hawaii with the underwater volcano. In this way, electrical power could be supplied to instruments that would monitor the seismic activity of Loihi. In addition, the laboratory has a small submersible that is being used to monitor and videotape the eruptions underwater, giving scientists the opportunity to observe and record never-before-seen events by going into the crater.

1. In your own words, state the central point of this selection.

_____

_____

_____

_____

_____

2. What is the main idea of the second paragraph?

_____

_____

_____

_____

_____

3. What supporting information does the writer use to develop the main idea of the second paragraph?

_____

_____

_____

_____

_____

4. How does the third paragraph of the selection relate to the central point?

_____

_____

_____

_____

_____

Thinking It Through

1. *In your own words, state the central point of this selection.*

   The central point is that people living on the main island of Hawaii would have to be brave because their island is so near the most active volcano on Earth. I came to this conclusion for several reasons. First, the title suggests that the selection is about people in Hawaii being brave. Second, the writer summarizes the selection's underlying idea in the first two sentences. Third, the writer gives reasons <u>why</u> the people would need to be brave: Loihi has been erupting for many years, it erupts often, and the earthquakes seem to be getting worse. Finally, the writer describes growing concern about the possible need for emergency evacuation.

2. *What is the main idea of the second paragraph?*

   The main idea is stated in the first sentence: Loihi has been erupting continuously for nearly 15 years. All the other sentences in the paragraph relate to the idea of Loihi's eruptions.

3. *What supporting information does the writer use to develop the main idea of the second paragraph?*

   The writer explains that Loihi's earthquakes have been generally weak until now but appear to be "increasing in magnitude and frequency." The writer tells how some recent earthquakes have measured between "4 and 5 on the Richter scale" and then describes the danger to Hawaii's people if a 6.8-magnitude earthquake were to occur.

4. *How does the third paragraph of the selection relate to the central point?*

   The third paragraph describes efforts to monitor Loihi's volcanic activity. These efforts relate to the idea that Hawaii's people may be in danger.

Skills Practice

Read the selection and answer the questions that follow.

Political Parties: Not the Force They Were

In New York State, as in many other parts of the country, political parties have lost some of their traditional strength. Various factors account for this change, including advances in technology, a weakening in party identification among voters, and reforms in government.

Technological advances have made political candidates less dependent on their parties than they were in the past. For example, through the use of television and, more recently, the Internet, candidates can reach millions of voters directly. Scientifically conducted polls allow candidates to sound out public opinion, helping them decide which issues to emphasize.

While candidates rely less on parties, many voters are less inclined to choose their candidates strictly along party lines. Moreover, the number of voters who identify themselves as party members has dropped. In a recent year, for example, the number of New York State voters enrolled in the state's five recognized political parties decreased by nearly 100,000.

Parties have also lost much of their ability to reward political allies. Today's party leaders cannot hand out government favors as easily as leaders of the past. In the 1870s, for example, party leaders generously awarded jobs and government contracts to those who demonstrated party loyalty. Government reform and the growth of the civil service have removed most government jobs and many contracts from the control of elected officials.

1. In your own words, state the central point of this selection.

   _____

   _____

   _____

   _____

2. How do the second and third paragraphs of the selection relate to the central point?

_____

_____

_____

_____

_____

3. What is the main idea of the last paragraph?

_____

_____

_____

_____

4. What supporting information does the writer use to develop the main idea of the last paragraph?

_____

_____

_____

_____

MAKING INFERENCES AND DRAWING CONCLUSIONS

SKILL FOCUS: All four parts of the Regents exam call on your ability to make inferences and draw conclusions and then use these inferences and conclusions to help you write an extended response. This Skill Builder focuses on developing your ability to apply inferential skills to informational selections that you read or hear.

As you read or listen to a selection, you gather and process information. When you combine this new information with knowledge you already have, you're able to make inferences and draw conclusions. These inferences and conclusions take you beyond the spoken or written word. They give you insight into the selection's meaning and purpose.

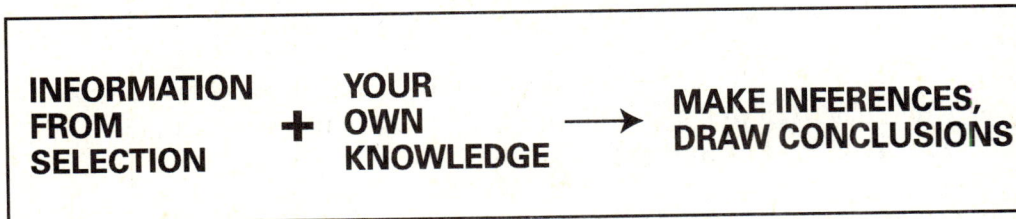

```
INFORMATION          YOUR                        MAKE INFERENCES,
FROM          +      OWN          ⟶              DRAW CONCLUSIONS
SELECTION            KNOWLEDGE
```

CONCEPTS TO UNDERSTAND

● To *infer* is to combine information you hear or read with your own knowledge and experience to make an educated guess. The process of reaching understandings that go beyond the spoken or printed word is called making inferences. Here's an example of an inference:

  Statement: Black clouds darkened the sky.
  Inference/conclusion: A storm is likely to occur. (You know that black clouds usually mean a storm is coming.)

● Inferences are based on facts, but go beyond facts. Often, you can draw more than one inference from a single statement or set of facts. Listeners and readers must use their judgment to draw the most reasonable inference. Here's an example:

  Facts: The phone rang ten times, but no one answered.
  Inference/conclusion:

     No one is at home.
        or

Whoever is at home doesn't want to answer.
or
Whoever is at home is unable to answer.

● Every paragraph has a main idea. This idea may or may not be directly stated. If it is not, you have to infer it. A main idea that is not directly stated is called an implied main idea.

? *Answer in your own words:* What does it mean to make an inference?

_____

_____

READING AND LISTENING STRATEGIES

Use the strategies below to make inferences and draw conclusions. All of the strategies that follow can improve your *reading* skills by helping you "read between the lines." In addition, you can apply most of these same strategies when *listening* to a speech or other informational selection, as you do for Part A of the Regents exam.

Strategies for Making Inferences and Drawing Conclusions

▶ **Think carefully about ideas and supporting facts, details, and examples.** Consider not just what they mean individually, but also how they fit together. Making inferences is a little like assembling a jigsaw puzzle. Once you fit all the pieces together, you're able to see the big picture. This picture may be the implied main idea of a single sentence or paragraph, or it may be the central point of a whole selection.

▶ **Watch for a pattern.** Why has the writer chosen to include certain facts, details, and examples? What do these choices tell you about the writer's purpose and point of view? Suppose, for example, that a writer describes numerous instances of a particular breed of dog attacking people. What point might the writer be making?

▶ **Consider the sequence of events.** Think about how events are related. What happened first? What happened next? Did one event lead to, or result from, another?

▶ **Watch for comparisons.** Writers often make a point by showing how people or things are alike or different or how they have changed. For example, a writer might contrast a hectic big city with a calm small town or compare the simplicity of 19th-century life with the complexity of modern-day living.

▶ **Consider choice of language.** Speakers and writers communicate a great deal through their choice of words. For example, compare the following sentences. How did changing three words alter the sentence's meaning?

◊ An *excited crowd greeted* the popular actor at the airport.

◊ A *wild mob attacked* the popular actor at the airport.

TRY THIS

Read the following selection and answer the questions. After you have finished, read the *Thinking It Through* section that follows to see how one student answered the questions.

Good Morning, Kids

It's Saturday morning. Across the nation, young children are sprawled in front of television sets. They're ready to view their favorite programs, the ones they see every Saturday and often watch during the week as well.

Images bombard these young viewers, fast-moving pictures filled with bright colors and accompanied by loud sounds. Crazed animated villains blow up buildings with ray guns or obliterate them with bombs. Evil super-robots demolish entire cities as people run screaming through the streets. Cartoon characters pound one another with mallets, shoot each other with shotguns, and fling each other off cliffs. Good guys do battle with bad guys, sometimes using fists and feet, other times using the latest in high-tech weaponry. The mayhem and murder are interrupted only by commercials selling action figures and fast food.

Research studies have shown that some of the most popular children's programs are five times more violent than shows televised during prime time. Some years ago, one study even identified a popular cartoon TV show as the single most violent program on television.

And adults wonder why children seem "desensitized" to violence and suffering in the real world, why kids sometimes respond with violence themselves. Spend an hour or two watching children's television, and the answer comes through as clearly as a gunshot.

1. What is the central point of this selection?

_____

_____

_____

_____

2. What is the main idea of the second paragraph?

_____

_____

_____

_____

3. For what audience and purpose do you think the writer wrote this selection?

_____

_____

_____

_____

_____

4. How did the writer's choice of language help to convey the writer's meaning?

_____

_____

_____

_____

Thinking It Through

1. *What is the central point of this selection?*

   The central point is that children's TV shows are so violent that it's not surprising kids become "desensitized" to real violence and sometimes act violent themselves. I came to this conclusion by thinking carefully about the facts, details, and examples that the writer provides. The pattern they suggest is of nonstop violent images. This pattern ties in directly with the ideas in the last paragraph.

2. *What is the main idea of the second paragraph?*

   The main idea is that Saturday morning children's programming consists of an almost constant flow of violent images.

3. *For what audience and purpose do you think the writer wrote this selection?*

   I think the writer probably wrote this selection to make parents and other adults aware of the nature of Saturday morning television.

4. *How did the writer's choice of language help to convey the writer's meaning?*

   The writer used words and phrases that are vivid and have a negative association, such as bombard, obliterate, screaming through the streets, and mayhem and murder. Such language helps stress the violent nature of the examples.

Skills Practice

Read the selection and answer the questions that follow.

Seeking Solutions to the Garbage Problem

Shopping for food a century ago was a very different experience from visiting a modern supermarket or convenience store. A family would travel to the general store where flour, sugar, and other basic items were sold in wooden barrels, cotton sacks, and stone containers. Today, food products of all sorts are packaged in cardboard boxes, plastic and glass containers, and aluminum cans. Food companies wrap these products in plastic and paper—often multiple layers—to preserve their freshness, to cushion them against damage, and just to make them look attractive to consumers.

All this packaging and wrapping ends up in the same place: the garbage. In fact, Americans discard nearly 200 million tons of garbage annually, much of it wrapping and packaging materials. This figure will only increase as the nation's population continues to grow.

What can be done with so much garbage? Existing landfills (garbage dumps) are running out of space, and not many new sites are available. Incinerators can burn some of the garbage, but their smoke pollutes the air, and some of the ash produced is toxic. Dumping garbage into the ocean pollutes sea waters.

Government officials, environmentalists, and many others discuss and debate various solutions to the garbage problem. Many people urge that new ways be found to recycle and reuse discarded materials. Others insist that additional methods for disposing of garbage must be devised. Still others suggest that the best first step in solving the problem would be for food and other companies to take a more responsible approach to packaging their products.

Meanwhile, garbage mounts up, environmental pollution continues, and shoppers continue to fill their carts with elaborately packaged convenience foods.

1. What is the central point of this selection?

   _____

   _____

   _____

   _____

   _____

2. In the first paragraph, how did making a comparison help the writer convey the paragraph's main idea?

   _____

   _____

   _____

   _____

   _____

3. What is the implied main idea of the third paragraph? How do you know?

_____

_____

_____

_____

3

ANSWERING THE MULTIPLE-CHOICE QUESTIONS FOR PART A

As you saw earlier, Part A of the Regents exam includes five or six multiple-choice questions. These questions focus on important aspects of the selection that your teacher reads aloud.

To answer the Part A questions, you'll use the strategies you've learned for effective listening and note-taking. You'll also apply your skills at recognizing key ideas *(Skill Builder 1)* and making inferences *(Skill Builder 2)*.

As in many other tests you've taken, the Regents exam multiple-choice questions generally take one of two forms: sentence completion or question and answer. Both forms of questions on the exam offer four answer choices. Here's an example of each form:

Sentence completion:

According to the speaker, the major purpose of political parties is to

      1   encourage the discussion of issues

      2   check on elected officials

      3   register voters

      4   win elections

Question and answer:

Who chooses elected officials?

      1   political parties

      2   political conventions

      3   pressure groups

      4   the voters

Strategies for Answering the Part A Multiple-Choice Questions

If you listen carefully to the oral selection and take good notes, you'll be well prepared to answer the multiple-choice questions for Part A. Here are some helpful tips:

▶ **Consult your notes whenever you need to.** Important ideas and information you've written down are likely to appear in the questions.

▶ **Try to recall the selection your teacher read and the way he or she read it.** Your memory is likely to store information that may not appear in your notes.

▶ **Read each question carefully.** Be sure you understand the question before considering the answers. Watch for particular words or phrases that offer clues to the correct answer.

▶ **Take a moment to think about the question before looking at the answers.** Try to think what the answer *should be*. This strategy works especially well with question-and-answer form questions.

▶ **Reread the question as needed.** Sometimes rereading the question with each possible answer is helpful, particularly with sentence-completion form questions.

▶ **Read, compare, and consider *all* the choices before picking one.**

▶ **Choose the *best* and *most complete* answer.**

▶ **Narrow your search.** If you're not sure which answer is correct, cross out choices you know are *incorrect*. Then focus your attention on the remaining choices.

▶ **Don't spend too much time on a troublesome question.** Make your best choice and move on to the next question. If you have time left over, you can return to the question you were unsure about. Also, you'll sometimes find that answering one question helps you answer another.

▶ **Answer every question.**

TRY THIS

NOTE: For this activity, you will need your teacher or a student to read the selection aloud.

Review the overview of the Part A prompt below, which you saw earlier in this chapter. Listen and take notes as your teacher reads the selection aloud twice. Save your notes for use *later* in this chapter.

Next, answer the multiple-choice questions that appear on page 50. After you've answered the questions, read the *Thinking It Through* section that follows to see how one student determined the correct answers.

Overview: For this part of the test, you will listen to a speech about the importance of seat belts, answer some multiple-choice questions, and write a response based on the situation described below. You will hear the speech twice. You may take notes anytime you wish during the readings.

STOP! DO NOT READ THE SELECTION BELOW. YOUR TEACHER WILL READ IT ALOUD.

Directions to READER:

1. Read the selection aloud.

2. Allow students a few minutes to look over their notes.

3. Read the selection a second time.

4. Give students time to clarify and expand their notes.

5. Allow students time to answer the multiple-choice questions.

My Own Son Didn't Listen

As a flight nurse employed by a hospital-based aeromedical helicopter service, I regularly respond to life-and-death situations. For 18 years I have flown to the scenes of some of the most terrible crashes you can imagine. But nothing in my experience or my training prepared me for what happened on this past Mother's Day weekend.

I was on duty when we received a request to respond to a head-on collision approximately 30 miles from Tulsa, Okla. En route to the scene it was reported by our communication center that this was a mass-casualty incident involving several vehicles. As we observed the scene from the air, we could see many victims lying on the highway and by the roadside. We hoped none had been ejected from their vehicles.

When we arrived, our crew was directed to an area where many of the victims were being stabilized. My partner and I were asked to assist with a young man who was in serious trouble. As I stepped into the ambulance I could see that he was already receiving cardiopulmonary resuscitation. As I moved in to help, I suddenly froze. I recognized the young man's shoes. They belonged to my 17-year-old son, Nik. In seconds my whole world crashed in around me. Nik was so gravely injured, I knew he was not going to survive.

Three of the four teenagers in the vehicle Nik was riding in were not wearing their seat belts. Two of the three unbelted passengers were killed: the driver and my son, who was in the back seat. The other unbelted back-seat passenger was ejected and seriously injured. The front-seat passenger, the only one wearing his seat belt, walked away with minor cuts and bruises.

I lost my son on Mother's Day weekend because he was not wearing his seat belt. Our family—and the families of more than 9,000 sons, daughters, mothers and fathers who will die this year because they were unbelted—will never be the same.

It is not just the families who suffer. The community pays a price as well. Those of us who buckle up are paying in higher health-care and insurance costs for those who don't. The hospital costs for treating unbelted crash victims are 50 percent higher than those for belted crash victims. And 85 percent of those inpatient costs are paid by society, not by the individual. Any way you look at it—the loss of human life or the financial strain on society—the results are catastrophic.

Despite the recent focus on the terrible problems of drunken driving or on newly identified problems such as aggressive driving, increasing seat-belt use is still the single most effective thing we can do to save lives on America's roadways. As a flight nurse and an emergency health-care giver, I have witnessed the difference a seat belt makes. The most satisfying part of my job is the opportunity to help save lives. The most difficult part is seeing unbelted children and adults who have been violently ejected from their vehicles or thrown into the windshield and knowing that their terrible injuries or death could have been prevented. The only reason Nik died was that he was not wearing his seat belt.

Based on my firsthand experience, I tried to drill into my four children the importance of wearing seat belts. When Nik was learning to drive, I had him take a driver's ed course sponsored by my auto-insurance company. We even made a visit to a young man recovering in an intensive-care unit who is now a quadriplegic because he wasn't wearing his seat belt.

I did everything I could think of to get Nik to buckle up. Unfortunately, the threat of serious injury or even death is not enough to persuade some people—especially young people, who believe they are invincible—to always buckle up.

The only proven way to get people who can't be convinced through public education to use a seat belt is a real threat of a ticket and fine. Belt use is about 15 percent higher in states with "standard" enforcement laws, where police officers treat failure to buckle up like every other traffic offense. In states with weak "secondary" enforcement, officers must first observe a motorist committing a traffic violation before ticketing for failure to use a belt. I feel certain that if Nik had known there was a real chance of getting stopped and given a ticket for not wearing his seat belt, he would still be alive today.

Ironically, in the months before my son's death, I had joined my local Safe Kids Coalition to help increase belt use by working to pass a standard belt law. While the challenge seemed great—belt use in Oklahoma was 48 percent—we were encouraged by the experiences of other states. Louisiana, which recently upgraded its belt law to standard enforcement, saw its belt use jump from 50 to 68 percent in just three years.

Through my advocacy work I also learned how weak belt laws leave innocent young children at risk. Adults who don't buckle up are telling children it's all right not to use a seat belt. More than 75 percent of the time, when the driver is unbelted, children and other passengers in that vehicle will be unbelted as well. If every state in the nation adopted a standard-enforcement law, we could save 1,900 lives and prevent more than 49,000 injuries a year.

After my son's funeral, I heard that Oklahoma's proposed belt law was in trouble. So I went to Oklahoma City to meet with the governor and several legislators. I told them my story and pleaded with them to do what they could to pass this bill. It passed, and I now know that it will save lives.

I have since told my story to the Ohio legislature, which is considering a stronger belt law similar to Oklahoma's. I plan to keep telling it because I think it's time we made protecting lives with seat belts as important as other traffic laws.

I know that when I go back to my job, each time I fly to a crash scene I will be reminded of the terrible day when I lost my son. But I also will carry a little hope that Nik's life can make a difference. And that by telling his story, it may help to improve our laws and save lives.

—Carolyn Hanig

Multiple-Choice Questions

Directions (1–6): Use your notes to answer the following questions about the passage read to you. Select the best suggested answer and circle its number. The questions may help you think about ideas and information you might use in your writing. You may return to these questions anytime you wish.

1 According to the speaker, people's failure to wear seat belts has resulted in

1 lower automobile prices
2 higher health-care and insurance costs
3 reduced driving speeds on highways
4 greater passenger comfort

2 The speaker implies that the most likely reason her son did not wear a seat belt is that

1 he did not take the threat of injury or death seriously enough
2 his parents had not warned him about the danger
3 the car he was in did not have seat belts
4 he had not taken a driver education course

3 Which statement about "standard" enforcement of seat-belt laws is true?

1 Under standard enforcement, the police must see a motorist commit a traffic violation before they can issue a ticket for not wearing a seat belt.
2 Under standard enforcement, the police treat failure to wear a seat belt like any traffic offense.
3 There is really no difference between standard enforcement and "secondary" enforcement.
4 Belt use is almost 10 percent higher in states with standard enforcement laws.

4 According to the speaker, Nik's life might have been saved if he had

1 taken driver's education in school
2 not sat in the back seat of the car
3 been driving the car that crashed
4 believed that he might be stopped and ticketed for not wearing a seat belt

5 If the driver of a vehicle does not wear a seat belt, the likelihood that passengers in the vehicle also won't wear belts is

1 less than 50 percent
2 about 65 percent
3 greater than 75 percent
4 greater than 90 percent

6 To give her story emotional impact, the speaker

1 begins by describing her feelings at the scene of the crash
2 explains that hospital costs are higher for unbelted crash victims than for belted victims
3 describes her meeting with Oklahoma governor
4 includes statistics about belt use in states that passed stricter laws

Thinking It Through

1 *According to the speaker, people's failure to wear seat belts has resulted in*

   1 *lower automobile prices*

   2 *higher health-care and insurance costs*

   3 *reduced driving speeds on highways*

   4 *greater passenger comfort*

   > *From listening to the selection and from the notes I took, I know right away that choice 2 is the correct answer. However, I consider the other choices just to be safe.*

2 *The speaker implies that the most likely reason her son did not wear a seat belt is that*

   1 *he did not take the threat of injury or death seriously enough*

   2 *his parents had not warned him about the danger*

   3 *the car he was in did not have seat belts*

   4 *he had not taken a driver education course*

   > *I remember that the speaker had tried to convince her son to wear a seat belt and also that she had him take driver's ed. Therefore, I can eliminate choices 2 and 4 and infer that choice 1 is the correct answer. I can also eliminate choice 3 because the selection did not include any such fact. Also, I know it's unlikely that a car wouldn't have belts.*

3 *Which statement about "standard" enforcement of seat-belt laws is true?*

1 *Under standard enforcement, the police must see a motorist commit a traffic violation before they can issue a ticket for not wearing a seat belt.*

2 *Under standard enforcement, the police treat failure to wear a seat belt like any traffic offense.*

3 *There is really no difference between standard enforcement and "secondary" enforcement.*

4 *Belt use is almost 10 percent higher in states with standard enforcement laws.*

From my notes, I know that "standard" enforcement is stronger than "secondary" enforcement. I also know that under secondary enforcement, police have to first see a motorist committing a violation before they can ticket the person for not wearing a belt. My notes also tell me that belt use is 15—not 10—percent higher in states with standard enforcement laws. The correct answer is choice 2.

4 *According to the speaker, Nik's life might have been saved if he had*

1 *taken driver's education in school*

2 *not sat in the back seat of the car*

3 *been driving the car that crashed*

4 *believed that he might be stopped and ticketed for not wearing a seat belt*

I see that this question is closely related to the central point of the selection. That is, the speaker believes that the only way to protect people like her son is to pass stronger belt laws. Therefore, choice 4 is most likely correct.

5 *If the driver of a vehicle does not wear a seat belt, the likelihood that passengers in the vehicle also won't wear belts is*

   1 *less than 50 percent*

   2 *about 65 percent*

   3 *greater than 75 percent*

   4 *greater than 90 percent*

> *Reviewing my notes, I find that choice __3__ is the correct answer. I double-check just to be sure, since the selection contained a number of statistics. I want to be sure I'm referring to the right one.*

6 *To give her story emotional impact, the speaker*

   1 *begins by describing her feelings at the scene of the crash*

   2 *explains that hospital costs are higher for unbelted crash victims than for belted victims*

   3 *describes her meeting with Oklahoma's governor*

   4 *includes statistics about belt use in states that passed stricter laws*

> *Reading this question carefully, I see the phrase "emotional impact." This phrase gives me an important clue. Thinking about the selection, I remember that it was the beginning that affected me most. That's the part where the speaker realizes that the victim in the ambulance is her own son. Of the four choices, only __1__ refers specifically to "feelings."*

Activity E: Evaluating Your Skills

Read for yourself the listening selection that your teacher read aloud: "My Own Son Didn't Listen," on pages 48–50. Then answer the questions below.

1. Review the notes you took and the multiple-choice questions you answered. How helpful were your notes in answering the questions? How could you have made your notes more helpful? Be specific.

    _____

    _____

    _____

2. Did you listen actively to the oral presentation? How could you have listened even more effectively?

_____

_____

_____

3. In what way is *listening* to a selection more of a challenge than *reading* one? What can you do to help yourself meet this challenge? Be specific.

_____

_____

_____

4. Share and compare your answers to the preceding questions with the answers of other students. What suggestions from other students did you find most helpful?

_____

_____

_____

4

PLANNING AND WRITING YOUR PART A RESPONSE

Remember, the extended response that you write for Part A will be based on a real-life situation that requires both listening and writing skills. Your response will call on your ability to analyze the listening selection and express your ideas in writing. However, it's important for you to know how your extended response will be scored.

Examining the Criteria as Applied to Part A

The readers who score your response for Part A will evaluate your paper holistically on the basis of the five criteria described in Chapter 1: meaning, development, organization, language use, and conventions.

SCORING CRITERIA

ORGANIZATION   DEVELOPMENT

MEANING

CONVENTIONS

LANGUAGE
USE

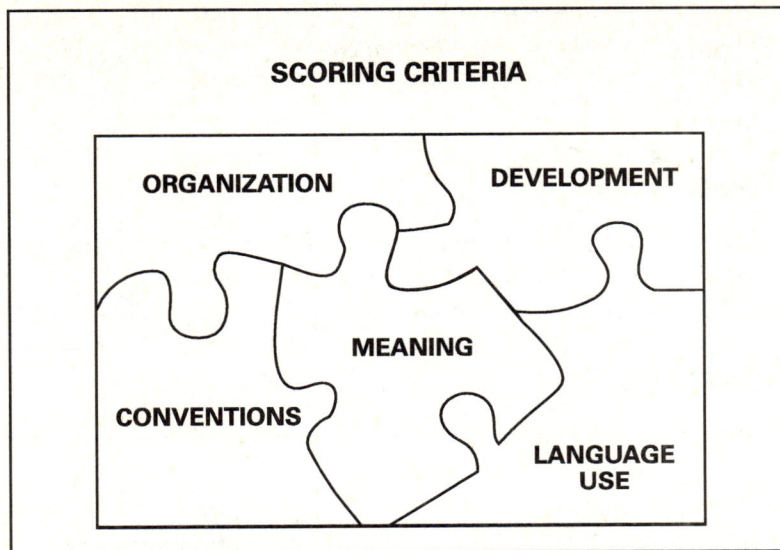

The following chart shows how the scoring criteria are applied specifically to Part A of the Regents English exam:

SCORING THE PART A EXTENDED RESPONSE

CRITERIA	WHAT YOUR PART A RESPONSE SHOULD SHOW
MEANING	• A solid understanding of the listening selection • Insightful connections between the content of the selection and the specific writing task
DEVELOPMENT	• Clear development of ideas • Effective use of specific and relevant supporting information
ORGANIZATION	• Clear, consistent focus • Logical and coherent structure
LANGUAGE USE	• Effective and engaging language that is appropriate for the specific audience and purpose • Varied sentence structure and length
CONVENTIONS	• Strong control of grammar, punctuation, spelling, and other elements of writing, with few errors

In the following pages, you'll learn how you can do well in Part A by paying careful attention to these criteria as you write. You'll also learn how planning before you write will help you collect, develop, and organize your ideas.

Thinking Ahead

When faced with a writing task, some students are afraid that they may be wasting time if they don't start writing at once. This is simply not true. The first step in the writing process is planning. Planning before writing will help you do your best on all parts of the Regents exam. Furthermore, *planning makes writing easier.*

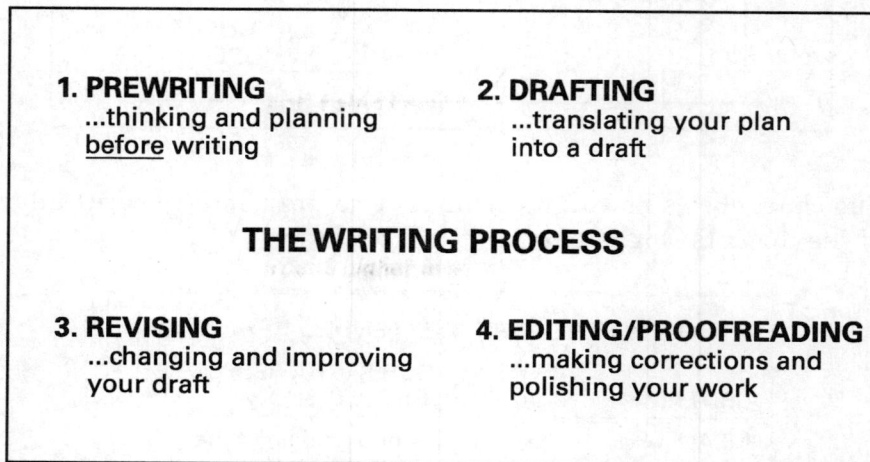

---

1. PREWRITING
...thinking and planning
<u>before</u> writing

2. DRAFTING
...translating your plan
into a draft

THE WRITING PROCESS

3. REVISING
...changing and improving
your draft

4. EDITING/PROOFREADING
...making corrections and
polishing your work

Now, let's focus on the parts of the Part A prompt that describe the response you will write: **The Situation, Your Task**, and **Guidelines**. Use these parts to guide both your planning and writing.

The Situation: You work as a volunteer for Safety First, a citizens' group for public safety. The group is launching a national campaign to reduce automobile-related injuries and fatalities. The director of Safety First has asked you to write an article for the *Safety First Newsletter* explaining the need to increase seatbelt use and suggesting how. This newsletter is read by high school students and their parents as well as state lawmakers across the nation. In preparation for writing your article, listen to a speech given by nurse Carolyn Hanig. Then use relevant information from this speech to write your article.

Your Task: Write an article for the *Safety First Newsletter* using relevant information from the speech to explain the need to increase seat-belt use and suggesting how.

Guidelines:

Be sure to

- Tell your audience what they need to know about the importance of wearing seat belts and how to increase belt use
- Use specific, accurate, and relevant information from the talk to support your discussion
- Use a tone and level of language appropriate for a newsletter read by students, parents, and lawmakers
- Organize your ideas in a logical and coherent manner
- Indicate any words taken directly from the talk by using quotation marks or referring to the speaker
- Follow the conventions of standard written English

Watch for Key Words

TIP

As you read the prompt, watch for verbs and other key words that provide clues to the writing task. For example, verbs such as *explain*, *tell*, and *show* suggest that your writing purpose will be to inform your readers about something. *Persuade, argue, recommend,* and *convince* suggest that you'll be writing to convey a point of view.

? *Fill in the blanks:* The five criteria that readers will use to score your written work are:

_____

_____

_____

▶ Read *The Situation, Your Task,* and *Guidelines* very carefully. Be sure you understand the specific writing task. Notice how the *Guidelines* tie in with the scoring criteria. For example, one guideline relates to organization, another to conventions, and so on.

▶ **Stay focused on your task, audience, and purpose.** To keep yourself on track, be sure you have a clear idea of what you're going to write. Refer back to the task, audience, and purpose that you jotted down before listening to the selection. Adjust or sharpen your focus as needed.

Look at the following example, and compare it with what you wrote for *Activity B* on page 22:

TASK: *write article for a newsletter*

AUDIENCE: *high school students, parents, state lawmakers across the*

nation

PURPOSE: *inform readers why seat-belt use is important, and suggest*

how to get people to wear belts

? *Be specific:* How does what you wrote for *Activity B* on page 22 differ from the example?

Developing, Supporting, and Organizing Your Ideas

To write an effective Part A response, you need to develop and support the points you make with specific information from the listening selection. Without supporting details, a writer's ideas carry little weight. Furthermore, unsupported ideas may not be clear to the reader.

As you're thinking about the ideas and information you'll present, also think about the best way to organize your response. Use **The Situation, Your Task,** and **Guidelines** to help you plan the most appropriate and logical organization. For writing to be logically organized, your ideas must flow in a way that makes sense and is easy for readers to follow. (See pages 148–149 for basic methods of organization.)

Q&A

How many ideas should I present, and how much supporting information should I include?

There's no fixed answer to this question. The number of ideas will vary depending on the particular prompt and on your approach to answering it. However, every idea that you do present must be developed with relevant and specific details from the listening selection. *You'll get a higher score by presenting a few ideas and supporting them well than by presenting many unsupported ideas.*

With your task, audience, and purpose clearly in mind, you're ready to plan your response. Referring to your listening notes as needed, jot down your thoughts on paper, using a simple list or outline format like this:

IDEA
Supporting detail
Supporting detail
Supporting detail

IDEA
Supporting detail
Supporting detail
Supporting detail

. . . and so on.

Of course, depending on the particular prompt, your rough outline may include more or fewer ideas or a different number of supporting details. You may also find it helpful to list more items than you need and then circle just the ones that are most useful.

Maybe you have an altogether different planning or outlining approach that works for you. That's fine. The important thing is that you take time to plan and think about your content before you begin writing.

Activity F: Making a Plan

1. On a sheet of paper, make a rough plan for an extended response to the prompt about seat-belt use. Keep your task, audience, and purpose in mind. Refer to your notes, the prompt, and the multiple-choice questions as needed.

2. Exchange papers with a partner, and evaluate each other's work. Be constructive and specific in your comments and suggestions.

Looking at a Sample Plan

Let's see how planning ahead helped one student shape a response to the Part A prompt about seat-belt use. Look at the sample plan below. Notice that the outline uses information that you would have in your listening notes. The outline also reflects ideas and information covered by the multiple-choice questions.

Later in this chapter, you'll see how the student translated this plan into a Part A extended response.

STUDENT'S PLAN FOR PART A RESPONSE

Note: For illustration purposes, this outline may be more detailed than yours would need to be. The plan you make for yourself need be only detailed enough for *you* to understand what you intend to write!

WHY IT'S IMPORTANT FOR DRIVERS AND PASSENGERS TO WEAR SEAT BELTS

(1) Wearing seat belts saves lives.

—About 9,000 people will die this year because they didn't wear belts

(2) People not wearing belts has caused higher health-care and insurance costs.

—Hospital costs for treating unbelted crash victims 50% higher than for belted victims

—85% of those costs paid by society, not individual

WAYS TO GET PEOPLE TO WEAR SEAT BELTS

(1) Communicate the buckle-up message!

—Adults should insist all passengers wear belts

—Drivers and other adults should themselves wear belts

—More than 75% of the time when driver isn't wearing belt, neither are children and other passengers

—Driver's ed courses should stress wearing belts

(2) Pass "standard" enforcement laws to make threat of getting a ticket and fine real

—"Threat of serious injury or even death not enough to persuade some people"

—Belt use about 15% higher in states with standard enforcement laws

—If all states had standard enforcement, would save 1,900 lives and prevent 49,000 injuries a year

Activity G: Evaluating a Plan

Answer the following questions about the student's plan. Before writing your answers, discuss your thoughts with a partner or a small group of students.

1. Overall, what are the strengths of the student's plan?

   _____

   _____

   _____

   _____

2. Give at least two examples of how the student made clear
   connections between the content of the selection and the specific
   writing task.

   _____

   _____

   _____

   _____

3. How has the student used the prompt to create a logical
   organizational structure?

   _____

   _____

   _____

   _____

4. Give at least two examples of how the student developed ideas with
   specific and relevant supporting details.

   _____

   _____

   _____

   _____

5. How will the student's plan make writing the response easier?

   _____

   _____

   _____

   _____

6. How has answering the multiple-choice questions helped the student focus on important ideas and information?

_____

_____

_____

_____

Activity H: Comparing Plans

Carefully compare the student's plan above with the rough plan you made for *Activity F* (page 59). Then answer the following questions.

1. What are the main differences you see between the two plans?

_____

_____

_____

2. In what ways do you think your plan is better than the student's plan? Be specific.

_____

_____

_____

3. In what ways is the student's plan stronger than yours? Again, be specific.

_____

_____

_____

4. Do you think that either of the two plans could be used to write an effective Part A response? Why or why not?

_____

_____

_____

_____

Don't Just Summarize

When you plan and write your response for Part A—or any of the other parts of the Regents exam—select your ideas and information with care. Don't just summarize or repeat what the selection says. Instead, _choose those details from the selection that best accomplish your specific writing purpose, and express them in your own words._

TIP

Keeping Your Writing Focused and Coherent

Once you have a plan, you're ready to start writing. To convey your ideas effectively, make your writing as focused and coherent as you can. Here's how:

► **Stick to the point.** _Focused_ writing has a clear and definite topic and _sticks to_ that topic. Focused writing omits ideas and information that are not related to the topic.

► **Use a clear and logical structure.** Connect your ideas and supporting information in such a way that readers can easily follow your thinking.

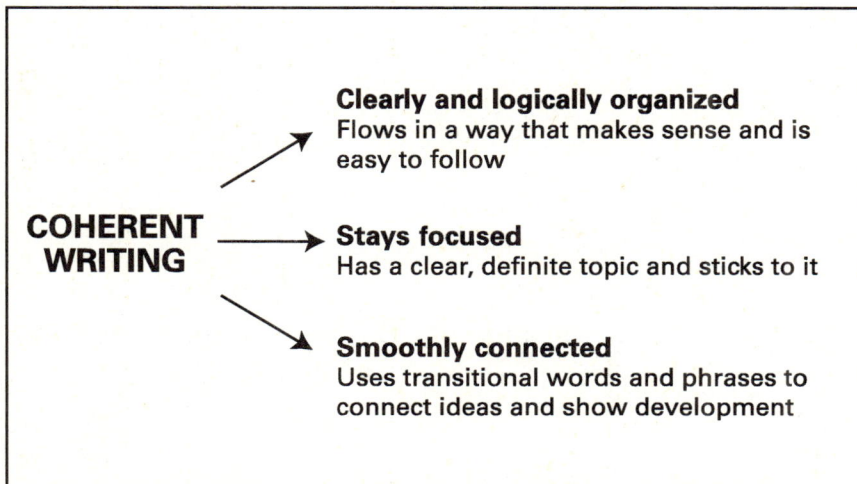

COHERENT WRITING →

Clearly and logically organized
Flows in a way that makes sense and is easy to follow

Stays focused
Has a clear, definite topic and sticks to it

Smoothly connected
Uses transitional words and phrases to connect ideas and show development

63

You can use *transitional words and phrases* to connect your ideas and help readers follow your organizational structure. Transitional words and phrases serve as guideposts, helping to give shape and direction to your writing. The chart below shows some examples. There are many others.

TRANSITIONAL WORDS AND PHRASES	
What the Word/Phrase Does	Examples
Indicates sequence	*first, second, third (and so on); next; finally*
Provides one or more examples	*for example, for instance, such as, one reason*
Adds information	*also, another, furthermore, in addition*
Indicates a consequence or conclusion	*because of, for this reason, therefore, due to*
Makes a comparison or signals a change in direction	*both, however, on the other hand*
Adds emphasis	*especially, in particular, in fact, most important*

Activity I: Identifying Transitional Words and Phrases

Circle the transitional word or phrase in each sentence. Then write what function the word or phrase serves (for example, "makes a comparison").

1. The role of New York's governor as policy maker for the state is an especially important responsibility.

   _____

2. Another responsibility of New York's governor is to prepare the state's annual budget.

   _____

3. Finally, the governor has the authority to pardon criminals convicted of committing state crimes.

   _____

4. Both the lieutenant governor of New York and the vice president of the United States must be prepared to assume leadership roles if necessary.

_____

5. The attorney general has a variety of responsibilities, such as upholding the state's business and labor laws.

_____

Making Your Writing Effective and Engaging

Your use of language determines not only how well you're able to communicate your ideas but also how involved your readers will be in what they're reading. _Engaging_ writing attracts and holds readers' interest. It _involves_ readers. Here are some tips to make your writing both effective and engaging:

▶ **Tailor your language to your specific audience.** An informal, breezy style might be fine when writing for your friends, but you'd probably want to use a more serious and formal style for a general audience.

▶ **Use language that is appropriate for your specific purpose.** If you're writing about a serious topic, use a serious voice and tone. If you're writing to persuade your audience, use language that gets your point across.

▶ **Be consistent in voice and tone.** Once you've decided on the appropriate approach, stick with it. Don't switch from formal to informal or serious to humorous.

▶ **Vary your sentences in structure and length.** Don't begin several consecutive sentences in the same way. Use a blend of short and long sentences throughout your response.

Q&A

Are voice and tone the same?

No, but they are related. Voice and tone are both components of writing style—the way in which you express your thoughts in words. Voice is what readers "hear" when they read your words. For example, a writer's voice, like a speaker's voice, may "sound" friendly or angry.

Tone is the attitude or viewpoint that you show toward your subject. For example, a writer's tone may be amused or annoyed.

Controlling Writing Conventions

In addition to other criteria, readers will consider conventions of writing when they evaluate your Part A response: grammar, punctuation, spelling, and other such elements. By having as few grammatical and mechanical errors as possible, you will help your audience focus on what you've written and understand the points you've made. In other words, your ability to communicate clearly is directly tied to your ability to control writing conventions.

Watch for errors both as you write and as you reread what you've written. When you're finished writing, proofread your work. Try to make your first writing as "clean" as possible. Consider such questions as these:

PUNCTUATION

✔ Have I used commas, apostrophes, and periods where needed?

✔ Have I used quotation marks appropriately?

CAPITALIZATION

✔ Have I capitalized the first word of every sentence?

✔ Have I capitalized all proper nouns?

GRAMMAR

✔ Have I written complete sentences?

✔ Have I avoided run-on sentences?

✔ Do my subjects and verbs agree?

SPELLING

✔ Have I spelled words correctly?

✔ Have I used the words that I meant to use (for example, *your / you're, there / their, to / too, affect / effect*)?

The ◆ Basics

QUOTATION MARKS

Use quotation marks to let readers know that you are quoting the exact words of a speaker or writer. Also use quotation marks to set off some titles.

◆ Use quotation marks to set off a *direct* quotation—the exact words of a speaker or writer. Do not use quotation marks with an *indirect* quotation—a restatement, or *paraphrase*, of a speaker's or writer's words.

◆ Direct quotation: "Every citizen should vote," the governor declared in his speech.

◆ Indirect quotation: The governor said that voting is the responsibility of all citizens.

◆ Direct quotation: The author describes traffic noise as "a miserable plague on society."

◆ Indirect quotation: The author objects, saying that traffic noise is a terrible thing.

◆ Commas and periods at the end of a quotation always go *inside* the quotation marks.

    "Just be patient," Ms. Tanelli said.
    Ms. Tanelli advised us to "just be patient."

◆ Use quotation marks to set off titles of short works, such as poems, articles, essays, stories, and songs. For *longer* works, such as books, plays, magazines, newspapers, and movies, use underlining.

◆ Short works: "Dreams" (poem), "How to Shop for a Computer" (magazine article), "The Pit and the Pendulum" (story), "Yesterday" (song)

◆ Longer works: The Grapes of Wrath (book), The Crucible (play), Sports Illustrated (magazine), The New York Times (newspaper), Star Wars (movie)

Activity J: Proofreading

The following excerpt comes from a student's Part A response. The excerpt contains at least ten errors that involve conventions of writing. Proofread the student's response, and identify and correct the errors. Use the questions listed on page 66 to help you.

Its no surprise that pet food and supplies represent big business in the United States. After all, nearly 40 percent of U.S. homes have at least one dog, and well over 30 percent of homes have one cat or more, there are about 70 million pet cats in all and about 60 million pet dogs.

Pet owners spend countless dollars on their animals some of this money buys necesities, such as food and heath care. Other dollars goes toward everything from sweaters for dogs to hammocks for cats. Some pet owners even send greetings cards from one pet to another!

Except for major illness. The greatest pet-related expense for owners of cats and dogs is food. In fact, in 1997 America's pet lovers spent about $10 billion on cat and dog food.

According to Dr. Rachel Menlo, president of the Hasbrook Pet Hospital, the amount of "animal dollars" spent has gotten way out of hand. "People have lost their perspective", Dr. menlo said in a recent speech By way of example, she pointed out that some well-to-do families spend more money on dog food than other familys can afford to spend on feeding their children.

From Plan to Part A Response: Taking a First Look

You've learned about various aspects of planning and writing a Part A extended response. Now let's see how the plan from page 60 translates into a response.

Note: Paragraph numbers have been added for reference purposes. They are not part of the paper.

(1) Wearing seat belts is not just important. It's <u>essential</u>.

(2) Seat belts save lives and prevent injuries. In fact, about 9,000 people will die this year because they didn't take the time to buckle up. Thousands more will be injured. These <u>preventable</u> casualties will include both drivers and passengers, adults and children.

(3) In addition to human suffering, failure to wear seat belts costs a high price in other ways. The costs of health care and insurance are much higher than they would be if everyone wore a seat belt. For example, hospital expenses for treating crash victims who had not been wearing their seat belt run about 50 percent higher than for victims who had buckled up.

Furthermore, society pays about 85 percent of those expenses, not the crash victims.

(4)   So, what can we do to get drivers and passengers to wear seat belts? First, driver's education courses should stress seat-belt use. Wearing a seat belt should be taught as an essential safe-driving practice, just like other safety rules. Second, adults should make sure that everyone they're riding with is belted. They themselves should serve as models too by wearing a seat belt. This is especially true of drivers. Research has shown that when a driver doesn't wear a seat belt, over 75 percent of the time passengers don't wear their belts either.

(5)   But what about people who know they should wear seat belts but still don't? As Carolyn Hanig said in her talk, "the threat of serious injury or even death is not enough to persuade some people." The way to get through to these people is to pass more "standard" enforcement laws. Standard enforcement is stronger than "secondary" enforcement. It treats failure to wear a seat belt like any traffic offense. Under secondary enforcement, drivers first have to commit some other violation before they can be stopped and ticketed for not wearing a seat belt. In states with standard enforcement laws, seat-belt use is about 15 percent higher than in other states. In addition, if all states had standard enforcement, about 1,900 lives a year could be saved and almost 49,000 injuries prevented.

(6)   The two best ways to get drivers and passengers to wear seat belts is to stress the buckle-up message and to pass standard enforcement laws. By getting more people to wear seat belts, we can save lives, prevent needless injuries, and cut health-care and insurance costs.

Activity K: Evaluating a Response for Audience, Purpose, and Language

For each question, rate the student's response on a scale of 1 to 5, with 5 being the highest rating. Then give specific reasons for your rating.

1. How appropriate is the student's response for the intended audience?

Rating: _____

Reasons:

_____

_____

_____

2. How well has the student accomplished the intended purpose?

Rating: _____

Reasons:

_____

_____

_____

3. Has the student used language that is effective, engaging, and appropriate?

Rating: _____

Reasons:

_____

_____

_____

4. Has the student used a consistent voice and tone?

Rating: _____

Reasons:

_____

_____

_____

Q&A

How many paragraphs long should my extended response be?

There's no set answer to this question. Responses vary widely, and some students write much longer paragraphs than others. In general, however, the "typical" response to receive a high score is about four or five paragraphs long. Responses of only a paragraph or two usually don't score as high.

Note, too, that there's more to this question than just numbers. Over the years, you may have learned certain organizational "formulas," such as "the three-paragraph paper" or "the five-paragraph essay." Or, maybe you learned that papers should start with an introductory paragraph and end with a clear conclusion.

Such guidelines are certainly helpful. However, no one approach will work for every writing task. Don't try to impose a formula that makes your writing sound artificial. Instead, choose the approach that most effectively accomplishes your specific writing purpose.

From Plan to Part A Response: Looking More Closely

Let's look at the student's Part A response in more detail. In this response, the student organized a newsletter article into six paragraphs. Paragraphs 1 and 2 could have been combined into one. However, the student chose to break out the first two sentences as a separate opening paragraph in order to capture the reader's attention more effectively.

The student is writing for a twofold purpose: to inform readers why seat-belt use is important and to suggest how to get people to wear belts. In paragraphs 2, 3, 4, and 5, the student clearly develops the ideas and specific supporting information needed to achieve this purpose.

The student helps structure the response by beginning both paragraph 4 and paragraph 5 with a question. These questions act as transitions, guiding readers along. For example, the question, "what can we do to get drivers and passengers to wear seat belts?" serves as a bridge from paragraph 3 to paragraph 4, taking readers from the idea of why belts are important to the idea of how to get people to wear them.

The final paragraph summarizes the student's central point and serves as a strong conclusion for the article.

Note also the following points:

● Nearly all the ideas and supporting information in the article come directly from the student's plan. The student adjusted and expanded the plan wording as necessary.

● The student's response shows a thorough understanding of the listening selection and makes strong connections between the selection content and the writing task.

71

- The article's organization has a clear and logical flow. The student uses transitional words and phrases throughout the article to link ideas and help readers follow the structure.

- The student stays focused on the topic and does not include irrelevant ideas or information.

- Sentences are varied in structure and length, which helps to engage reader interest.

Start and End Strongly

Whether you're writing an article, an essay, or another type of composition, give extra attention to your first and last paragraphs. Your opening paragraph should hook readers and make them want to read more. Your final paragraph should leave readers with something to think about.

TIP

Activity L: Examining a Part A Response

Answer the following questions about the student's response.

1. Suppose the student had not wanted to begin paragraph 4 with a question. Write a topic sentence for paragraph 4 that the student might have used in place of the question.

_____

_____

_____

2. In paragraph 5, the student includes a direct quotation from the author, Carolyn Hanig. What main idea does this quotation help to support?

_____

_____

_____

3. Give three examples of transitional words or phrases. Explain what function each word or phrase serves. (You may want to refer back to the *Transitional Words and Phrases* chart on page 64.)

_____

_____

_____

4. Review the chart on page 55, *Scoring the Part A Extended Response*. If you were a reader evaluating the student's response, how would you rate it? Give specific reasons for your answer.

_____

_____

_____

Use All the Steps of the Writing Process

TIP

Remember that the writing process consists of *four* steps: prewriting, drafting, revising, and editing/proofreading. Carrying out those last two steps can make a big difference in the quality of your work.

Always reread and think about what you've written. Ask yourself how you can improve it. Look for ways to express your ideas as clearly and completely as possible.

Activity M: Writing an Extended Response

Using the plan you created in Activity F along with the suggestions and student examples provided in this section, write your own extended response on a separate sheet of paper. Look back at **Your Task** and **Guidelines** on page 57 before you write. Make revisions as needed and submit it to a classmate or teacher for evaluation based on the questions in Activity K on page 70.

5

CHAPTER REVIEW

Look back at the various lists, boldfaced items, boxes, and charts to quickly review many of the important ideas presented. You'll also find it helpful to review Chapter 1. Here are a few key points to get your review started:

- Read the prompt carefully, and think about each part of it. The prompt summarizes what you have to do for Part A, identifies your audience and purpose, and describes the extended response you will have to write.

- Listen actively to the selection your teacher reads. This means concentrating on what you hear and making a conscious effort to process the information.

- Take clear, concise, and complete notes as you listen. You can refer to your notes when you answer the multiple-choice questions and when you write your response.

- Plan before you write. Planning helps you organize your ideas and makes writing easier.

- To write an effective response, develop and support your ideas with specific and relevant information from the listening selection. Use the prompt to help you plan the most appropriate and logical organization.

- Remember that ideas and information important enough to be addressed by the multiple-choice questions may also be important enough to include in your written response.

PRACTICE FOR SESSION ONE, PART A

The test and activities that follow will give you an opportunity to practice and develop the skills you'll need to do well on Part A of the Regents English exam. But don't limit yourself to just these activities. Identify your particular strengths and weaknesses. If you know you need to improve in a certain area—taking notes, for example, or organizing a written response—practice on your own, or ask your teacher for help.

PRACTICE TEST (SESSION ONE, Part A)

NOTE: For this activity, you will need your teacher or a student to read the selection aloud.

Directions to READER:

1. Give students time to read the Part A prompt below.

2. Read aloud the selection that appears on pages 77–78.

3. Allow students a few minutes to review the prompt and look over their notes.

4. Read the selection a second time.

5. Give students time to clarify and expand their notes.

6. Direct students to answer the multiple-choice questions and then proceed to write their extended response.

Overview: For this part of the test, you will listen to a speech about alternative sources for paper, answer some multiple-choice questions, and write a response based on the situation described below. You will hear the talk twice. You may take notes anytime you wish during the readings.

> **The Situation:** As president of the Environmental Awareness Club, you have been asked to prepare an article for the Earth Day edition of the junior high school newspaper, making students aware of possible alternatives to trees as a source for paper. In preparation for writing your article, listen to a speech about so-called tree-free papers. Then use relevant information from the speech to write your article.

Your Task: Write an article for the Earth Day edition of the junior high school newspaper using relevant information from the speech to explain that there are alternatives to trees as a source for paper.

Guidelines:

Be sure to
- Tell your audience what they need to know to help them understand the alternatives to trees as a source for paper
- Use specific, accurate, and relevant information from the talk to support your discussion
- Use a tone and level of language appropriate for an article for a junior high school newspaper
- Organize your ideas in a logical and coherent manner
- Indicate any words taken directly from the talk by using quotation marks or referring to the speaker
- Follow the conventions of standard written English

Multiple-Choice Questions

Directions (1–6): Use your notes to answer the following questions about the passage read to you. Select the best suggested answer and circle its number. The questions may help you think about ideas and information you might use in your writing. You may return to these questions anytime you wish.

1 Papers that are "tree-free"

   1 don't cost anything
   2 are not made from wood fibers
   3 come from government-owned forests
   4 are manufactured only in foreign countries

2 The speaker identifies all of the following as possible benefits of making paper from sources other than trees except

   1 reduced deforestation
   2 decreased use of pesticides and other chemicals
   3 more jobs for agricultural workers
   4 increased industrial production

3 The speaker implies that

   1 trees will no longer be used for papermaking in the future
   2 tree-free paper is likely to become more widely accepted
   3 tree-free paper is the best paper for printing office documents
   4 the use of tree-free paper will eliminate agricultural waste

4 The speaker points out that kenaf is

   1 a useful alternative resource but one with limited availability

   2 a highly profitable source of writing paper
   3 a fiber that was widely used in paper production before 1870
   4 a crop that will probably replace cotton and okra

5 According to the speaker, agricultural wastes

   1 have already replaced wood fiber as the main papermaking source
   2 are less promising than crop fibers as an alternative paper source
   3 are in short supply
   4 are available in many parts of the country for use in making paper products

6 What is the most likely reason that the speaker talks about elephant-dung paper?

   1 to show that Zambia's paper industry is more efficient than that of the United States
   2 to illustrate how paper companies are seeking new ways to increase their profits
   3 to emphasize that there are many papermaking alternatives to cutting down trees
   4 to demonstrate that elephants can play a key role in the papermaking industry

---

After you have finished these questions, review **The Situation** and read **Your Task** and the **Guidelines**. Use scrap paper to plan your response. Then write your response.

STOP! DO NOT READ THE SELECTION BELOW. YOUR TEACHER WILL READ IT ALOUD.

Tree-Free Papers Are Taking Root

When most people hear about paper made from fibers other than wood, their first reaction is, "If it's not made from wood, what's it made from?"

The answer: Just about anything, it seems.

For years, a handful of companies have been refining papermaking using a wide range of fibers derived from plants, or from agricultural or manufacturing waste products. The idea is that doing so may reduce deforestation; use fewer pesticides, herbicides, bleaches, and other potentially problematic chemicals; and possibly generate jobs for loggers, cotton growers, tobacco farmers, and others in troubled agricultural sectors.

Tree-free papers that were once found only in natural-products stores or gift catalogs are slowly but surely taking root in mainstream commerce. Major newspapers are now testing paper made in part from non-wood fibers. Some of the world's largest paper companies, including Weyerhaeuser, International Paper and Crane, are experimenting with papers made from alternative resources.

Tree-free fibers fall into two distinct categories:

annual crop fibers, notably kenaf, a herbaceous annual related to cotton and okra, whose plants can reach 12–18 feet in about five months.

agricultural wastes, including everything from grasses and grain stalks to corn starch and sugar beets. These represent a lot of untapped fibers: some 160 million tons of ag wastes are burned or landfilled each year, says the U.S. EPA. Some states, like California, have banned further burning of these wastes.

Tree-free advocates are quick to point out that wood fibers have been used only for the past 125 or so years to make paper. Prior to 1870, most paper was made from hemp or flax fibers, or cotton fibers from rags or fabric scraps.

No organization is yet calculating sales figures for tree-free papers. The American Forest Products Association, the paper industry's principal trade group, barely acknowledges tree-free's existence. Indeed, it hasn't made much of a dent in the market. My estimate puts North American tree-free paper sales at well under 2,000 tons a year—less than 0.01% of the roughly 30 million tons of printing and writing paper sold in a typical year.

Still, a growing number of companies are finding a role for tree-free paper. Bank of America, Esprit, Patagonia, Bridgestone Bicycles, Fetzer Vineyards, J.C. Penney, The Gap, and Sony are among those that have used tree-free papers in company documents. Kinko's, the copying and printing chain, offers tree-free papers at select stores, and is evaluating the potential for expanded use.

Crops vs. Wastes

The differences between crop fibers and ag wastes are significant, as far as their economic viability and environmental impacts. According to a variety of experts, ag wastes present far more opportunities and far fewer challenges.

Consider kenaf; at first glance, it appears attractive: It can produce up to five times as much dry fiber per acre as Southern pine, according to the U.S. Agricultural Department data. But this simple comparison doesn't reflect all of the tradeoffs between any two fiber sources. In any given situation, one must evaluate the entire process of growing, harvesting and processing fiber to identify the greenest alternative. Only a few regions of the country have the ideal growing conditions for kenaf. In contrast, many regions have a steady supply of agricultural waste that could be turned into valuable paper products. And sometimes, environmental experts still pick a well-managed forest as the best source of fiber for paper, safeguarding biodiversity, while using the least energy and fewest chemicals to produce paper.

Kenaf can also play a special role in increasing paper recycling. "I see kenaf as an incredible enhancer," says Emily Miggins, director of Rethink Paper, an initiative of the San Francisco-based Earth Island Institute that works with industry, nonprofits, and others to reduce the use of virgin wood fiber in the U.S. paper industry. She explains that kenaf's superior tensile and tear strength make it ideal to mix with lowgrade, mixed-paper waste — "junk mail," newsprint and the like. "Throw in 15% to 25% kenaf and you can bring that waste paper back to its original life," she says.

Meanwhile, a succession of ecoentrepreneurs are demonstrating just how many ingredients can substitute for tree-based fibers. You can now buy paper made from bamboo, banana stalks, cereal straw, coffee bean residue, denim scraps, hemp, old money and sugar cane, among many other things.

And then there's Dale Lewis, proprietor of Matuvi Paper Works, in Zambia's Luangwa Valley. Lewis, a Wildlife Conservation Society researcher, has worked with native people to make paper using office paper, cardboard — and elephant dung.

It's scarcely a vision of the future. The dung-paper is intended primarily to underscore the value of living elephants to the local economy. But it also demonstrates that the fibers of tomorrow can come from the trunk of more than one living thing.

—Joel Makower

Evaluating a Part A Response

Exchange papers with a partner. Referring to the chart on page 55, *Scoring the Part A Extended Response,* evaluate your partner's written response on the basis of the five criteria.

Be as *positive, constructive, and specific* as you can in your comments and suggestions. Your goal is to help your partner improve his or her skills.

MEANING:_____

_____

_____

_____

DEVELOPMENT:_____

_____

_____

_____

ORGANIZATION:_____

_____

_____

_____

LANGUAGE USE:_____

_____

_____

_____

CONVENTIONS:_____

_____

_____

_____

Improving and Polishing Your Part A Response

Use your partner's comments to help you revise, edit, and polish your paper. Make whatever changes you think are necessary to improve your work.

For additional practice, two actual Regents exams appear at the end of this book.

CHAPTER 3

Reading and Writing for Information and Understanding

1

UNDERSTANDING THE SESSION ONE, PART B TASKS

For Session One, Part B of the Regents Comprehensive Examination in English, you will read an informational selection accompanied by one or more graphs, charts, diagrams, or other visual materials. The text and the visual materials are meant to work together. You may take notes as you read the selection and look at the visual materials.

Next, you'll answer ten multiple-choice questions about the selection and the related visual materials. Finally, you'll write an extended response—such as an article or essay—based on your understanding and analysis of the information.

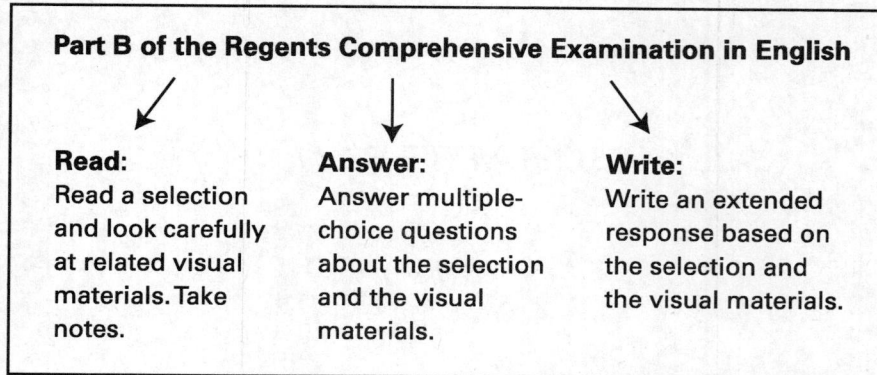

Part B of the Regents Comprehensive Examination in English

Read:	**Answer:**	**Write:**
Read a selection and look carefully at related visual materials. Take notes.	Answer multiple-choice questions about the selection and the visual materials.	Write an extended response based on the selection and the visual materials.

☀ A QUICK LOOK ☀

What is Part B testing me on?

Part B tests your ability to understand, analyze, and respond to information from two sources, one textual, the other visual.

How is Part B similar to other parts of the exam?

Part B, like most other parts, requires you to answer multiple-choice questions and then write an extended response. Part B has several more questions than Part A.

How does Part B differ from other parts of the exam?

Part B is the only part of the test that requires you to respond to a combination of textual and visual materials.

Examining the Session One, Part B Prompt

Part B of the Regents exam resembles Part A. However, while in Part A of the actual test you never see the oral selection in print, Part B includes the actual reading selection.

Look at the typical Part B prompt below. It consists of six elements:

- Directions
- The Situation
- Your Task
- Guidelines
- The reading selection with related visual materials
- Multiple-choice questions about the selection and the visual materials (Note: The multiple-choice questions appear on pages 132 and 133.)

*NOTE: For now, just look over the prompt to get a feel for it. **Do not read the selection yet**. You will refer back to this prompt and the selection later in the chapter.*

PART B

Directions: Read the article and study the diagrams on the following pages, answer the multiple-choice questions, and write a response based on the situation described below. You may use the margins to take notes as you read and scrap paper to plan your response.

The Situation: A newspaper editorial poked fun at people for taking too seriously the idea that an asteroid could collide with Earth. The editorial writer told readers not to "mistake Hollywood fiction for fact" and insisted that "there's nothing we can do about such things anyway." You decided to write a reply to the editorial, discussing the very real danger that asteroids pose and explaining that there are actions to be taken.

Your Task: Write a response to the newspaper editorial. Using relevant information from the article *and* the diagrams, discuss the danger that asteroids pose and how to deal with it.

Guidelines:

Be sure to
- Tell your audience what they need to know about the danger that asteroids pose to Earth
- Discuss appropriate actions to prepare for and deal with this danger
- Use specific, accurate, and relevant information from the article *and* the diagrams to support your discussion
- Use a tone and level of language appropriate for a newspaper
- Organize your ideas in a logical and coherent manner
- Indicate any words taken directly from the article by using quotation marks or referring to the author
- Follow the conventions of standard written English

Whew!

The mile-wide asteroid heading for Earth proved to be a cosmic false alarm, but that's no reason not to start planning for the next one

"It scares me," said Jack Hills, an astronomer at the Los Alamos National Laboratory. "It really does." He and the rest of the world had good reason to be worried. Astronomer Brian Marsden at the Harvard-Smithsonian Center for Astrophysics had just announced that a newly discovered asteroid a mile wide
5   was headed for Earth and might pass as close as 30,000 miles in the year 2028.

"The chance of an actual collision is small," Marsden reported, "but not entirely out of the question."

An actual collision? With a mile-wide asteroid? It sounded like the stuff of science fiction and grade-B movies. But front-page stories and TV news-
10 casts around the world soon made clear that the possibility of a direct hit and a global catastrophe well within the lifetime of most people on Earth today was all too real.

Then suddenly, the danger was gone. Barely a day later, new data and new calculations showed that the asteroid, dubbed 1997 XF11, presented no threat
15 at all. It would miss Earth by 600,000 miles—closer than any previously observed asteroid of that size but a comfortable distance. Still, the incident focused attention once and for all on the largely ignored danger that asteroids and comets pose to life on Earth. As Los Alamos senior scientist Greg Ca-navan put it, paraphrasing Dr. Samuel Johnson, "Nothing so clears the mind
20 as the sight of the gallows."

XF11 was discovered last Dec. 6 by astronomer Jim Scotti, a member of the University of Arizona's Spacewatch group, which scans the skies for un-discovered comets and asteroids. Using a 77-year-old telescope equipped with an electronic camera, he had recorded three sets of images, 30 minutes apart,
25 of a small sector of the night sky. The digitized images, fed into a computer programmed to look for objects moving against the background of fixed stars, revealed an asteroid that Scotti, in an E-mail to Marsden, described as stand-ing out "like a sore thumb."

Marsden promptly posted Scotti's data on the Harvard Center's Website,
30 making them available to other astronomers. In early March, those data and newer observations by two Japanese amateur astronomers and a Texas scien-tist were fed into the Harvard Center's number-crunching orbit predictor, which spat out the 30,000-mile "miss distance" that led Marsden to make his dramatic announcement.

35 For a brief but exciting 24 hours, the big asteroid commanded everyone's attention. Astronomer Hills calculated that an asteroid the size of XF11 col-liding with Earth at more than 38,000 m.p.h. would explode with the energy of 300,000 megatons—nearly 20 million times the force of the bomb that leveled Hiroshima. If it hit in the ocean, he predicted, it would cause a tsunami
40 (commonly called a tidal wave) hundreds of feet high, flooding the coastlines of surrounding continents. "Where cities stood," he said, "there would be only mudflats." A land hit, he calculated, would blast out a crater at least 30 miles across and throw up a blanket of dust and vapor that would blot out the sun "for weeks, if not months."

45 Then, as abruptly as the asteroid mania began, it was over. Jet Propulsion Lab astronomer Eleanor Helin, rummaging through some photographic plates taken in 1990, found previously overlooked images of XF11. Combining the asteroid's position eight years ago with the current readings, three groups working independently arrived at the same conclusion: the miss distance was

50   actually 600,000 miles, and the chance of XF11's hitting Earth in 2028 was zero, or as JPL astronomer Don Yeomans declared, "less than zero."

The worldwide sigh of relief was almost palpable. The threat of asteroid strikes, however, still looms over the planet, which has been hit many times in the past by large objects raining down from space. Evidence of these ancient

55   impacts is everywhere: more than 150 craters pock Earth's surface, some clearly visible, some that can be seen only from aircraft or satellites, others long buried or on the ocean bottom.

By far the most notorious of these craters is the circular feature 120 miles in diameter discovered below the northern tip of Mexico's Yucatán Peninsula.

60   This monster crater is believed to be the impact site of a six-to-eight-mile-wide comet or asteroid that struck 65 million years ago and wiped out the dinosaurs and some 70% of Earth's other species.

While these catastrophic events seem remote and unreal, there are plenty of more recent reminders that Earth's neighborhood in space is still teeming

65   with mountain-size rocks and the occasional wayward comet. Arizona's spectacular Meteor Crater, for one, was gouged out only 50,000 years ago by an iron asteroid. The impact and explosion blasted a hole nearly three-quarters of a mile across and 700 feet deep. Today it could destroy a city.

Much more recently, in 1908, an asteroid or a chunk of a comet less than

70   200 feet across roared into the atmosphere and exploded some five miles above the unpopulated Tunguska region of Siberia. The blast, estimated at tens of megatons, devastated an area of several hundred square miles, knocking down trees, starting fires and killing reindeer. Had it occurred over a large city, hundreds of thousands would have died.

75   And two years ago, an asteroid about 1,500 feet across was discovered just four days before it sped by at 58,000 m.p.h., missing Earth by only 280,000 miles. If it had hit, the resulting explosion would have been in the 3,000-to-12,000-megaton range—equivalent, as the late astronomer Gene Shoemaker put it, to "taking all of the U.S. and Soviet nuclear weapons, putting them in a

80   pile and blowing them up."

Scientists agree that it is only a matter of time before another celestial hulk hits home. "It's like a game of cosmic darts," said astronomer Clark Chapman on the PBS show *Nova*. "It could just as likely happen tomorrow as some day 300,000 years from now."

85   But what really worries astronomers is the devil they don't know. While they estimate that perhaps as many as 2,000 asteroids larger than a kilometer (six-tenths of a mile) across either cross or come close to Earth's orbit, they have discovered and tracked fewer than 200 of them. "We simply don't know where the other objects are," says JPL astronomer Helin. "But the ones that

90   have been discovered," she warns, "certainly suggest that we could someday face a surprise encounter with a large, unseen object." The significance of the kilometer size? An impact of anything that large, scientists believe, would cause not just a regional but a global catastrophe.

95   Almost as worrisome are the estimated 300,000 asteroids larger than 300 feet wide that also come perilously near or intersect Earth's orbit; each could inflict Tunguska-like damage over a large region. The number of Earth-crossing asteroids larger than 60 feet across, says University of Arizona astronomer Tom Gehrels, could be as high as 100 million. A hit by any one of them could destroy a large city.

100   Gehrels heads Spacewatch, Scotti's astronomy group and one of two such teams dedicated exclusively to the discovery of threatening "near-Earth objects" (NEOS). The other group, called NEAT (for near-Earth asteroid tracking), is run by Helin and uses an Air Force telescope atop a mountain on Maui, Hawaii.

105   Strapped for funds—NASA contributes only $1.8 million annually to asteroid hunting—astronomers fear it will take decades to discover most of the larger objects. With only a few million more dollars a year, they say, and with access to the other two Air Force satellite-tracking telescopes, most of the kilometer-wide and larger asteroids could be identified and tracked within 10
110   years.

    What if one or more of these asteroids are found to be a serious threat? Scientists generally agree on the best strategy for avoiding disaster: launch a rocket to intercept the intruder and, at the very least, change its orbit. If the asteroid is small and detected many years and orbits before its predicted
115   impact, the solution would be straightforward. "You apply some modest impulse to the asteroid at its closest approach to the sun," says Los Alamos' Canavan. "The slight deflection that results will amplify during each orbit, ensuring that the asteroid misses Earth by a wide margin." That little push, he notes, could be provided by conventional high explosives.

120   For objects 300 feet or larger and detected late in the game, however, nuclear weapons may well be the only answer. If XF11 had been discovered only 90 million miles away and on a beeline toward Earth, for example, the equivalent of a 1-megaton explosion would have been necessary to shove it into a safe orbit. Had it first been spotted at just a tenth of that distance, a
125   100-megaton blast would have been needed to turn it away.

    If the incoming asteroid is composed largely of iron, a nearby or even a surface explosion would present no problem. But if the asteroid is rocky, a blast, particularly an ill-planned one, might well shatter it into chunks, each a potential danger to a terrestrial region or metropolitan area.

130   For that reason, Earth's defenders, if they have the luxury of time, would prefer to send a robot craft to rendezvous with a threatening asteroid and determine its composition and mechanical strength before dispatching a nuke to the scene. Physicist Edward Teller suggests that this is what we should do, just for practice, when XF11 passes far from Earth two years from now. Other
135   defensive plans being bandied about at the Los Alamos and Lawrence Livermore national labs involve more exotic devices, such as neutron bombs or netlike arrays of interconnected tungsten balls.

140

Yet none of these defensive measures can be effective without adequate warning. And given the large numbers of undiscovered NEOS still out there, says David Morrison at NASA's Ames Research Center, an asteroid strike could take place with far less than a 30-year warning. Indeed, says Morrison ominously, "the most likely warning time would be zero." —*With reporting by Dan Cray/Los Angeles and Dick Thompson/ Washington*

—Leon Jaroff

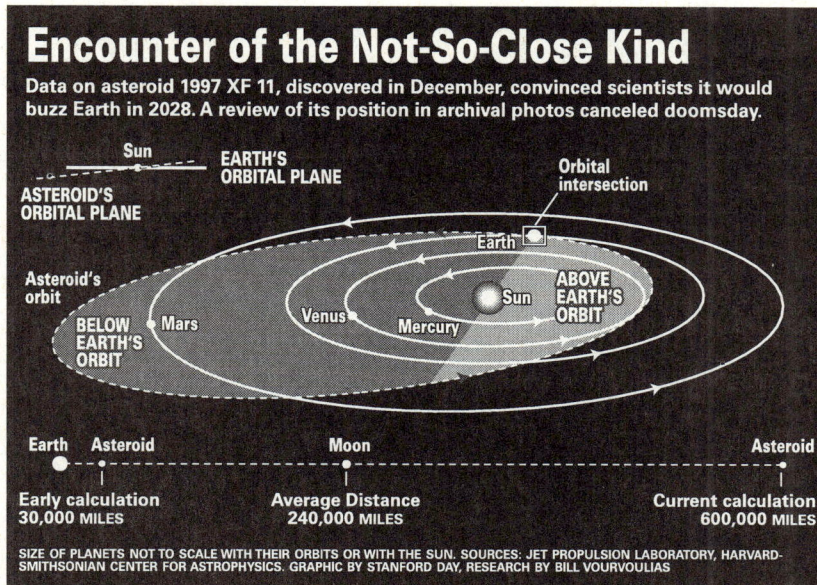

Diagram 1

Diagram 2

As in Part A, each element of the prompt has a specific purpose:

- **Directions** summarizes the tasks you'll do for Part B.
- **The Situation, Your Task,** and **Guidelines** describe in detail the extended response you will write.
- *The reading selection and related visual materials* serve as your information source for both the multiple-choice questions and the written response.
- The *multiple-choice questions* highlight key information and ideas in both the selection and the visual materials.

Let's look at these elements more closely.

Directions provides an overview. For this prompt, you'll have four tasks: (1) read an article, (2) study diagrams, (3) answer questions about the article and the diagrams, and (4) write a response.

> **Directions**: Read the article and study the diagrams on the following pages, answer the multiple-choice questions, and write a response based on the situation described below. You may use the margins to take notes as you read and use scrap paper to plan your response.

Note that the prompt tells you to *study* the diagrams. This is important, because *the readers who score your Part B response will expect you to combine information from both the textual and visual materials.*

The prompt also suggests that you take notes as you read. As in Part A, you can refer to your notes both when you answer the multiple-choice questions and when you write your response.

The next parts of the prompt describe the particular situation, state your writing task, and define your audience:

The Situation: A newspaper editorial poked fun at people for taking too seriously the idea that an asteroid could collide with Earth. The editorial writer told readers not to "mistake Hollywood fiction for fact" and insisted that "there's nothing we can do about such things anyway." You decided to write a reply to the editorial, discussing the very real danger that asteroids pose and explaining that there are actions to be taken.

Your Task: Write a response to the newspaper editorial. Using relevant information from the article **and** the diagrams, discuss the danger that asteroids pose and how to deal with it.

Note that the word *and* is in boldface type. This is a reminder that you must use information from both textual *and* visual materials to do well on Part B of the Regents exam.

Practice Synthesizing Information

TIP

Synthesize means to "combine parts or elements into one whole." For Part B of the Regents exam, you have to synthesize information from two sources: a reading selection and a graph, diagram, table, or other visual material.

Practice synthesizing information whenever you read a textbook, magazine, or newspaper. Think about how the textual and visual materials work together. What do the visual materials add to the text? How does combining textual with visual information make ideas and information easier to understand?

The Part B prompt may identify your audience specifically, or you may have to *infer* who your audience is. For example, in this case you will be writing for a "local newspaper," so you can assume your audience consists of adults and young people in the general population.

? *Complete the sentence:* To "infer who your audience is," you need to combine information you read in the prompt with your own _____ to make an educated guess.

After **Your Task**, the prompt provides specific writing guidelines. As you know from the previous chapter, these guidelines relate to the five scoring criteria: meaning, development, organization, language use, and conventions.

Guidelines:

Be sure to

- Tell your audience what they need to know about the danger that asteroids pose to Earth
- Discuss appropriate actions to prepare for and deal with this danger
- Use specific, accurate, and relevant information from the article *and* the diagrams to support your discussion
- Use a tone and level of language appropriate for a newspaper
- Organize your ideas in a logical and coherent manner
- Indicate any words taken directly from the article by using quotation marks or referring to the author
- Follow the conventions of standard written English

The first two items on this list clarify your writing task as well as your writing purpose. For this prompt, your writing purpose is to inform readers about the danger posed by asteroids and discuss how "to prepare for and deal with this danger."

The remaining guidelines on the list are essentially the same as the guidelines in the Part A prompt. The only important difference is the reference here to using *two* sources of information—"article and diagrams"—rather than one.

After the reading selection and accompanying visuals, the last section of Part B consists of eight to ten multiple-choice questions. As in Part A, this section has its own directions, reminding you that the multiple-choice questions may prove helpful when you write your response:

Directions: Answer the following questions. The questions may help you think about ideas and information you might use in your writing. You may return to these questions anytime you wish.

Following the multiple-choice questions, the prompt advises you to "review *Your Task* and the *Guidelines*" and to use scrap paper to plan before writing your response.

Activity A: Examining a Part B Prompt

A portion of a Part B prompt appears below. Read the prompt, and answer the questions that follow.

Directions: Read the text and study the graphs on the following pages, answer the multiple-choice questions, and write a response based on the situation described below. You may use the margins to take notes as you read. You may use scrap paper to plan your response.

The Situation: A statewide anti-drug organization has invited high school students to submit essays for its magazine. You decided to write an essay discussing causes of teenage drug use and approaches to counteract these causes.

Your Task: Write an essay for the antidrug group's magazine. Using relevant information from the text *and* the graphs, discuss causes of teenage drug use and approaches to counteract these causes.

Guidelines:

Be sure to

- Tell your audience what they need to know about causes of teenage drug use
- Discuss approaches to counteract causes of teenage drug use
- Use specific, accurate, and relevant information from the text *and* the graphs to develop your discussion

1. What are your two sources of information for both the multiple-choice questions and the written response?

   _____

   _____

   _____

2. What four tasks does the **Directions** paragraph explain that you will have to do?

   _____

   _____

3. What is your specific writing task?

_____

_____

_____

4. For what audience will you be writing?

_____

_____

5. What is your writing purpose?

_____

_____

_____

2

EFFECTIVE READING AND NOTE-TAKING FOR PART B

In the previous chapter, you learned strategies to help you take notes while *listening* to the Part A oral presentation. You can use, or adapt, many of the same strategies as you read the selection and study the visuals for Part B of the Regents exam.

Strategies for Reading the Part B Selection

Remember that the reading selection and the visual materials work together. Here are some suggestions to help you get the most from both:

▶ **Keep in mind *why* you're reading.** Before reading the selection, be sure you fully understand the prompt. The prompt makes clear your purpose for reading. After reading the prompt, jot down your specific writing task, your audience, and your writing purpose, just as you did for Part A. Here's an example based on the prompt you saw in *Activity A* on page 93:

TASK: write essay for a magazine

AUDIENCE: general population, mainly adults

PURPOSE: inform readers about causes of teenage drug use and

approaches to counteract these causes

▶ **Skim the multiple-choice questions.** *Before* reading the selection, take a minute to look over the multiple-choice questions. They will alert you to important information to watch for as you read the selection and study the visual materials.

▶ **Read with care.** Think about the central point of the selection. Identify main ideas, and look for important supporting facts and details in the text *and* in the visual materials.

▶ **Reread portions of text that are not clear to you.** Don't skip sentences or paragraphs that seem difficult. Instead, reread them and try to grasp their meaning. You may need to reread some portions of text more than once.

Note-Taking Tips for Part B

Unlike Part A, Part B gives you the actual selection to read. So you may be wondering: *If I have the selection, why should I bother to take notes?*

The notes you take will help you zero in on key parts of the text and quickly identify the most significant ideas and information. Furthermore, the process of taking notes will help you better understand what you're reading.

Here's how to use your note-taking skills to do your best on Part B of the Regents exam:

▶ **Be organized.** As in Part A, use a simple outline form. Your outline for Part B can be less detailed than your outline for Part A because you have the actual selection to refer to.

▶ **Be concise.** Keep your notes brief, simple, and clear. Write words and phrases that will help you focus on *the most important* ideas and information in the selection and the visual materials.

▶ **Underline or circle information.** You may find it helpful to underline important points in the selection itself. However, don't get carried away and underline *too many lines*.

▶ **Highlight connections between text and visual materials.** Make note of places in the text that link directly to the visual materials. For example, suppose you have a graph showing population growth in New York. As you read the selection, you come upon a paragraph that describes New York's population growth. In the margin next to that paragraph, jot down something like, *See graph!*

▶ **Use shortcuts.** Remember to use abbreviations and symbols rather than whole words.

Clear notes:
easy to read and understand

Concise notes:
brief and to the point

**Three C's of
Effective Note-Taking**

Complete notes:
include the most important
ideas and information

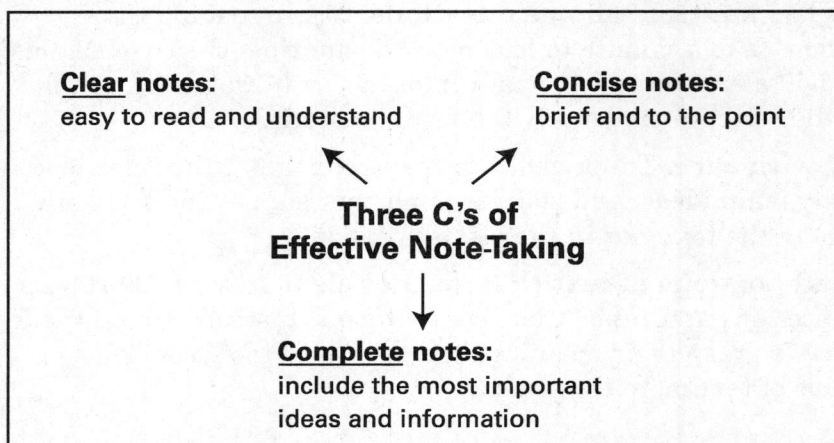

Activity B: Identifying Task, Audience, and Purpose

Carefully review the prompt that appears on page 85. Identify the specific writing task, audience, and writing purpose. (You may want to look back at the example on page 21.)

*TASK:*_____

_____

*AUDIENCE:*_____

_____

*PURPOSE:*_____

_____

Keeping Notes Brief

To keep your notes for the Part B reading selection brief, you need to be selective about what you write. Your goal is to jot down as little as possible—but enough to be helpful.

Read paragraphs 1–6 of the selection—reproduced below—and compare the text with the sample student notes taken in the margin. What information does the student include? What does the student omit? What shortcuts does the student use?

Whew!

Astron said asteroid headed for Earth

—1 mi. wide

The mile-wide asteroid heading for Earth proved to be a cosmic false alarm, but that's no reason not to start planning for the next one

    "It scares me," said Jack Hills, an astronomer at the Los Alamos National Laboratory. "It really does." He and the rest of the world had good reason to be worried. Astronomer Brian Marsden at the Harvard-Smithsonian Center for Astrophysics had just announced that a newly discovered asteroid a mile wide was headed for Earth and might pass as close as 30,000 miles in the year 2028. "The chance of an actual collision is small," Marsden reported, "but not entirely out of the question."

—pass within 30,000 mi. in 2028

An actual collision? With a mile-wide asteroid? It sounded like the stuff of science fiction and grade-B movies. But front-page stories and TV newscasts around the world soon made clear that the possibility of a direct hit and a global catastrophe well within the lifetime of most people on Earth today was all too real.

—chance of <u>collision</u>, "global catastrophe"

Then suddenly, the danger was gone. Barely a day later, new data and new calculations showed that the asteroid, dubbed 1997 XF11, presented no threat at all. It would miss Earth by 600,000 miles—closer than any previously observed asteroid of that size but a comfortable distance. Still, the incident focused attention once and for all on the largely ignored danger that asteroids and comets pose to life on Earth. As Los Alamos senior scientist Greg Canavan put it, paraphrasing Dr. Samuel Johnson, "Nothing so clears the mind as the sight of the gallows."

Revised est. would miss by 600,000 mi.

—"comfortable distance" but closer than any other big asteroid

—showed that <u>danger</u> is real

XF11 was discovered last Dec. 6 by astronomer Jim Scotti, a member of the University of Arizona's Spacewatch group, which scans the skies for undiscovered comets and asteroids. Using a 77-year-old telescope equipped with an electronic camera, he had recorded three sets of images, 30 minutes apart, of a small sector of the night sky. The digitized images, fed into a computer programmed to look for objects moving against the background of fixed stars, revealed an asteroid that Scotti, in an E-mail to Marsden, described as standing out "like a sore thumb."

Marsden promptly posted Scotti's data on the Harvard Center's Website, making them available to other astronomers. In early March, those data and newer observations by two Japanese amateur astronomers and a Texas scientist were fed into the Harvard Center's number-crunching orbit predictor, which spat out the 30,000-mile "miss distance" that led Marsden to make his dramatic announcement.

For a brief but exciting 24 hours, the big asteroid commanded everyone's attention. Astronomer Hills calculated that an asteroid the size of XF11 colliding with Earth at more than 38,000 m.p.h. would explode with the energy of 300,000 megatons—nearly 20 million times the force of the bomb that leveled Hiroshima. If it hit in the ocean, he predicted, it would cause a tsunami (commonly called a tidal wave) hundreds of feet high, flooding the coastlines of surrounding continents. "Where cities stood," he said, "there would be only mudflats." A land hit, he calculated, would blast out a crater at least 30 miles across and throw up a blanket of dust and vapor that would blot out the sun "for weeks, if not months."

—Hit at 38,000 mph would explode w/energy of 300,000 megatons

—20 mill times Hirosh bomb!

—hit ocean: huge tidal wave

—hit land: 30 mi. crater & dust block sun for weeks/ months

As you compare the marginal notes with the actual selection, note the following important points:

- The student reduced six paragraphs to these lines of notes.

- The student included only what was most important and relevant: key words and phrases, main ideas, important facts and details.

- The student did not take notes for every paragraph. For example, the student made no specific notes for paragraphs 4 and 5 because the student did not think they had any information important enough to write down.

- The notes are concisely written. The student used phrases rather than whole sentences, and also shortened or abbreviated words.

- The student used quotation marks to identify direct quotations (the writer's exact words).

Make Note of Key Terms and Examples

TIP

When taking notes, write down the meaning of key terms that are new to you. You'll also find it useful to include an example or two, as appropriate. For instance, as you read a science selection, you might jot down the definition of *cloning*, along with a couple of examples of animals that scientists have successfully cloned.

Activity C: Taking Notes

Read and take notes for the selection on pages 85–89. You may write your notes in the margin or on separate paper. (For paragraphs 1–6, take your own notes or use those that appear above.) Use the strategies you've learned for effective reading and note-taking. You will refer back to your notes later in this chapter.

Activity D: Improving Note-Taking Skills

Pair up with another student. Exchange the notes you took for *Activity C*, and evaluate each other's work. Be constructive and specific in your comments and suggestions. Your goal is to help your partner improve his or her skills. Here are some guidelines:

- Do the notes accurately reflect the selection's most important and relevant ideas and information? What ideas and information should be included but are not?

- Are the notes as concise as they might be? How could they be made more concise?

- Are the notes well organized? How could the organization be improved?

- Are the notes clear and easy to understand? How could they be made clearer?

3

OBTAINING INFORMATION FROM VISUAL MATERIALS

Visual materials support, illustrate, or otherwise complement reading selections. Part B of the Regents exam may include any of a wide range of visual materials. You may, for example, see one or more of the following:

- a line graph, bar graph, pie chart, or pictograph

- a diagram, table, or chart

- some other kind of visual, such as a picture, map, or schedule

All these visual materials have one thing in common: they present information. Carefully studying these visual materials will enable you to understand, analyze, and interpret the information they present—and use it when you write your response.

Applying the Basics

The kinds of visual materials that appear on the Regents exam will be familiar to you. You've seen similar materials in textbooks, newspapers, and magazines.

You can apply the following guidelines to any visual material you'll find on the Regents exam:

▶ **Get a sense of the whole.** Begin by reading the title and looking over the visual material. Ask yourself what kind of information is being presented. Try to get a clear sense of the *whole* before studying its parts.

▶ **Read the printed words.** Read any captions, descriptive labels, headings, or subheadings.

▶ **Watch for explanations**. Look for such explanatory items as footnotes, keys, and distance scales.

▶ **Consider the purpose.** Think about the *purpose* of the visual material and its *relationship* to the reading selection. Why is the visual material there? What information does it add to the text? Does it help you visualize a concept? Does it clarify information that appears in the text?

Understanding Graphs

Graphs present numerical information visually. They help you "see" what numbers or statistics mean. Graphs can show:

- when a trend is increasing, decreasing, or remaining the same.
- how quantities change over time.
- how one kind of *data* (information) relates to, or compares with, another.

There are several different kinds of graphs: line graphs, bar graphs, circle graphs, and pictographs.

In a **line graph**, points represent data. These points are connected by a line to illustrate a trend. Some line graphs contain more than one line, so you can compare two related trends.

In the line graph that follows, one line shows the growth of the total U.S. population from 1950 to 2000. The other line shows the growth in labor force (people working or looking for work). Notice that the abbreviation *(est)* under the year 2000 tells you that the data for that year is estimated.

Increases in Size of the U.S. Population and Labor Force

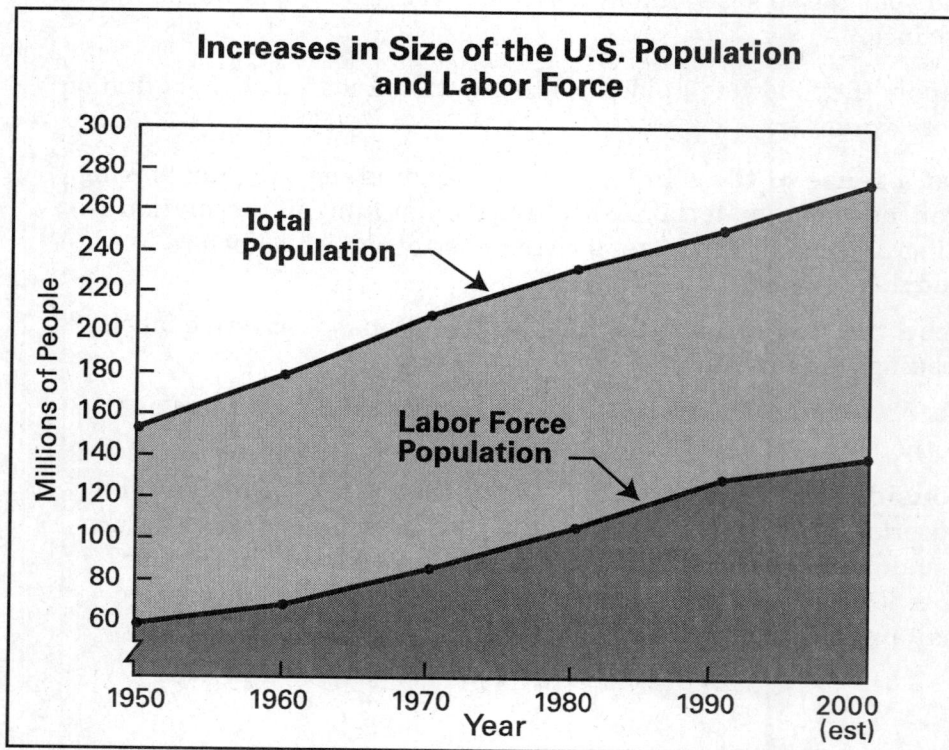

LINE GRAPH

100

Activity E: Interpreting a Line Graph

Use the line graph above to answer the questions.

1. As the U.S. population has grown, what has happened to the labor force?

   _____

   _____

2. Between 1990 and 2000, the total population is estimated to grow from about 250 million to about 275 million. During that same period, what is expected to happen to the labor force population?

   _____

   _____

Pay Attention to Units of Data

Graphs use many different units of data. For example, a graph may express data in terms of *dollars, tons,* or *miles.* Graphs also differ in amounts shown. For instance, a financial graph may express money in *dollars, thousands of dollars,* or *millions of dollars.* Similarly, a graph may represent changes that occurred over a time period of *months, years,* or even *centuries.* Graphs may show actual amounts, estimated amounts, or a combination of both.

Always study graphs carefully, and think about what specific units of data are shown.

TIP

A **bar graph** uses horizontal or vertical bars to represent data. Two examples appear below. Notice that the second bar graph includes an explanatory key.

Fastest-Growing Occupations, 1992-2005

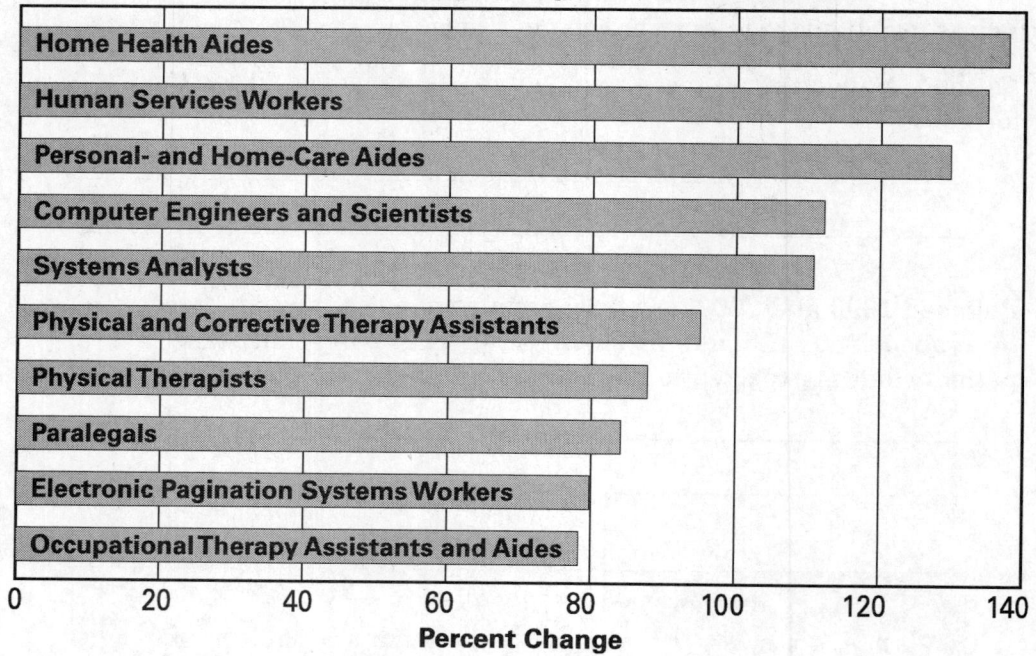

Occupations of Employed Workers, 1950, 1970, and 1995

BAR GRAPHS

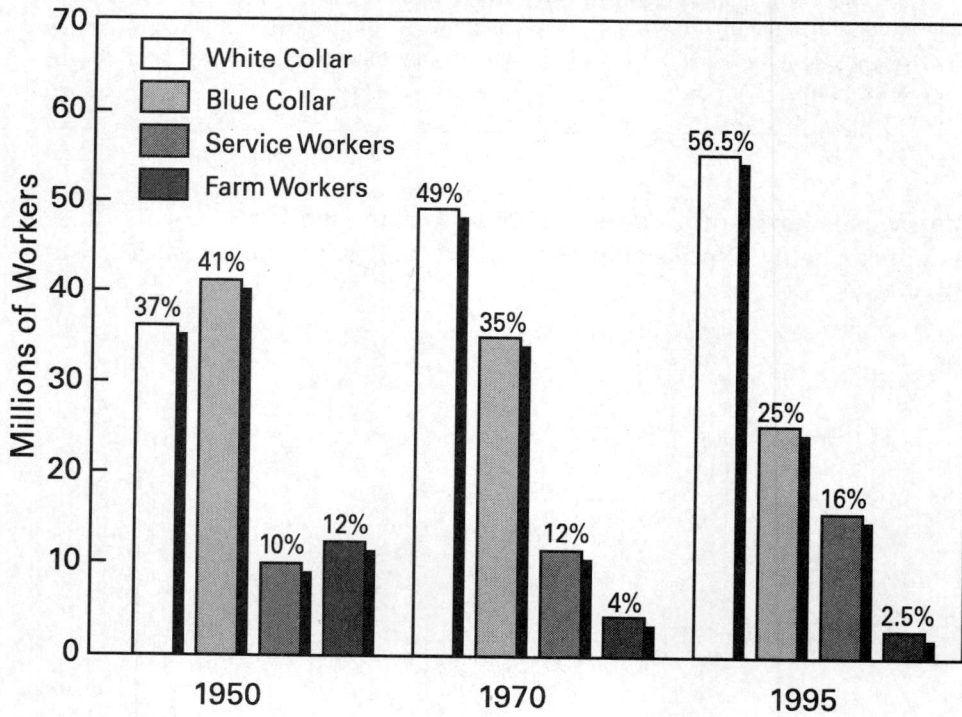

Bar graphs are particularly useful for comparing data. For example, the second bar graph compares occupations in three different years—1950, 1970, 1995—and among four kinds of workers—white collar, blue collar, service workers, and farm workers.

Activity F: Interpreting Bar Graphs

Use the bar graphs above to answer the questions.

1. *(Refer to the first bar graph.)* Between 1992 and 2005, which *three* groups of occupations are expected to grow most quickly?

   _____

   _____

   _____

2. *(Refer to the first bar graph.)* Between 1992 and 2005, by what percent is the need for physical therapists expected to grow?

   _____

   _____

   _____

3. *(Refer to the second bar graph.)* In 1950, blue collar workers outnumbered white collar workers. How did this situation change over the next 45 years?

   _____

   _____

   _____

4. *(Refer to the second bar graph.)* What trend can you observe in the need for service workers between 1950 and 1995?

   _____

   _____

   _____

PREPARING FOR THE REGENTS COMPREHENSIVE EXAMINATION IN ENGLISH

A **circle graph**—also called a **pie chart**—uses a circle to represent a whole (100%) and pie-shaped wedges to represent portions or percentages of that whole. Here's an example:

Sources of Federal Government Income

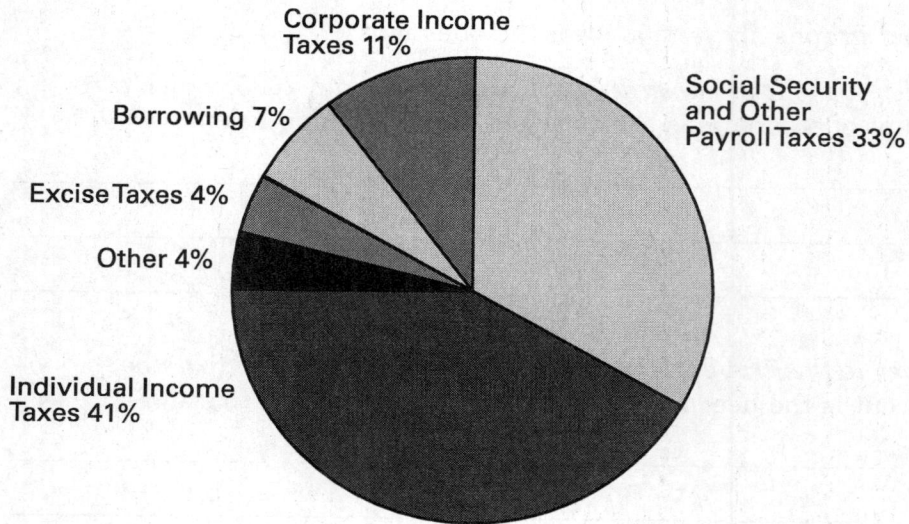

Corporate Income Taxes 11%

Social Security and Other Payroll Taxes 33%

Borrowing 7%

Excise Taxes 4%

Other 4%

Individual Income Taxes 41%

CIRCLE GRAPH (PIE CHART)

Activity G: Interpreting a Circle Graph

Use the circle graph above to answer the questions.

1. What does the entire circle represent?

   _____

   _____

2. What was the government's greatest source of income? What percentage did this source represent?

   _____

   _____

A **pictograph** uses pictures or symbols to represent quantities of data. Each symbol represents one item or a specified number of items. When a fractional part of the symbol is shown, it represents a portion. For example, in the pictograph below, each symbol stands for one person, and a partial symbol means less than one person. Thus, in 1990 the average number of persons per household was about 2.5.

Average Number of Persons per U.S. Household, 1790–1990

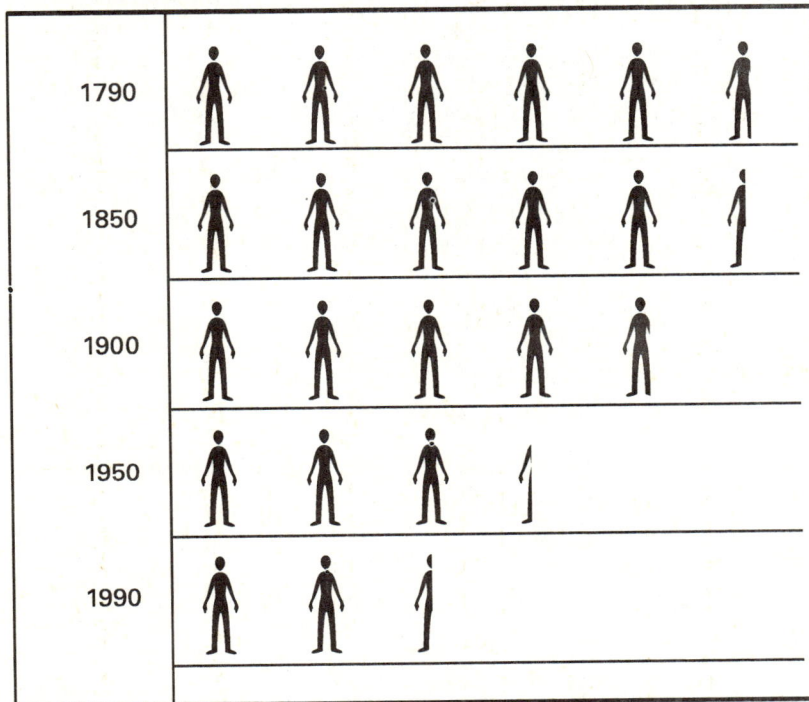

PICTOGRAPH

Activity H: Interpreting a Pictograph

Use the pictograph above to answer the questions.

1. What was the average number of persons per household in 1850?

   _____

   _____

2. How has the average number of persons per household changed during the time period shown?

   _____

   _____

Q & A

What kind of notes should I take for the Part B visual materials?

The answer to this question depends on the prompt and on the visual materials. Some materials are clear enough for you to quickly find the information you need without having to take notes. You may, however, want to circle or underline certain key data. You may also want to include in your notes a specific reference to the visual material. For example, you might jot down something like, *See graph for highest %.*

In other instances, you'll find it helpful to jot down important trends or facts that you see in the visual materials, *especially* if they relate directly to main ideas in the text. Suppose, for example, that both the prompt and the reading selection focus on the importance of exercise to good health. An accompanying graph shows that the more people exercise, the fewer visits they pay to the doctor. You might want to make note of key information from the graph for use in your extended response.

Understanding Diagrams, Tables, and Other Visual Materials

There are many kinds of diagrams, tables, and charts. They help you visualize information, make comparisons, and draw conclusions.

A **diagram** is an illustration that explains how something works or shows the parts of a whole. Some diagrams provide information about an object, such as an automobile engine or a computer. Other diagrams provide information about a process, such as how a bill becomes a law or how to administer first aid. Diagrams usually have descriptive labels or captions that provide important information.

Look at the examples that follow. Which diagram illustrates an object? Which illustrates a process? What information do the labels provide? Which diagram has an explanatory caption?

REMOTE CONTROL for a TV

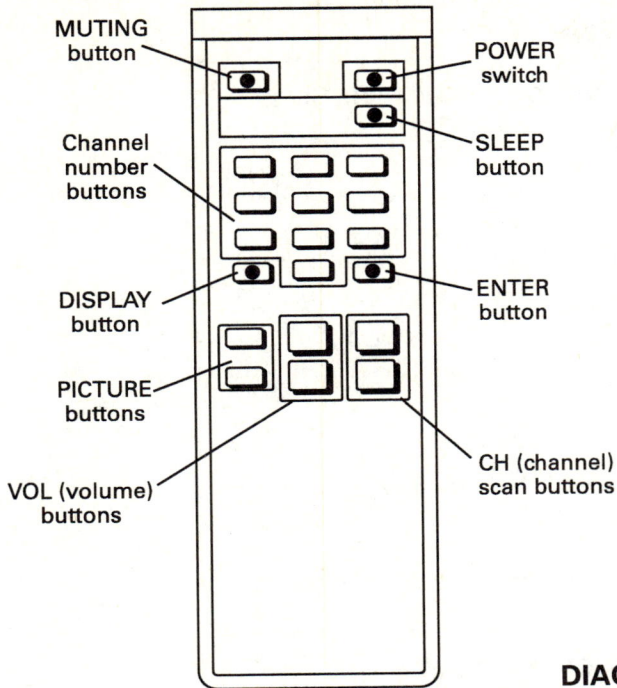

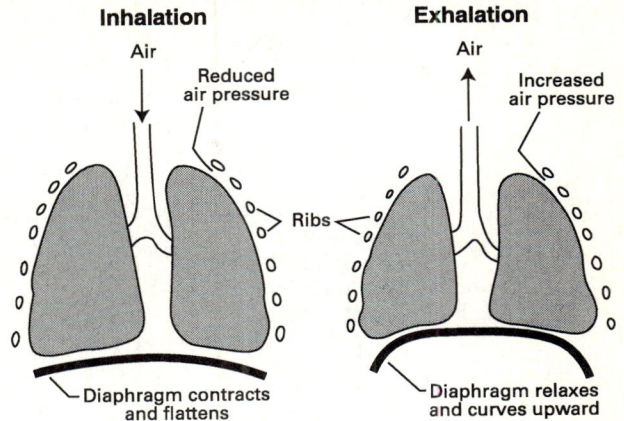

MUTING button

POWER switch

SLEEP button

Channel number buttons

DISPLAY button

ENTER button

PICTURE buttons

VOL (volume) buttons

CH (channel) scan buttons

Inhalation

Air

Reduced air pressure

Exhalation

Air

Increased air pressure

Ribs

Diaphragm contracts and flattens

Diaphragm relaxes and curves upward

Breathing Movements

The *diaphragm* is a membrane of muscle and tissue located between the chest cavity and the abdominal cavity. It is used during *inhalation* (breathing in) and *exhalation* (breathing out).

DIAGRAMS

Activity I: Interpreting a Diagram

Use the *Breathing Movements* diagram above to answer the questions.

1. How does the caption help you understand the diagram? Be specific.

_____

_____

2. Based on the diagram, what differences can you see between inhalation and exhalation?

_____

_____

107

A **table** is an arrangement of rows and columns designed to show information *in a concise, easy-to-understand form.* Here are two examples:

THE WORLD'S LARGEST MULTINATIONAL CORPORATIONS (IN BILLIONS OF U.S. DOLLARS)

Company	Home Country	Sales	Profits	Assets	Market Value
Ford Motor	U.S.	$128.4	$5.3	$219.4	$29.9
General Motors	U.S.	155.0	5.7	198.6	52.9
General Electric	U.S.	60.1	4.7	194.5	98.9
Toyota Motor	Japan	109.0	1.2	116.3	72.2
Royal Dutch/Shell	Neth.	94.9	6.2	108.0	107.6
Hitachi	Japan	76.4	1.1	102.3	31.7
EXXON	U.S.	99.7	5.1	87.9	88.7
IBM	U.S.	64.1	3.0	81.1	54.5
British Petroleum	UK	50.7	2.4	48.6	38.8
Mobil	U.S.	59.0	1.8	41.5	39.4
Nestle	Switz.	41.6	2.4	34.5	40.7

Source: Forbes, July 17, 1995

TABLES

INVENTIONS AND INNOVATIONS OF THE INDUSTRIAL REVOLUTION

Date	Inventor	Contribution
1787	John Fitch (Connecticut)	First U.S. steamboat
1787	Oliver Evans (Pennsylvania)	First high-pressure steam engine in U.S.
1798	Eli Whitney (Massachusetts)	System of interchangeable parts for guns
1807	Robert Fulton (Pennsylvania)	First commercially successful steamboat
1829	Joseph Henry (New York)	Improved electromagnet (used in telegraphs and, later in doorbells, buzzers, relay switches)
1830	Peter Cooper (New York)	First U.S. steam locomotive
1835	Samuel Colt (Connecticut)	First repeating pistol (revolver)
1844	Samuel F. B. Morse (Massachusetts)	First telegraph
1846	Richard M. Hoe	Rotary printing press
1846	Elias Howe (Massachusetts)	First sewing machine

To understand a table, first read the title. The title tells you what information the table contains. In the first table above, notice that the title also tells you that the numbers in the table refer not to dollars, but to *billions* of dollars.

The *rows* of a table go across from left to right. The *columns* go up and down. The uppermost row of the table contains the column headings. These headings show what information is being compared. To obtain specific information, find the appropriate column heading, and then move your finger across, up, or down as necessary to locate the information you want.

Here's an example. Suppose that in the first table above you wanted to know IBM's sales. First, find IBM in the *Company* column. Then move your finger across to the *Sales* column. You'll see that IBM's sales are $64.1 billion ($64,100,000,000).

Here's a slightly different example using the same table. Suppose you wanted to know which multinational corporation had the greatest profits. First, move your finger down the *Profits* column until you find the biggest number: $6.2. Now move your finger from 6.2 across to the *Company* column. You'll see that Royal Dutch/Shell had the greatest profits—$6.2 billion ($6,200,000,000).

Activity J: Reading Tables

Use the tables above to answer the questions.

1. *(Refer to the first table.)* Which corporation had the greatest sales?

   _____

   _____

2. *(Refer to the first table.)* Which two corporations are Japanese companies?

   _____

   _____

3. *(Refer to the second table.)* Who invented the first U.S. steam locomotive? In what year?

   _____

   _____

Like a table, a **chart** shows information in a concise, visual form. Charts have various uses. One of the most common uses is to help readers visualize organizational structure. Here's an example:

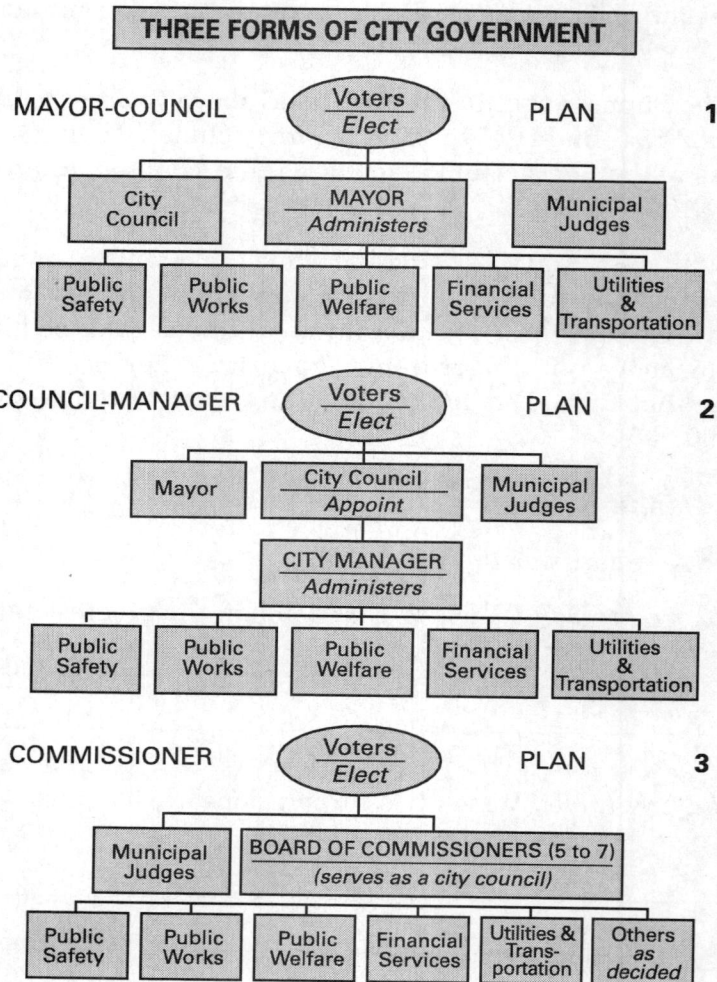

THREE FORMS OF CITY GOVERNMENT

MAYOR-COUNCIL   *Voters Elect*   PLAN   **1**

- City Council
- MAYOR *Administers*
- Municipal Judges
  - Public Safety
  - Public Works
  - Public Welfare
  - Financial Services
  - Utilities & Transportation

COUNCIL-MANAGER   *Voters Elect*   PLAN   **2**

- Mayor
- City Council *Appoint*
- Municipal Judges
  - CITY MANAGER *Administers*
    - Public Safety
    - Public Works
    - Public Welfare
    - Financial Services
    - Utilities & Transportation

COMMISSIONER   *Voters Elect*   PLAN   **3**

- Municipal Judges
- BOARD OF COMMISSIONERS (5 to 7) *(serves as a city council)*
  - Public Safety
  - Public Works
  - Public Welfare
  - Financial Services
  - Utilities & Transportation
  - Others *as decided*

CHART

Activity K: Using a Chart

Study the chart above. Then answer the question.

If you were writing about types of city government, how could this chart help you?

_____

_____

_____

In addition to those you've seen, there is a wide range of other visual materials, from pictures and maps to schedules and time lines. Some materials blend the features of different kinds of illustrations. For example, the map below includes some of the sort of information often presented in a chart or table. Notice how the numbers help you match areas on the map with the industries in those areas.

INDUSTRIES OF NEW YORK STATE

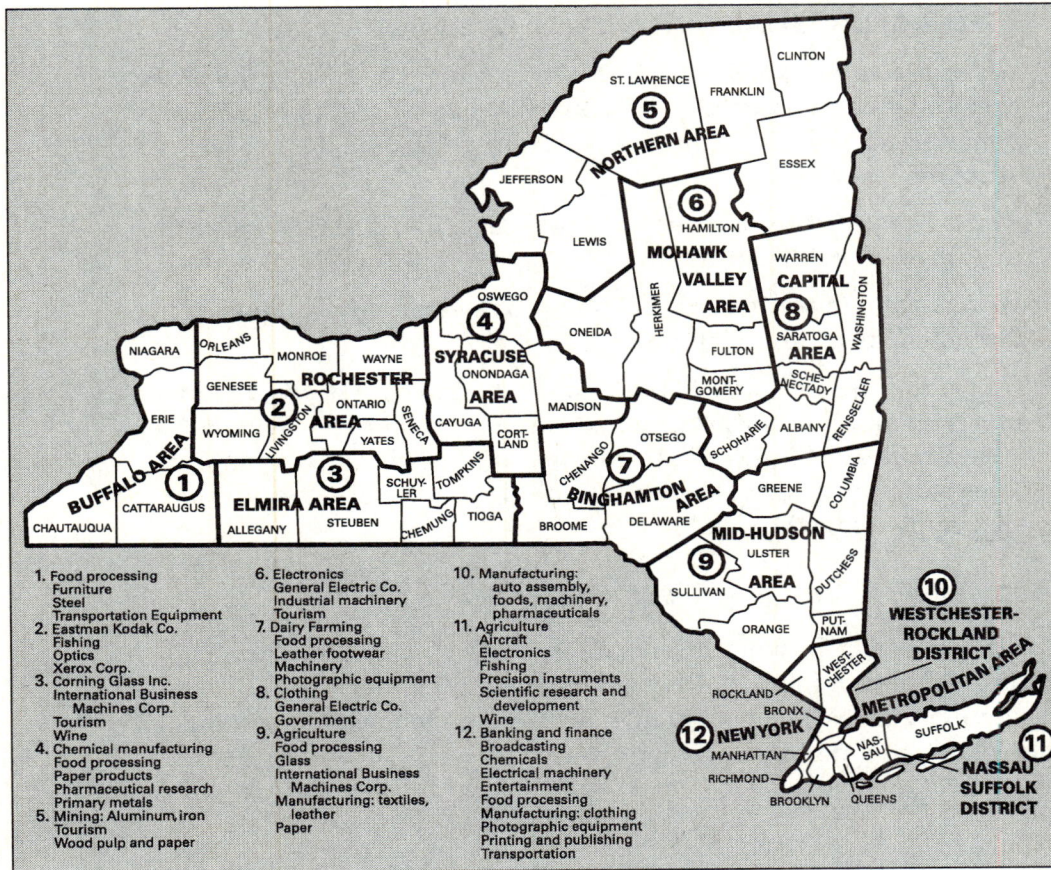

1. Food processing
   Furniture
   Steel
   Transportation Equipment
2. Eastman Kodak Co.
   Fishing
   Optics
   Xerox Corp.
3. Corning Glass Inc.
   International Business
      Machines Corp.
   Tourism
   Wine
4. Chemical manufacturing
   Food processing
   Paper products
   Pharmaceutical research
   Primary metals
5. Mining: Aluminum, iron
   Tourism
   Wood pulp and paper

6. Electronics
   General Electric Co.
   Industrial machinery
   Tourism
7. Dairy Farming
   Food processing
   Leather footwear
   Machinery
   Photographic equipment
8. Clothing
   General Electric Co.
   Government
9. Agriculture
   Food processing
   Glass
   International Business
      Machines Corp.
   Manufacturing: textiles,
      leather
   Paper

10. Manufacturing:
      auto assembly,
      foods, machinery,
      pharmaceuticals
11. Agriculture
    Aircraft
    Electronics
    Fishing
    Precision instruments
    Scientific research and
       development
    Wine
12. Banking and finance
    Broadcasting
    Chemicals
    Electrical machinery
    Entertainment
    Food processing
    Manufacturing: clothing
    Photographic equipment
    Printing and publishing
    Transportation

Activity L: Using a Map

Use the map above to answer the questions.

1. Which areas of New York offer job opportunities in manufacturing?

   _____

2. Which areas of New York offer opportunities in food processing?

   _____

3. Suppose you were writing about where in New York to live to have the widest choice of jobs. How could the map help you?

_____

_____

Whatever visual materials you find in Part B of the Regents exam, remember to apply the following basic guidelines:

FOR ALL VISUAL MATERIALS . . .

✔ *Get a sense of the whole.* Begin by reading the title and looking over the visual material. Ask yourself what kind of information is being presented. Try to get a clear sense of the whole before studying its parts.

✔ *Read the printed words.* Read any captions, descriptive labels, headings, or subheadings.

✔ *Watch for explanations.* Look for such explanatory items as footnotes, keys, and distance scales.

✔ *Consider the purpose.* Think about the purpose of the visual material and its relationship to the reading selection. Why is the visual material there? What information does it add to the text? Does it help you visualize a concept? Does it clarify information that appears in the text?

Activity M: Examining Visual Materials

Work with a partner for this activity. Search newspapers, magazines, and books for examples of four *different* kinds of visual materials accompanying text. For each example, answer the following questions on a separate sheet of paper. Be specific in your answers.

1. What is the purpose of the visual material?

2. What information does the visual material provide that is not in the accompanying text?

3. How does the visual material help you understand the *textual* information presented?

> **Note What Visual Data the Questions Ask About**
> Two or three of the Part B multiple-choice questions will
> probably deal with the visual materials. These questions are
> likely to focus on important facts, trends, or other information.
> This information may be clearly shown in the visual materials or
> it may be implied. Either way, the information may be important enough to in-
> corporate into your extended response.
>
> **TIP**

Activity N: Using Supporting Information from Visual Materials in Your Writing

1. Use specific information from any of the visual materials on pages 100–111 to write a paragraph in which you *inform* readers about something. (Example: Use information from the diagram on page 107 to inform readers about the breathing process.)

2. Use specific information from any of the visual materials on pages 100–111 to write a paragraph in which you *persuade* readers about something. (Example: Use information from the bar graphs on page 102 to persuade readers that the job market is changing.)

Activity O: Using Textual and Visual Materials Together

Review the prompt on page 85 and the work you did for *Activity B* (page 96) and *Activity C* (page 98). Then study the two diagrams that accompany the selection on page 89. Answer the following questions.

1. How does Diagram 1, "Encounter of the Not-So-Close Kind," relate to the article?

   _____

   _____

   _____

2. How does Diagram 1 help you to better understand the article?

   _____

   _____

   _____

3. How does Diagram 2, "When the Sky Falls," relate to the article?

_____

_____

_____

4. What information does Diagram 2 add to the text?

_____

_____

_____

5. The prompt's **Guidelines** direct you to:

● Tell your audience what they need to know about the danger that asteroids pose to Earth.

● Discuss appropriate actions to prepare for and deal with this danger.

● Use specific, accurate, and relevant information from the article **and** the diagrams to support your discussion.

What information from the diagrams could you use to develop your response to the prompt? Be specific.

_____

_____

_____

_____

USING CONTEXT CLUES TO DETERMINE MEANING

SKILL FOCUS:

The first three parts of the Regents exam call on your ability to use context clues to help you determine the meaning of words and phrases. This Skill Builder focuses on developing your ability to use context clues as you read any selection.

As you read, you may encounter words or phrases whose meaning is either unfamiliar or unclear to you. In a science article, for example, a writer may use technical terms that you've never seen before. Or, a writer may use a word that has more than one definition, and you're not sure which meaning applies. In such situations, you can use context to help you determine meaning.

CONCEPTS TO UNDERSTAND

- **Context** refers to the words that come before and after a particular word or phrase.

- You can figure out the meaning of a word or phrase by examining its context. The context may include just a few words, the entire sentence, or a paragraph or more.

- The same word or phrase may have different meanings in different contexts. One meaning may be *literal* (using words in their usual sense) while another is *figurative* (using words in an imaginative way to create an effect). For example, compare the meaning of the word *disaster* in the following sentences. Which is literal, and which is figurative?

  The explosion was the worst *disaster* ever to occur in this town, injuring 29 people and causing extensive property damage.

  The blind date I had Friday night was such a total *disaster* that I couldn't wait for the evening to end.

  ? *Be specific in your answer:* How is the *literal* meaning of a word or phrase different from the *figurative* meaning?

  _____

  _____

READING STRATEGIES

Use the strategies below to determine meaning through context clues. All of these strategies can improve your reading skills by helping you better understand ideas and information. Note, too, that you can apply many of these strategies when you *listen* to an informational selection, as you do for Part A of the Regents English exam.

Strategies for Using Context Clues to Determine the Meaning of Unfamiliar Words

► **Look for *descriptive information* that suggests what the unfamiliar word means.**

Example:

The children were so *rambunctious* that the babysitter could scarcely control them.

("The babysitter could scarcely control them" is descriptive information. *Rambunctious* means wild and noisy.)

► **Look for an *explanation* of the word.** Writers often explain or define a term the first time it appears.

Example:

The musician performed her next song with a *balalaika,* a stringed instrument that resembles a guitar.

► **Look for *examples* that will help you figure out the word's meaning.**

Example:

The stew was so tasteless that we added salt, pepper, mustard, ketchup, and all the other *condiments* we could find.

("Salt, pepper, mustard, ketchup" are examples. *Condiments* are seasonings, spices, sauces, and the like used to make food flavorful.)

► **Look for a *synonym* (a word that means the same or almost the same) that clarifies the unfamiliar word's meaning.**

Example:

The witness gave a detailed account of the crime, but the accused man told a different *version* of events.

(*Account* and *version* are synonyms.)

▶ **Look for an *opposite or contrast* that helps to show the unfamiliar word's meaning.** Contrasts are often, but not always, signaled by such words as *but, not, although, unlike, either . . . or.*

> *Example:*
>
> Unlike her *loquacious* sister, Kim hardly spoke at all.
>
> (The word *unlike* signals that Kim and her sister are opposites. *Loquacious* means talkative.)

▶ **Look at *nearby sentences.*** Remember that context is not limited to just one sentence. If necessary, also look at preceding and following sentences for context clues.

> *Example:*
>
> The guidance counselor warned students not to *procrastinate*. The application deadline was rapidly approaching. "Don't put off until tomorrow what you can do today," she told them.
>
> (*Procrastinate* means to put off doing things.)

TRY THIS

Use context clues to figure out the meaning of each italicized word or phrase. Write your definition of the word or phrase in the space provided. After you have finished, read the *Thinking It Through* that follows to see how one student defined the words.

1. Most people can't afford to shop in that store because the prices are *exorbitant*.

   _____

   _____

2. Amazingly, the actress moved through the crowd unrecognized. She was traveling *incognito,* wearing old clothes and large, dark glasses that hid most of her face.

   _____

   _____

3. We had planned to spend the day swimming and biking. However, the *inclement* weather forced us to remain indoors.

   _____

   _____

4. This game was not a close contest as previous encounters between the two teams had been. In fact, this game was an embarrassing *rout*. Many of the disgusted fans left before it was over. They had seen enough.

   _____

   _____

5. He tore open the envelope and read the letter. His broad grin *reflected* his instant happiness.

   _____

   _____

6. The octopus and the squid are both *invertebrates,* having no backbone.

   _____

   _____

7. I enjoy losing myself in pleasant *reveries*. My daydreams are brief vacations from the stresses of life.

   _____

   _____

8. For its first three years, the small company was spending more money than it was earning. Finally, in its fourth year, the company began operating *in the black*.

   _____

   _____

9. As a teen, Justin was calm and easygoing. As he grew older, though, he became increasingly *irascible*. By the age of 30, Justin often lost his temper at the slightest frustration.

   _____

   _____

10. She loves to read, *devouring* five or more books every month.

_____

_____

Thinking It Through

1. *Most people can't afford to shop in that store because the prices are exorbitant.*

   Since most people can't afford to shop in the store, it must be unusually

   expensive. The dictionary tells me that my thinking is on the right track.

   Exorbitant means "beyond what's reasonable or usual."

2. *Amazingly, the actress moved through the crowd unrecognized. She was traveling* incognito, *wearing old clothes and large, dark glasses that hid most of her face.*

   The fact that the actress was not recognized because of her clothing and

   glasses helps me to figure out that incognito means "in disguise."

3. *We had planned to spend the day swimming and biking. However, the* inclement *weather forced us to remain indoors.*

   Inclement must mean "stormy," because that's the kind of weather that

   would keep people from going outdoors.

4. *This game was not a close contest as previous encounters between the two teams had been. In fact, this game was an embarrassing* rout. *Many of the disgusted fans left before it was over. They had seen enough.*

   The first sentence tells me that the game was not close. The next two

   sentences explain that the game was so embarrassingly one-sided that

   fans left in disgust. As I figured out and the dictionary confirmed, a rout is

   "a total or overwhelming defeat."

5. *He tore open the envelope and read the letter. His broad grin* reflected *his instant happiness.*

I know that the verb <u>reflect</u> has more than one meaning. For example, a person can reflect on a problem, and a mirror can reflect someone's face. From this context, though, I know that the meaning of reflect here is "to show or express."

6. *The octopus and the squid are both* invertebrates, *having no backbone.*

Descriptive information in the sentence plus the octopus and squid examples tell me that an <u>invertebrate</u> must be "an animal that doesn't have a backbone."

7. *I enjoy losing myself in* reveries. *My daydreams are brief vacations from the stresses of life.*

<u>Daydreams</u> in the second sentence appears to be a synonym for <u>reveries</u>. The dictionary tells me that my thinking is correct: a reverie is "a pleasant daydream."

8. *For its first three years, the small company was spending more money than it was earning. Finally, in its fourth year, the company began operating* in the black.

The first sentence tells me that the company was losing money for three years. The second sentence tells me that things changed in the fourth year, so I assume that <u>in the black</u> must mean that the company was no longer losing money. The phrase <u>in the black</u> means "making a profit."

9. *As a teen, Justin was calm and easygoing. As he grew older, though, he became increasingly* irascible. *By the age of 30, Justin often lost his temper at the slightest frustration.*

   I can tell that <u>irascible</u> must mean the opposite of calm and easygoing.

   (And the word <u>though</u> acts as a signal word.) The last sentence confirms

   my thinking. <u>Irascible</u> means "easily angered" or "quick-tempered."

10. *She loves to read,* devouring *five or more books every month.*

    The verb <u>devour</u> is another word with more than one meaning. Usually, it

    refers to eating something, but here it's used in a figurative way. The

    dictionary definition of <u>devour</u> in this context is "to take in eagerly or

    greedily with the eyes, ears, or mind."

Skills Practice

Use context clues to figure out the meaning of each italicized word. Write your definition of the word in the space provided.

1. The howling of the wolves was *incessant* throughout the night. The nervous campers remained awake, keeping their fire burning brightly.

   _____

   _____

2. The photographer captured wonderful images of the *macaw,* showing the parrot's brilliant colors and long tail.

   _____

   _____

3. The inventor's machines, though clever, produced only *mediocre* results.

   _____

   _____

4. The label on the bottle said that the cat's medicine was highly *palatable*. However, my cat took one taste and ran out of the room.

_____

_____

5. The queen had spared no expense on the banquet. Few of the guests had ever attended such a *sumptuous* dinner.

_____

_____

6. The driver *vehemently* denied that the collision had been his fault. He insisted that the light had been green. The police officer told him to stop shouting and try to calm down.

_____

_____

7. The President said the political situation in the Middle East was extremely *volatile*. Recent events had left the whole region unstable, and no one could predict what might happen next.

_____

_____

8. A *vociferous* crowd filled the stadium, their cheers and shouts growing ever noisier as the game approached its final minutes.

_____

_____

9. As soon as the ceremony *commenced,* the huge sign above the stage crashed to the ground. It was not a promising start to the afternoon.

_____

_____

10. The mountain proved far more challenging than any of the climbers had expected. After the snowstorm, the climbers did finally manage to reach the *pinnacle,* but they were all utterly exhausted.

_____

_____

DISTINGUISHING BETWEEN FACTS AND OPINIONS

SKILL **F**OCUS: Whether you're listening to a Part A oral selection, reading a Part B text selection, or writing an extended response, it's important to distinguish facts from opinions. This Skill Builder focuses on developing your ability to distinguish between facts and opinions in informative and persuasive writing.

Writers use facts to develop and support their ideas. However, writers often mix facts with opinions. Although the two can sometimes be difficult to tell apart, they are very different. In order to read or write effectively, you must be able to distinguish between facts and opinions.

CONCEPTS TO UNDERSTAND

● A **fact** is something that is known to be true. Facts are based on objective information that can be verified. A *statement of fact* can be proved.

● Some facts can be proved by verifying them with a reliable source, such as a reference book or a knowledgeable person: *Albany is the capital of New York.* Other facts can be proved simply by observation: *Three women entered the room.*

● An **opinion** is a belief, judgment, or conclusion based on what someone thinks. A *statement of opinion* cannot be proved or disproved. An opinion is sometimes referred to as a *nonfact.*

● There are various kinds of opinions, such as personal beliefs, thoughts and feelings, and predictions. Here are a few examples:

Belief: The Metropolitan Museum of Art is the finest art museum in the country.

Thought/feeling: The Yankees aren't playing as well this year as they did last year.

Prediction: The Democratic candidate is sure to win the election.

● Opinions alone cannot prove a point because you can agree or disagree with an opinion. Writers must use facts to support their opinions and prove their arguments. These facts may come from printed materials (such as books and newspaper articles), from visual materials (such as graphs and tables), or from other sources.

OPINION

FACT   FACT   FACT

Writers use facts to support their opinions and make persuasive arguments

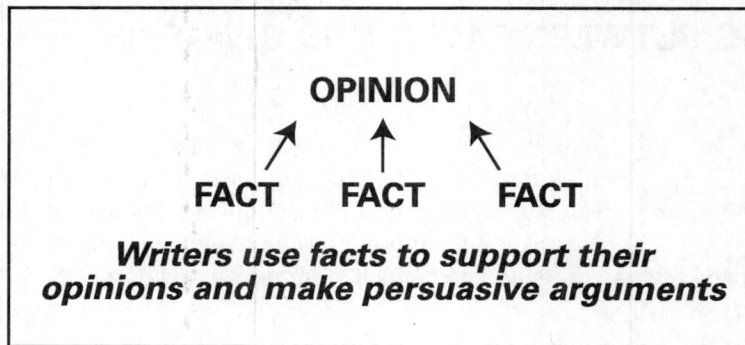

? *Answer in your own words:* What is the difference between a fact and an opinion?

_____

_____

_____

READING STRATEGIES

Use the strategies below to distinguish between facts and opinions. All of these strategies can improve your reading and comprehension skills. In addition, recognizing the difference between facts and opinions will help you to be a stronger *writer*.

Strategies for Distinguishing Between Facts and Opinions

► **Think critically about what you read**. Don't assume a statement is true just because it's in print. Ask yourself: Is the statement based on objective information that can be verified? Or, is the statement simply an expression of the writer's thoughts or beliefs—a statement with which you could disagree?

Opinion: The Hudson River is the most beautiful river in New York. (You might disagree with this statement, believing that some other river is more beautiful than the Hudson.)

Fact: The Hudson River is the largest river in New York. (This fact can be verified by checking an encyclopedia or other reference source.)

► **Watch for statements that predict the future**. Statements about events that may or may not occur in the future are usually opinions because they cannot be proved or disproved. Such predictions are usually expressed in the future tense.

Opinion: Within 10 years, this corporation will be the leading manufacturer in the state. (This is a prediction that may or may not come true. *Will be* is future tense.)

Fact: The new highway is scheduled to be in operation by the year 2010. (This is a factual statement because it's telling what the *schedule* calls for, not making a prediction. The fact can be verified by checking the schedule.)

▶ **Be alert for signal words**. Certain words may signal that a writer is expressing an opinion. Read carefully, however, because such signal words do not necessarily mean that a sentence contains no facts. Also keep in mind that writers may express opinions *without* using signal words.

Words that *may* signal an opinion include:

think	suspect	may	least	impossible
believe	predict	might	most	likely
feel	should	best	greatest	possibly
expect	must	worst	finest	probably

Opinion: I believe that the mayor won the election because voters wanted to put a woman in office. (The word *believe* signals that the writer is expressing an opinion. Someone else may have a different opinion as to why the mayor won the election.)

Fact and opinion: New York City is the largest city in the United States and the greatest. (New York City is "the largest city"—that's a verifiable fact. Whether it's also "the greatest," however, is a matter of personal opinion.)

▶ **Look for supporting information.** When you encounter a statement of opinion, look for facts that support it. Often the statement of opinion is the topic sentence of a paragraph and is followed by supporting facts.

Opinion (topic sentence): People should not drive when they are taking medication.

Supporting facts: Some doctor-prescribed medications contain narcotic drugs. Even "harmless" over-the-counter drugs can cause drowsiness and impair a person's driving ability and judgment.

TRY THIS

Identify each of the following statements as a fact or an opinion. After you have finished, read the *Thinking It Through* that follows to see how one student replied.

1. Nelson Rockefeller was governor of New York from 1959 to 1973.

    _____

2. Nelson Rockefeller was probably New York's most outstanding governor.

    _____

3. It's impossible to find better hiking trails in New York than the ones in the Adirondacks.

    _____

4. Many mountain peaks in the Adirondacks reach a height of 4,000 feet.

    _____

5. The huge amount of traffic in New York's major cities has created an air pollution problem.

    _____

6. New York will solve its air pollution problems within the next ten years.

    _____

7. The mayor of New York City has too much power.

    _____

8. New York City's chief executive is the mayor.

    _____

9. Vermont, Massachusetts, and Connecticut border New York on the east.

    _____

10. I think that more New Yorkers will travel to Massachusetts this summer than to Vermont.

    _____

Thinking It Through

1. *Nelson Rockefeller was governor of New York from 1959 to 1973.*

   This is a fact. It can be checked in an encyclopedia or other reference book.

2. *Nelson Rockefeller was probably New York's most outstanding governor.*

   This is an opinion. Someone else might disagree, believing that another governor was better than Nelson Rockefeller. The sentence contains two signal words: <u>most</u> and <u>probably</u>.

3. *It's impossible to find better hiking trails in New York than the ones in the Adirondacks.*

   This is the writer's opinion. The statement can't be proved or disproved, and other people may disagree with it. I notice that the sentence contains the signal word <u>impossible</u>.

4. *Many mountain peaks in the Adirondacks reach a height of 4,000 feet.*

   This is a fact. It can be checked in a reference book.

5. *The huge amount of traffic in New York's major cities has created an air pollution problem.*

   This is true. It is a fact that can be checked either by looking at reference materials or by talking with a knowledgeable person.

6. *New York will solve its air pollution problems within the next ten years.*

   This is an opinion. It is a prediction that may or may not happen. I notice that the sentence uses future tense.

7. *The mayor of New York City has too much power.*

    This is the writer's opinion. It can't be proved or disproved, and someone else may feel differently. This sentence does not contain any signal words.

8. *New York City's chief executive is the mayor.*

    This is a fact. It can be checked in a reference book.

9. *Vermont, Massachusetts, and Connecticut border New York on the east.*

    This is true. It is a fact that can be easily checked by looking at a map.

10. *I think that more New Yorkers will travel to Massachusetts this summer than to Vermont.*

    This is a statement of opinion. The writer is making a prediction about the future (will travel is future tense), which may or may not turn out to be true.

Skills Practice

A. Identify each of the following statements as a fact or an opinion.

1. *Hamlet* is Shakespeare's best work and possibly the greatest play ever written.

    _____

2. Construction of the Erie Canal began in 1817, but the canal did not open until 1825.

    _____

3. People who drive aggressively should lose their licenses and be required to pay large fines.

    _____

4. The Soviet Union launched *Sputnik,* the first artificial satellite, in 1957.

　　　 _____

5. Hundreds of years ago, the Inca empire of South America extended some 3,000 miles and included as many as 7 million people.

　　　 _____

6. It's likely that a woman will become President within the next ten years.

　　　 _____

B. Read the following paragraph, taken from a student's essay. The student has taken a position and supported that position with facts. Identify each sentence in the paragraph as either a fact or an opinion.

(1) Present legal restrictions on the sale of firearms are not strong enough. (2) It is much too easy to obtain guns, and there are just too many guns around. (3) Guns result in about 2,000 accidental deaths a year. (4) More than half of the people killed are under 19 years of age. (5) In addition, there are about 12,000 gun murders each year. (6) We would all be better off if absolutely no guns were allowed in this country.

(1) _____

(2) _____

(3) _____

(4) _____

(5) _____

(6) _____

C. Express your opinions in the space provided. Then support each opinion with three facts. Write your opinions and your supporting facts in complete sentences. Be sure your statements of fact are based on objective information that can be verified.

1. An *opinion* that I have about high school:

   _____

   Three *facts* that support my opinion:

   (a) _____

   _____

   (b) _____

   _____

   (c) _____

   _____

2. An *opinion* that I have about a favorite sport, hobby, or interest:

   _____

   Three *facts* that support my opinion:

   (a) _____

   _____

   (b) _____

   _____

   (c) _____

   _____

4

ANSWERING THE MULTIPLE-CHOICE QUESTIONS FOR PART B

Part B of the Regents exam includes ten multiple-choice questions, several more than in Part A. The Part B questions focus on important ideas and information in the reading selection and accompanying visual materials.

For the Part B questions, you'll apply the strategies you've learned for effective reading and note-taking. You'll also use what you've learned about obtaining information from visual materials.

Strategies for Answering the Part B Multiple-Choice Questions

To answer the Part B multiple-choice questions, you'll use many of the same basic strategies you used for Part A. The difference is that in addition to your notes, you'll have the actual selection to refer to, as well as the visual materials. Here are some tips for answering the questions:

▶ **Consult your notes and/or the reading selection as needed.** Important ideas and information in your notes are likely to appear in the questions. However, don't rely only on your notes. You'll need to refer to the selection to answer some of the questions.

▶ **Use the visual materials.** Some questions will refer specifically to the visual materials. However, you'll find that studying the visual materials will also help you answer some other questions as well.

▶ **Read each question carefully.** Be sure you understand the question before considering the answers. Be alert for particular words or phrases that offer clues to the correct answer.

▶ **Use the context.** If the question refers to one or more specific lines of text, reread those lines before trying to answer. Also, review the surrounding context, especially when a question refers to just one line.

▶ **Take a moment to ponder the question before looking at the answers.** Try to think what the answer should be. This strategy works especially well with question-and-answer form questions.

▶ *Reread* **the question as needed.** Sometimes rereading the question with each possible answer is helpful, particularly with sentence-completion form questions.

▶ **Read, compare, and consider** *all* **the choices before picking one.**

▶ **Choose the** *best* **and** *most* **complete answer.**

▶ **Narrow your search.** If you're not sure which answer is correct, cross out choices you know are wrong. Then focus your attention on just the remaining choices.

▶ **Don't spend too much time on a troublesome question.** Make your best choice and move on to the next question. If you have time left over, you can return to the question you were unsure about.

▶ **Answer every question.**

TRY THIS

Review the Part B prompt, reading selection, and visual materials on pages 85–89. Also review the notes you took for *Activity C* (page 98). Next, answer the multiple-choice questions. After you've answered the questions, read the *Thinking It Through* that follows to see how one student determined the correct answers.

Multiple-Choice Questions

Directions (7–16): Answer the following questions by selecting the best answer and circling its number. The questions may help you think about ideas and information you might use in your writing. You may return to these questions anytime you wish.

7 The incident involving asteroid 1997 XF11 called attention to the fact that

  1 Earth is in danger of being hit by objects from space
  2 asteroids cannot strike Earth
  3 scientists are well prepared to cope with any objects that may fall from space
  4 astronomers cannot measure space distances

8 The text (lines 67–68) implies that if the "iron asteroid" had struck more recently, it would have

  1 done less damage
  2 created a much bigger crater
  3 cost many lives in Arizona
  4 destroyed all of Arizona

9 The article compares the impact of an asteroid with the

  1 force of a tropical storm
  2 explosive power of a bomb
  3 strength of a tidal wave
  4 intensity of a laser

10 Scientists believe that an asteroid striking Earth in the future is

  1 something that is not likely to occur
  2 an event that happens only in movies
  3 a fifty-fifty possibility
  4 an event that is sure to happen sometime

11 In line 85, what does "the devil they don't know" refer to?

  1 unknown asteroids
  2 asteroid 1997 XF11
  3 Earth's orbit
  4 comets

12 The article implies that astronomers think

  1 all dangerous space objects have been identified
  2 there is little benefit to be gained from tracking asteroids
  3 defensive measures require little or no advance warning.
  4 more money should be spent on identifying and tracking space objects

13 What is the main point of the article?

　1 Asteroids may have struck Earth in the past but will not do so again.
　2 Earth should be better prepared to cope with the danger of objects from space.
　3 Only asteroids composed mainly of iron pose a serious threat to Earth.
　4 Asteroids must be destroyed as soon as they are identified.

14 Scientists would use a "robot craft" (line 131) to

　1 set off a nuclear device
　2 change the path of an incoming asteroid
　3 plan the best defensive measures
　4 block the path of an incoming asteroid

15 What does Diagram 1 ("Encounter of the Not-So-Close Kind") show?

　1 Astronomers' revised calculations were almost the same as their early figures.

　2 At first it appeared that the asteroid would come even closer to Earth than the moon was.
　3 The orbit of the asteroid was nearly identical with the orbit of Mars.
　4 The asteroid was likely to collide with the sun.

16 According to Diagram 2 ("When the Sky Falls"), scientists

　1 are considering various defense measures against space objects
　2 already have five devices to use in defense of Earth if needed
　3 would use nuclear weapons as their first choice for defense
　4 are currently trying out five methods of defense against space objects they have identified

Thinking It Through

7 *The incident involving asteroid 1997 XF11 called attention to the fact that*

　1 *Earth is in danger of being hit by objects from space*

　2 *asteroids cannot strike Earth*

　3 *scientists are well prepared to cope with any objects that may fall from space*

　4 *astronomers cannot measure space distances*

From reading the selection, I know right away that choice 1 is probably correct. However, I carefully consider all the choices to be sure. I know choice 2 is wrong, since many asteroids have struck Earth in the past. Choice 3 is also incorrect because one point the article makes is that scientists really aren't well prepared. Choice 4 is wrong, too, because it's not a conclusion that can be drawn from the incident.

8 *The text (lines 67–68) implies that if the "iron asteroid" had struck more recently, it would have*

   1 *done less damage*

   2 *created a much bigger crater*

   3 *cost many lives in Arizona*

   4 *destroyed all of Arizona*

After carefully rereading lines 67–68, I can infer that choice 3 is correct. If the asteroid that struck Arizona 50,000 years ago hit today, the "impact and explosion" would be the same. However, today Arizona is a populated state, which of course it wasn't 50,000 years ago. Therefore, I can eliminate choices 1 and 2 as not logical. The text says that today the asteroid "could destroy a city." Therefore, choice 4 doesn't apply either.

9 *The article compares the impact of an asteroid with the*

   1 *force of a tropical storm*

   2 *explosive power of a bomb*

   3 *strength of a tidal wave*

   4 *intensity of a laser*

From my notes, I see that the text made a comparison with "the bomb that leveled Hiroshima" (lines 36–39). I also recall that an astronomer in the article said something about an asteroid exploding with as much power as all the U.S. and Soviet nuclear weapons blowing up (lines 77–80). Therefore, I'm sure that choice 2 is the correct answer.

10 *Scientists believe that an asteroid striking Earth in the future is*

    1 *something that is not likely to occur*

    2 *an event that happens only in movies*

    3 *a fifty-fifty possibility*

    4 *an event that is sure to happen sometime*

> *I know right away that the first two choices are wrong. I can eliminate the third choice, too, especially after rereading that "scientists agree that it is only a matter of time . . ." (lines 81–82). Choice <u>4</u> is the correct answer.*

11 *In line 85, what does "the devil they don't know" refer to?*

    1 *unknown asteroids*

    2 *asteroid 1997 XF11*

    3 *Earth's orbit*

    4 *comets*

> *After carefully rereading the sentence containing the phrase "the devil they don't know" <u>and</u> the following few sentences, I know that the correct answer is choice <u>1</u>. According to the text, astronomers estimate that maybe 2,000 large asteroids approach Earth. However, they've identified and tracked fewer than 200. This makes the scientists worry about "a surprise encounter" (line 91) with "the devil they don't know"—one of the unknown asteroids.*

135

12 *The article implies that astronomers think*

    1 *all dangerous space objects have been identified*

    2 *there is little benefit to be gained from tracking asteroids*

    3 *defensive measures require little or no advance warning*

    4 *more money should be spent on identifying and tracking space objects*

> *I know at once that choice 1 is wrong, so I can eliminate it. Choices 2 and 3 are also wrong, because the article makes clear that defensive measures require advance warning, and tracking would be needed to provide such warning. Choice 4 is definitely an idea implied in the paragraph that begins on line 105, so I'm sure that's the correct answer.*

13 *What is the main point of the article?*

    1 *Asteroids may have struck Earth in the past but will not do so again.*

    2 *Earth should be better prepared to cope with the danger of objects from space.*

    3 *Only asteroids composed mainly of iron pose a serious threat to Earth.*

    4 *Asteroids must be destroyed as soon as they are identified.*

> *From my reading I can conclude that choice 2 is correct. This is the central point of the whole selection. I also know that choices 1 and 3 are not right. Choice 4 is also wrong: it wouldn't be practical to destroy every single asteroid identified, and the article doesn't suggest doing so.*

14 Scientists would use a "robot craft" (line 131) to

1 set off a nuclear device

2 change the path of an incoming asteroid

3 plan the best defensive measures

4 block the path of an incoming asteroid

The context again helps me here. The sentence referring to the "robot craft" explains the purpose of such a craft. By rereading a paragraph or two, I can conclude that choice 3 is correct. If the robot craft determines that an approaching asteroid is rocky, a defensive measure other than a nuclear blast might be more effective. Besides, the other answer choices do not reflect information in the text.

15 What does Diagram 1 ("Encounter of the Not-So-Close Kind") show?

1 Astronomers' revised calculations were almost the same as their early figures.

2 At first it appeared that the asteroid would come even closer to Earth than the moon was.

3 The orbit of the asteroid was nearly identical with the orbit of Mars.

4 The asteroid was likely to collide with the sun.

Studying the diagram, I see that the early calculation of the asteroid's distance from Earth was 30,000 miles. This is much closer than the 240,000-mile average distance of the moon. Therefore, I know that choice 2 is the correct answer. Looking at the other possible answers, I can also see that none of the other choices is supported by the information in the diagram.

16 *According to Diagram 2 ("When the Sky Falls"), scientists*

  1 *are considering various defense measures against space objects*

  2 *already have five devices to use in defense of Earth if needed*

  3 *would use nuclear weapons as their first choice for defense*

  4 *are currently trying out five methods of defense against space objects they have identified*

> After comparing the answer choices, I take another close look at Diagram 2. The diagram text explains that scientists are "exploring" various ideas and that the five ideas in the diagram are "under discussion." The diagram does not say that the devices shown are already in use or that they all even exist. Therefore, I can eliminate choices 2 and 4. Choice 1 is the correct answer. Choice 3 is not supported by the diagram.

Activity P: Evaluating Your Skills

Review the notes you took and the multiple-choice questions you answered. Then respond to the questions below. Be specific in your answers.

1. How helpful in answering the questions were the notes that you took? How could you have made your notes more useful?

2. Did you read the selection and study the diagrams carefully enough? What could you have done to further improve your understanding of the textual and visual materials?

3. Share and compare your answers to the preceding questions with the answers of other students. What suggestions from other students did you find most helpful?

_____

_____

_____

5

PLANNING AND WRITING YOUR PART B RESPONSE

As you've seen, Part B of the Regents exam asks you to analyze a combination of textual and visual materials. You'll use information that you obtain from these materials to write an extended response. Your response will be based on a given situation and written for a specific purpose.

Examining the Criteria as Applied to Part B

Just as for Part A, readers will evaluate your response for Part B holistically on the basis of five criteria: meaning, development, organization, language use, and conventions.

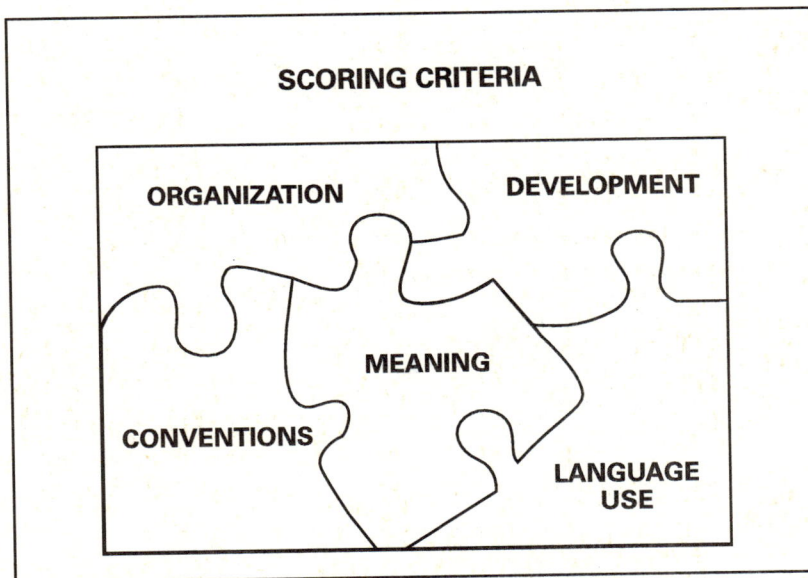

SCORING CRITERIA

ORGANIZATION

DEVELOPMENT

MEANING

CONVENTIONS

LANGUAGE USE

The chart below shows how the scoring criteria are applied specifically to Part B of the exam. You'll see that the evaluation for Part B is almost the same as that for Part A. However, there are two main differences: (1) your

Part B response is based on *reading* a selection, not listening to one, and (2) you have to use information from a combination of textual and visual sources.

SCORING THE PART B EXTENDED RESPONSE

CRITERIA	WHAT YOUR PART B RESPONSE SHOULD SHOW
MEANING	• A solid understanding of both the textual and visual materials • Insightful connections between the content of the textual and visual materials and the specific writing task
DEVELOPMENT	• Clear development of ideas • Effective use of specific and relevant supporting information from both textual and visual materials
ORGANIZATION	• Clear, consistent focus • Logical and coherent structure
LANGUAGE USE	• Effective and engaging language that is appropriate for the specific audience and purpose • Varied sentence structure and length
CONVENTIONS	• Strong control of grammar, punctuation, spelling, and other elements of writing, with few errors

---

In the following pages, you'll learn how to plan and write an effective Part B response that takes into account these criteria.

? *Fill in the blanks:* The language you use when you write your response should be appropriate for the specific _____ and _____.

Getting Started

As you read in the previous chapter, the writing process begins with planning. Planning makes writing easier and helps you write a clear, complete, and well-organized response.

Look again at the Part B prompt from earlier in this chapter. Just as with Part A, you can use **The Situation**, **Your Task**, and **Guidelines** to guide you as you plan and write your response:

The Situation: A newspaper editorial poked fun at people for taking too seriously the idea that an asteroid could collide with Earth. The editorial writer told readers not to "mistake Hollywood fiction for fact" and insisted that "there's nothing we can do about such things anyway." You decided to write a reply to the editorial, discussing the very real danger that asteroids pose and explaining that there are actions to be taken.

Your Task: Write a response to the newspaper editorial. Using relevant information from the article and the diagrams, discuss the danger that asteroids pose and how to deal with it.

Guidelines:

Be sure to
- Tell your audience what they need to know about the danger that asteroids pose to Earth
- Discuss appropriate actions to prepare for and deal with this danger
- Use specific, accurate, and relevant information from the article and the diagrams to support your discussion
- Use a tone and level of language appropriate for a newspaper
- Organize your ideas in a logical and coherent manner
- Indicate any words taken directly from the article by using quotation marks or referring to the author
- Follow the conventions of standard written English

To begin planning, you can follow the same guidelines you used to plan your Part A response:

▶ **Carefully read *The Situation, Your Task,* and *Guidelines*.** Be sure you understand exactly what you have to write. Think about how the *Guidelines* relate to the various scoring criteria.

▶ **Maintain your focus on task, audience, and purpose.** Look back at the task, audience, and purpose that you jotted down before reading the selection. Make any adjustments that may be necessary to sharpen your focus.

Use Specific, Accurate, Relevant Information

Notice that the **Guidelines** for both Part A and Part B call for "specific, accurate, and relevant information." These words—*specific, accurate, relevant*—are important to keep in mind as you plan and write your response. Using supporting information that is too general, that is inaccurate, or that does not relate directly to your task and purpose will lower your score.

TIP

Developing and Organizing Your Content

For your Part B written response, you'll need to develop and support your ideas with specific information from the reading selection and the accompanying visual materials. Use **The Situation, Your Task,** and **Guidelines** to guide you as you plan what ideas and information to include and how best to organize your content.

The Basics box on pages 148–149 shows three possible ways to organize content. Choose the approach that you feel will be most effective. Just be sure that your response has a logical, coherent structure that makes it easy for readers to follow your flow of ideas. You may also find it helpful to review the basics of essay structure, which are discussed in *The Basics* box on pages 223–224.

Keep your task, audience, and purpose firmly in mind as you set about planning your response. Jot your thoughts down on paper just as you did when planning your Part A response. However, instead of referring only to listening notes as you did for Part A, you can refer to the actual reading selection, the visual material, and your notes as you develop your plan.

Use a simple list or outline format like the one shown below from Chapter 2, or use whatever planning or outlining approach you think will work best for the particular content.

> IDEA
> Supporting detail
> Supporting detail
> Supporting detail
>
> . . . and so on.

Include in your plan as many ideas and as much supporting information as you think you need to answer the prompt. Remember, this is just a plan: you can adjust it as you work.

Refer to

→ **your notes**

→ **the reading selection**

→ **the visual materials**

as you plan and write your Part B response.

Keep in mind that the main ideas you present should be developed with specific, accurate, and relevant information from the textual and visual materials. As noted in Chapter 2, you'll get a higher score by presenting a few ideas and supporting them well than by presenting numerous ideas with little or no supporting information.

Activity Q: Making a Plan

1. On a sheet of paper, make a rough plan for an extended response to the prompt about asteroids.

2. Exchange papers with a partner. Evaluate each other's work. Be constructive and specific in your comments and suggestions.

Looking at a Sample Plan

Let's see how planning ahead helped one student shape a response to the Part B prompt about asteroids. Look at the sample plan below. You'll see that the student's outline includes information from both the textual and visual materials as well as information highlighted by the multiple-choice questions. Later, you'll read a Part B extended response based on this plan.

STUDENT'S PLAN FOR PART B RESPONSE

Note: For illustration purposes, this outline may be more detailed than yours would need to be. *The plan you make for yourself need be only detailed enough for* you *to understand what you intend to write!*

ASTEROIDS POSE REAL DANGER TO EARTH

(1) Recent event involving asteroid 1997 XF11 called attention to danger

—Scientists first thought asteroid might pass as close as 30,000

miles

—Would have come much closer than the moon (240,000 miles)

(2) Space objects have often hit Earth in past

—More than 150 craters on Earth's surface

—Asteroid created Meteor Crater in Arizona 50,000 years ago

—Had asteroid hit today, would have killed many people

—1908: space object exploded over Siberia

—Devastated large area

—Had explosion occurred over populated area, many would have died

—Two years ago, large asteroid missed Earth by just 280,000 miles

—Had it hit, explosion would have been like "taking all of the U.S. and Soviet nuclear weapons, putting them in a pile and blowing them up."

(3) Scientists agree: sooner or later another space object will hit Earth

(4) Most asteroids that approach Earth's orbit are unknown

—Example: Scientists have identified and tracked only about 200 out of estimated 2,000 asteroids larger than a kilometer. (That's just 10%!)

—Estimated 300,000 asteroids larger than 300 ft. wide

—Maybe 100 million asteroids bigger than 60 ft. across

THERE ARE ACTIONS TO TAKE TO PREPARE FOR AND DEAL WITH ASTEROID DANGER

(1) Invest more money in "asteroid hunting"

—Make greater effort to find and track at least larger asteroids

—The better our early-warning system is, better able we'll be to take defensive action

—We should "practice" defending against nearby asteroids—such as 1997 XF11

(2) Options for dealing with approaching asteroids

—Intercept with rocket to either change path or destroy

—For very big or very close asteroid may need to use nuclear weapons

—Use robot craft to analyze asteroid before taking action

—Don't want to blow up rocky asteroid because falling chunks could

be deadly

—Attach "solar sail"

—Deflect with laser beams

Activity R: Evaluating a Plan

Answer the following questions about the student's plan. Before writing your answers, discuss your thoughts with a partner or a small group of students.

1. Overall, what are the strengths of the student's plan?

   _____

   _____

   _____

   _____

2. Give at least three examples of how the student made clear connections between the content of the reading selection and the specific writing task.

   _____

   _____

   _____

   _____

3. Give at least two examples of how the student made clear connections between the content of the visual materials and the specific writing task.

   _____

   _____

   _____

   _____

4. How has the student used the prompt to create a logical organizational structure?

_____

_____

_____

_____

5. Give at least three examples of how the student developed ideas with specific and relevant supporting details.

_____

_____

_____

_____

6. How will the student's plan make writing the response easier?

_____

_____

_____

_____

7. How has answering the multiple-choice questions helped the student focus on important ideas and information?

_____

_____

_____

_____

Activity S: Comparing Plans

Carefully compare the student's plan above with the plan you made for *Activity Q* (page 143). Then answer the following questions.

1. What are the main differences you see between the two plans?

_____

_____

_____

_____

2. In what ways do you think your plan is better than the student's plan? Be specific.

_____

_____

_____

_____

3 In what ways is the student's plan stronger than yours? Again, be specific.

_____

_____

_____

_____

4. Do you think that either of the two plans could be used to write an effective Part B response? Why or why not?

_____

_____

_____

_____

The ◆ Basics

METHODS OF ORGANIZATION

How best to organize the content of an extended response will depend on your task and purpose. For example, if you're writing an essay warning people about the dangers of smoking cigarettes, you may want to present your ideas in order of importance. However, if you're explaining how you yourself managed to quit smoking, you would probably describe events in the order they happened.

◆ Three basic methods of organization are summarized below. You can use these methods to organize the paragraphs that, together, develop your *central point.* You can also use these methods to organize the information *within* individual paragraphs—that is, the information that supports a paragraph's main idea.

◆ Your response may not fit neatly into one particular organizational pattern. You may have to combine or blend methods, or use different methods in different paragraphs. You may have to devise an approach tailored specifically to the particular prompt. No matter what structure you choose, your response should have a logical flow, and your ideas should be smoothly connected.

◆ To use *order of increasing importance/interest,* arrange ideas and supporting information in order from the least important/interesting to the most important/interesting. This form of organization is effective when you want to build to a conclusion or climax.

Order of Increasing Importance/Interest

third most important idea →

  second most important idea →

    most important idea of all

◆ To use *order of decreasing importance/interest,* arrange ideas and supporting information in order from the most important/interesting to the least important/interesting. This approach works well when you want to lead off with a strong point and then add additional points.

Order of Decreasing Importance/Interest

most important idea →

  second most important idea →

    third most important idea

148

◆ To use *chronological order*, present events or information in time order, usually moving forward in time. You can use this form of organization to show sequence—for example, how one event leads to another.

Chronological (Time) Order

what happened first →

      what happened next →

            what happened after that

Writing a Focused, Coherent Response

As you translate your Part B plan into a written response, keep two key words in mind: *focus* and *coherence*. Review the following diagram, from Chapter 2:

COHERENT WRITING

→ **Clearly and logically organized**
Flows in a way that makes sense and is easy to follow

→ **Stays focused**
Has a clear, definite topic and sticks to it

→ **Smoothly connected**
Uses transitional words and phrases to connect ideas and show development

? *Fill in the blanks:* Coherent writing is clearly and logically _____ . It stays focused on a _____ .

Transitional words and phrases help to make your writing coherent. You can use them at the beginning of a sentence to link that sentence with the preceding one. You can similarly use transitional words and phrases in the middle or at the end of a sentence.

149

Study the chart below. This chart is an expanded version of the one you saw in Chapter 2.

TRANSITIONAL WORDS AND PHRASES

What the Word/Phrase Does	Examples
Indicates sequence	*first, second, third (and so on), next, finally, after, before, while, during, later on, then, meanwhile, at last, after a while, immediately*
Provides one or more examples	*for example, for instance, such as, one reason, in particular*
Adds information	*also, another, furthermore, in addition, and, besides, too, as well*
Indicates a consequence or conclusion	*because of, for this reason, therefore, consequently, as a result, finally, lastly*
Makes a comparison or signals a change in direction	*both, however, on the other hand, but, although, even though, otherwise, on the contrary*
Adds emphasis	*especially, in particular, in fact, above all, most important*
Indicates position	*above, across, before, behind, beside, below, farther, in front of, inside, nearby, next to, outside, over, under*

? *Fill in the blanks:* Transitional words and phrases may appear at the _____, in the _____, or at the _____ of a sentence.

As you write your response for Part B—*and* your responses for the other three parts of the Regents exam—you can use transitional words and phrases to carry out several functions:

- Guide readers from one sentence or paragraph to the next.
  Example:

  Committee members estimated the cost of the construction project. *Later on,* they revised their calculations based on additional information.

  "Later on" guides readers forward in time.

- Show how one idea or detail relates to another.
  Example:

  > The steering wheel had a serious defect. *Consequently,* the manufacturer recalled hundreds of thousands of cars.

  > "Consequently" indicates that the defect led to the recall.

- Signal a shift in focus.
  Example:

  > Researchers continued to evaluate new medications for the disease. *Meanwhile,* patients eagerly awaited news of an effective treatment.

  > "Meanwhile" indicates a shift in focus from "researchers" to "patients."

Often you'll want to use a transitional *sentence* to link paragraphs. Such a sentence may appear at the beginning or end of a paragraph. Here's an example:

> Artists in ancient Greece and Rome typically had low status in society. Some were even slaves, whose artwork was dictated by the wishes of their master. By the Middle Ages, artists had begun to advance in status. They were generally recognized as craftsmen.

> *Not until the 15th century, however, did artists truly begin to gain high status.* Renaissance artists were well regarded, even though rich patrons largely controlled the work that the artists did.

The second paragraph begins with a transitional sentence: *Not until the 15th century, however, did artists truly begin to gain high status.* This sentence guides readers forward in time and also signals a significant shift in artists' status. Note, too, that the transitional word *however* appears in the middle of the sentence.

Activity T: Using Transitional Words and Phrases

In the following paragraphs, add transitional words or phrases to guide readers smoothly from sentence to sentence. Use the words and phrases shown in the box. Use each one only once.

in addition	furthermore	for example
	as a result	however

According to estimates, perhaps eighty million species live on our planet. Only a fraction of these have been identified. _____ *(signals change in direction)*, scientists fear that the number of plant and animal species is rapidly decreasing. The relentlessly expanding human population is consuming the land and other natural resources that these species need to survive. _____ *(indicates a consequence)*, earth's diversity is declining. _____ *(adds information)*, the tragedy of this situation goes beyond the elimination of plants and animals. Species are disappearing at such a fast rate, that people will not even be aware of the potential benefits they have lost forever. _____ *(provides example)*, researchers have identified various plants that are valuable in treating diseases. Some of these plants are already near extinction. _____ *(adds information)*, many other useful plants will vanish before we even have a chance to learn of their value.

Q & A

What kinds of supporting information should I use to develop my ideas?

As a writer, you can support and develop your ideas with facts, reasons, examples, details, statistics, anecdotes, quotations, or any combination of these. How best to develop your ideas depends on your specific task and purpose and, of course, on what information and details you have available for use.

Your choice of details also involves judgment. For example, if your purpose for Part B is to present a convincing argument, you'll want to support your argument with strong facts from the textual and visual materials. However, if the selection includes a particularly dramatic quotation, you might want to use that quotation to add impact to your argument.

Using Appropriate Tone and Language

In the previous chapter, you read about the importance of tailoring your language to your audience in order to make your writing effective and engaging. As you've seen, the **Guidelines** for both Part A and Part B highlight this idea by directing you to "use a tone and level of language appropriate for" the particular task and audience. You may, for example, be asked to write an article for a community newsletter, an essay for a school newspaper, or a persuasive argument for a group of administrators.

Determining what tone and language is appropriate is a matter of judgment and common sense. For example, jokes and slang expressions may be fine for a humorous essay aimed at junior high school students. However, they would not be appropriate for a serious newspaper editorial about banning nuclear weapons. Similarly, expressions such as "what I think is" and "I'm writing to tell you that" are fine if you're writing a letter to a friend. However, using the first person—*I*—is generally not appropriate for newspaper articles and the like.

The readers who score your Part B response will expect your writing to show that you are thinking about your specific audience. So, choose your words with care.

Activity U: Evaluating Tone and Language

Compare the two sample student paragraphs below. Then answer the questions that follow. Work with a partner for this activity.

Sample A

It's time to extend the school year to twelve months. Giving students two or three months off each year does no one any good, except for the people who own summer camps, hotels, and amusement parks. Between the end of one school year and the start of the next, students forget much of what they've learned. Consequently, for the first several weeks of every school year, teachers have to review past lessons instead of moving ahead to new material.

Sample B

I really think it's about time to extend the school year to twelve months. Giving kids a bunch of weeks off each year is dumb, although I'm sure that the people who own summer camps, hotels, and amusement parks think it's way cool because they're raking in big bucks. Between the end of one school year and the start of the next, kids' minds totally empty out. So what happens? You guessed it: teachers have to go back over old stuff instead of pouring on the new material.

1. How would you describe the writer's tone and language in Sample A?

   _____

   _____

   _____

2. How would you describe the writer's tone and language in Sample B?

_____

_____

_____

3. Give at least three specific examples of differences in word choice that make the two paragraphs different.

_____

_____

_____

4. Which of the two paragraphs would be more appropriate for an essay directed at an adult audience? Why?

_____

_____

_____

Activity V: Proofreading Practice

The following excerpt comes from a student's Part B response. The excerpt contains at least seven errors that involve conventions of writing. Proofread the paragraph, and identify and correct the errors. (Refer to the questions on page 66.)

Women have made great progres in reducing the inequality between men's and womens sports. A major step forward was the 1972 passage of a law known as Title IX this important law required schools to provide girls and boys equal opportunitys with regard to school sports programs. In the 25 years following passage of title IX, the number of high school girls in varsity sports rose 500 percent. as one high school senior commented: Title IX opened the doors to the sports arena, and women came charging in!"

154

From Plan to Part B Response: Taking a First Look

Let's see how the student's plan from pages 143–145 translates into a Part B response.

Note: Paragraph numbers have been added for reference purposes. They are not part of the paper.

(1) Asteroids pose a very real, maybe even catastrophic, danger to our planet. A recent event showed just how real that danger is. Astronomers spotted an asteroid that they first thought might come within 30,000 miles of Earth. To picture just how near that is, consider that our moon is 240,000 miles away! As things turned out, scientists revised their first estimates and figured out that the asteroid would not pass as close as they had thought. However, the incident should remind us of several important facts.

(2) First, many space objects have struck Earth in the past. The evidence of this includes 150 craters on Earth's surface. In Arizona, the huge Meteor Crater was formed about 50,000 years ago by an asteroid. If that asteroid had hit today, many people would have died. This century, a space object exploded over Siberia. Had the explosion happened over a more populated area, it would have killed hundreds of thousands of people. Furthermore, only two years ago a large asteroid missed our planet by just 280,000 miles. If it had struck Earth, the explosion, in one astronomer's words, would have been like "taking all of the U.S. and Soviet nuclear weapons, putting them in a pile and blowing them up."

(3) Scientists agree that sooner or later another space object will hit Earth. There are thousands of asteroids moving through space. Some are large, while others are small. However, only a tiny number have been identified. Any of them could come our way, maybe without warning.

(4) Even though the danger is real, Earth need not be a defenseless target. There are actions we can take to defend ourselves. To begin, we should invest more money in identifying and tracking asteroids, especially big ones. Obviously, the more we know about approaching space objects and the sooner we know it, the better able we will be to defend ourselves. Next, we should develop effective defenses. For example, we could send a rocket to intercept an approaching asteroid. The rocket could either change the asteroid's path or destroy it. We need to be careful, though. If we blow up a rocky asteroid, we could end up showering Earth with deadly chunks of rock. To avoid this possibility, we could send a robot craft in advance to analyze the coming asteroid.

(5) There are other possible options. For example, some scientists have proposed attaching a giant sail to an approaching object. Solar wind could then carry the object away from Earth. Another possibility is the use of lasers to deflect the object. None of these options can work, though, if we don't have a good early-warning system in place. And the first step to developing such a system is to recognize that the danger of space objects hitting Earth is real.

Activity W: Evaluating a Response for Audience, Purpose, and Language

For each question, rate the response on a scale of 1 to 5, with 5 being the highest rating. Then give specific reasons for your rating.

1. How appropriate is the student's response for the intended audience?
   Rating: _____
   Reasons:

   _____

   _____

   _____

2. How well has the student accomplished the intended purpose?
   Rating: _____
   Reasons:

   _____

   _____

   _____

3. Has the student used appropriate tone and language?
   Rating: _____
   Reasons:

   _____

   _____

   _____

4. Has the student used language that is effective and engaging?
   Rating: _____
   Reasons:

   _____

   _____

   _____

From Plan to Part B Response: Looking More Closely

Let's look at the student's Part B response in greater detail. The student has written a five-paragraph essay responding to the newspaper editorial. The purpose of the essay is, first, to inform readers about the danger asteroids pose and, second, to discuss how to prepare for and deal with this danger.

The student devotes the first three paragraphs to informing readers about the asteroid danger and then uses paragraphs 4 and 5 to discuss how to deal with the danger. The student clearly develops the main idea of each paragraph with specific supporting information, drawn from both the reading selection text and the accompanying diagrams.

The student captures the reader's attention with a dramatic opening sentence about the reality of the danger that asteroids pose. This idea—which is central to the entire essay—is echoed in the final sentence of the essay, which also serves as a strong closing sentence.

Note the following specific points:

- The essay's ideas and supporting information come from the student's plan and/or from the selection. The student adjusted, expanded, and added to the plan wording as necessary. For example, paragraph 5 includes two sentences describing the use of a giant sail as a defensive measure. However, the plan merely mentioned the idea of a "solar sail." The student had to refer back to Diagram 2 to obtain the details.

- The essay does not include every detail that appears in the plan or in the selection. Rather, the student chose the information and ideas that were most significant, most relevant, and would best accomplish the specific writing purpose. Note, too, that the essay does not just summarize or repeat selection content. Instead, the essay expresses key information from the selection in the student's own words.

- The student's response shows a thorough understanding of the textual and visual materials and makes strong connections between the content of these materials and the writing task.

- The essay is organized clearly, logically, and coherently. The student uses transitional words, phrases, and sentences to connect ideas and help readers follow the content flow. For example, the last sentence of paragraph 1 leads students directly into paragraph 2.

- Sentences are varied in structure and length, which helps to engage and hold the reader's interest.

Activity X: Examining a Part B Response

Answer the following questions about the student's response.

1. The student used the incident involving asteroid 1997 XF11 as the basis of the opening paragraph. Do you think this was an effective way to begin the essay? Why or why not?

   _____

   _____

   _____

2. Paragraph 2 starts with a topic sentence. What is the main idea that this sentence states?

   _____

   _____

   _____

3. What specific details does the student use to support the main idea of paragraph 2?

_____

_____

_____

4. What is the main form of organization the student uses in paragraph 2: order of increasing importance, order of decreasing importance, or chronological order?

_____

_____

_____

5. Suppose you wanted to divide paragraph 4 into two shorter, separate paragraphs. How would you break up the content?

_____

_____

_____

6. Give five examples of transitional words or phrases. Explain what function each word or phrase serves. (You may want to refer back to the *Transitional Words and Phrases* chart on page 150.)

_____

_____

_____

7. The student includes a direct quotation in paragraph 2. What idea in the essay does this quotation help to support?

_____

_____

_____

8. Review the chart on page 140, *Scoring the Part B Extended Response.* If you were a reader evaluating the student's response, how would you rate it? Give specific reasons for your answer.

_____

_____

_____

Use Your Time Wisely

Remember to carry out all four steps of the writing process: prewriting, drafting, revising, and editing/proofreading. After you've written your response, reread what you've written and revise, edit, and polish it. Proofread for errors, and look for ways to strengthen your language. For example, change vague words to specific words, and use active, not passive, constructions.

TIP

Activity Y: Writing an Extended Response

Using the plan you created in *Activity Q* on page 143 along with the suggestions and student examples provided in this section, write your own extended response on a separate sheet of paper. Make revisions as needed and submit it to a classmate or teacher for evaluation.

6

CHAPTER REVIEW

Look back at the various lists, boldfaced items, boxes, and charts to quickly review many of the important ideas presented. You'll also find it helpful to review Chapters 1 and 2. Here are a few key points to get your review started:

- Session One, Part B of the Regents exam requires you to use information from a combination of two sources: a reading selection and a graph, diagram, table, or other visual material.

- Think about the purpose of the visual material and its relationship to the reading selection.

- The notes you take should help you zero in on important ideas and information in the textual and visual materials. Keep your notes brief and concise.

- Support the ideas in your extended response with "specific, accurate, and relevant information" from the textual and visual materials.

- Your response should flow logically, using an organizational approach that you think will work best. Your structure may not fit neatly into one particular pattern, so you may need to blend organizational methods or use an approach tailored specifically to the prompt.

- Use transitional words, phrases, and sentences to help make your writing coherent.

PRACTICE FOR SESSION ONE, PART B

The test and activities that follow will give you an opportunity to practice and develop the skills you'll need to do well on Part B of the Regents English exam. But don't limit yourself to just these activities. Practice on your own, or ask your teacher for help.

PRACTICE TEST (SESSION ONE, PART B)

Directions: Read the text and study the graph and table on the following pages, answer the multiple-choice questions, and write a response based on the situation described below. You may use the margins to take notes as you read and scrap paper to plan your response.

> **The Situation**: You are a member of the youth advisory board of a national driver safety organization. You have been asked to write a report recommending what principles should be stressed in driver education programs.

Your Task: Write a report for a national driver safety organization. Using relevant information from the text *and* the graph and table, discuss factors that cause motor vehicle accidents and recommended principles to be stressed in driver education programs.

Guidelines:

Be sure to
- Tell your audience what they need to know about factors that cause motor vehicle accidents
- Explain what principles you believe should be stressed in driver education programs
- Use specific, accurate, and relevant information from the article *and* the graph and table to support your discussion
- Use a tone and level of language appropriate for a report to be submitted to a national driver safety organization
- Organize your ideas in a logical and coherent manner
- Indicate any words taken directly from the article by using quotation marks or referring to the author
- Follow the conventions of standard written English

What Makes a Safe Driver?

According to National Highway Transportation Safety Agency, approximately three-quarters of the more than 6 million motor vehicle collisions which occur on U.S. highways annually are caused by drivers' attention being diverted in the moments before collision. Despite every device that auto manufacturers can
5   provide to ensure car safety, it is primarily the driver of a vehicle who ultimately determines whether or not a car or truck will be involved in an accident. Many factors play a part in traffic fatalities, including the amount of alcohol consumed before getting behind the wheel, the age of the driver, and the speed of the vehicle. The U.S. General Accounting Office study, *Factors Affecting Involvement*
10   *in Vehicle Crashes*, Washington, DC, 1994, revealed that, when other factors are controlled, driver characteristics far outweigh vehicle factors in predicting a crash.

Alcohol Impairment

The use of alcohol as a contributing factor in fatal traffic accidents has been steadily decreasing since 1982, most likely because of tougher enforcement of liquor and DWI laws in most states and the raising of the drinking age to 21. In 1982,
15   about 57 percent of all traffic fatalities involved an intoxicated driver (this includes motorcyclists). NHTSA reported that 41 percent of all traffic deaths in 1995 involved a person who was legally intoxicated (blood alcohol concentration of 0.10 or higher) — more than 17,270 alcohol-related fatalities.

The highest rates of intoxication were for drivers in their early 20s. About
20   35 percent of all drivers ages 21 through 24 involved in a fatal accident were legally drunk. The rate of intoxication decreased steadily with age, and only about 6.8 percent of drivers on the road over age 65 involved in fatal accidents were drunk.

In its 1996 survey, *Prevention Magazine* found that 17 percent of drivers
25   said they sometimes drive after drinking. Men were about twice as likely as women (23 percent vs. 12 percent) to say that they sometimes drive after drinking. Unfortunately, heavy drinkers were the most likely to drive after drinking.

FIGURE 1
Driving at or Below the Speed Limit

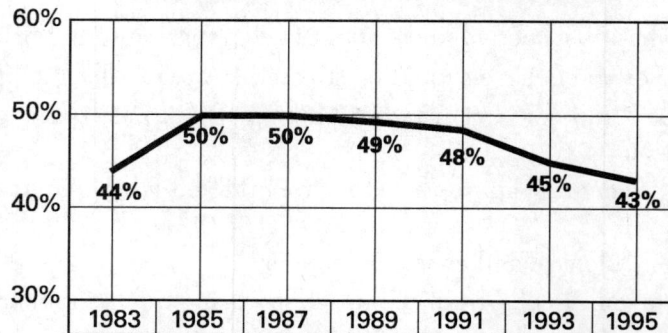

Source: *Auto Safety in America*, Prevention Magazine, Emmaus, PA, 1996

162

Young Drivers and Accidents

30

The youngest drivers, those under age 20, are the most accident-prone. Accident rates decrease between ages 25 and 34 and then gradually increase between ages 35 and 74. After the driver reaches 74, the accident rate increases sharply.

35

40

Young drivers between the ages of 16 and 24 are disproportionately high contributors to traffic accidents and highway deaths. Young drivers also pose the greatest loss for insurers. According to the AAA Foundation for Traffic Safety, about 75 percent of young driver citations are issued for speeding, young males consistently have more costly claims, and in addition to speeding, principal factors involved in young driver accidents are losing control of the vehicle and rear-ending the car in front. The AAA also reports that insurance companies are reducing the number of young policy holders covered under traditional coverage by sending them to more costly risk insurers.

FIGURE 2

IMPROPER DRIVING REPORTED IN ACCIDENTS, 1995*

Kind of Improper Driving	Fatal Accidents	Injury Accidents	All Accidents
Total	**100.0%**	**100.0%**	**100.0%**
Improper driving	**68.1**	**73.5**	**75.5**
Speed too fast or unsafe	19.8	13.9	14.0
Right of way	15.2	25.5	22.9
Failed to yield	10.2	18.1	17.0
Disregarded signal	3.0	5.0	4.0
Passed stop sign	2.2	2.4	1.9
Drove left of center	9.1	2.4	2.2
Made improper turn	2.3	2.8	4.2
Improper overtaking	1.5	1.3	1.5
Followed too closely	0.5	7.0	7.2
Other improper driving	19.7	20.7	23.6
No improper driving stated	**31.9**	**26.5**	**24.5**

*Based on reports from 20 state traffic authorities

Source: *Accident Facts, 1996 Edition*, National Safety Council, Itasca, IL, 1996

45

Many young people object to being penalized with high insurance rates and are proposing "age-free" insurance policy programs. Under such policies, young beginning drivers would be required to pass rigorous driver education courses and sign contracts agreeing to abide by safety belt laws, drinking-and-driving laws, and other safety behaviors. In return, they would pay higher premiums for a specified time and then be eligible for refunds if they lived up to the contract terms.

50

Citing inadequate driver training as contributing toward teenage driving error, several organizations, such as the National Highway Traffic Safety

163

Administration, the Insurance Institute for Highway Safety, and the National Association of Independent Insurers, support "graduated licensing" for the future. Under such a program, teens would not go directly from learner's permit to adult license. Rather, there would be an intermediate stage involving more restrictions and greater supervision during a teen's most dangerous driving years, from 16 to 18. The aim is to control and monitor their progress toward full driving privileges as restrictions are lifted when drivers gain added experience and maturity.

Older Drivers and Accidents

As the U.S. population matures, an increasing number of older drivers will be on the road. The U.S. General Accounting Office (*Factors Affecting Involvement in Vehicle Crashes,* Washington, DC, 1994) reported that when the miles they drive are considered, elderly persons are disproportionately involved in collisions, particularly two-vehicle collisions. The National Safety Council has found that there are definite crash patterns among older drivers. They often fail to yield the right of way and sometimes do not pay attention to, or do not see, signs and signals.

Senior citizens' driving skills may diminish in other ways, including functional losses in vision, reaction time, and the speed of information processing. They often have more difficulty with backing and parking maneuvers. Older drivers have the most accidents making left turns across traffic. The American Automobile Association's Foundation for Traffic Safety notes, however, that it is not chronological age but the driver's overall functional ability which predicts driving difficulties. This means that one cannot assume that a driver who is age 60 is necessarily more able to drive than one who is 75.

Older people enjoy the freedom and independence of driving their own cars as much as anyone else. In looking toward the future, when many more senior citizens will be on the road, the AAA has sponsored a study which is developing guidelines for a "grade" licensing program — a license that carries some restrictions. Several states are already experimenting with these licenses which attempt to balance the risks and safety needs of older drivers and others. The goal of the program is to help elderly drivers maintain their mobility for as long as they can safely do so.

Obeying the Speed Limit

The *Prevention Magazine* 1996 annual study on American behavior revealed that less than half (43 percent) of Americans who drive claim they always stay within the speed limit. A majority (55 percent) say they sometimes or never adhere to speed laws. (See Figure 1.) Careful observance of speed laws is more prevalent among older drivers. Along with age, income and education are determining factors in compliance with speed laws. As income and education levels increase, compliance with speed laws declines. Men are more likely than women to break speed laws.

Accidents and Driver Error

Most accidents on the road result from the interaction of three factors — the driver, the vehicle, and the road conditions. While motorists have little or

95 no control over highway conditions and usually cannot predict whether their vehicles will perform correctly, they can control the way they drive. Cellular telephone use in a moving vehicle increases the risk of having an accident four-fold — the same risk as when a person's blood alcohol level is at the legal limit. Figure 2 lists types of improper driving that resulted in injuries or fatal accidents in 1995.

100 Right-of-way mistakes and speeding cause the most accidents and fatal injuries. The National Safety Council estimates that 76 percent of all accidents were caused by some type of driver error. Of collisions between motor vehicles, angle-collisions (collisions which are not head-on, rear-end, rear-to-rear, or side-swipe) cause most deaths, while rear-end collisions generate the most nonfatal injuries and injury accidents.

Multiple-Choice Questions

Directions (7–16): Answer the following questions. Select the best suggested answer and circle its number. The questions may help you think about ideas and information you might use in your writing. You may return to these questions anytime you wish.

7 About three-quarters of motor vehicle crashes occur when drivers

1 make improper turns
2 drive too fast
3 are distracted just before a collision
4 fail to yield the right of way

8 Alcohol use as a contributing factor to car crashes

1 increased between 1982 and 1995
2 is a marked problem with drivers in their early 20s
3 tends to increase with driver age
4 affects a greater percentage of women than men

9 Which drivers are most likely to have an accident?

1 drivers under age 20
2 drivers between ages 25 and 34
3 drivers between ages 35 and 59
4 drivers in their 60s

10 The text implies that speeding is a particular problem with

1 young male drivers
2 older drivers
3 female drivers
4 drivers with limited education

11 The text implies that "graduated licensing" (line 52) would

1 improve driver safety among senior citizens
2 reduce alcohol use as a contributing factor to collisions
3 improve the skills of all drivers
4 produce more experienced and mature teen drivers

12 According to the American Automobile Association, the factor that best predicts the likelihood of driving difficulties is

1 whether or not the driver is a senior citizen
2 the driver's overall ability to function
3 whether the driver is male or female
4 the condition of the driver's vehicle

13 According to the text, the most important factor determining whether or not a driver will have an accident is

  1 how the driver operates the vehicle
  2 the age of the driver
  3 roadway conditions
  4 how many years the driver has had a license

14 The text (lines 94–96) implies that talking on a cellular phone while driving is

  1 safe if the driver is careful
  2 against the law
  3 as risky as drinking before driving
  4 the leading cause of fatal collisions

15 What general conclusion can you draw from Figure 1?

  1 The percentage of drivers who obey speed limits changes dramatically from year to year.
  2 Drivers tend to exceed the speed limit.
  3 Most drivers drive at or below the speed limit.
  4 More drivers obey speed limits in the 1990s than in the 1980s.

16 According to Figure 2, what percentage of fatal accidents are *not* caused by improper driving?

  1 about 68 percent
  2 about 20 percent
  3 about 27 percent
  4 about 32 percent

After you have finished these questions, review **The Situation** and read **Your Task** and the **Guidelines**. Use scrap paper to plan your response. Then write your response.

Evaluating a Part B Response

Exchange papers with a partner. Referring to the chart on page 140, *Scoring the Part B Extended Response,* evaluate your partner's written response on the basis of the five criteria.

Be as *positive, constructive, and specific* as you can in your comments and suggestions. Your goal is to help your partner improve his or her skills.

*MEANING:*_____

_____

_____

_____

_____

*DEVELOPMENT:*_____

_____

_____

_____

_____

*ORGANIZATION:*_____

_____

_____

_____

_____

*LANGUAGE USE:*_____

_____

_____

_____

_____

CONVENTIONS: _____

_____

_____

_____

_____

_____

Improving and Polishing Your Part B Response

Use your partner's comments to help you revise, edit, and polish your paper. Make whatever changes you think are necessary to improve your work.

For additional practice, two actual Regents exams appear at the end of this book.

CHAPTER 4

Reading and Writing for Literary Response

1

UNDERSTANDING THE SESSION TWO, PART A TASKS

For Session Two, Part A of the Regents Comprehensive Examination in English, you will read two literary selections. They may be short, complete selections or excerpts from longer works. The two texts will share a common topic or theme, but they will represent two different *genres,* or types of literature. For example, you may read a poem and a short story, a novel excerpt and a memoir, or a literary essay and a play excerpt. You may take notes as you read the selections.

Next, you'll answer ten multiple-choice questions about the two literary selections. Finally, you'll write an essay based on your understanding and analysis of the selections.

Part A of the Regents Comprehensive Examination in English

Read:
Read two literary selections. Take notes.

Answer:
Answer multiple-choice questions about the selections.

Write:
Write an essay about the two selections.

✺ A QUICK LOOK ✺

◆ *What is Part A testing me on?*

Part A tests your ability to understand and analyze two literary selections and write an essay about them. Part A also tests your understanding of how authors use literary elements and techniques.

◆ *How is Part A similar to other parts of the exam?*

Like most other parts of the test, Part A requires you to answer multiple-choice questions and then write an extended response.

◆ *How does Part A differ from other parts of the exam?*

Unlike the two parts of Session One, Session Two, Part A deals with literary rather than informational selections. Also, Part A specifies that your response take the form of "a unified essay."

Examining the Session Two, Part A Prompt

Although Session Two, Part A of the Regents exam resembles the two parts of Session One, Part A differs in several ways. First, the Part A prompt does not have **The Situation** section. Second, the **Guidelines** section of the prompt is different from the **Guidelines** section in Session One. Third, Part A includes two separate (but related) reading selections.

Look at the typical Part A prompt that begins on page 174. It consists of the following elements:

- Directions
- Your Task
- Guidelines
- Two reading selections

Multiple-choice questions about the selections appear later in the chapter.

NOTE: For now, just look over the prompt to get a feel for it. **Do not read the selections yet.** *You will refer back to this prompt and the selections later in the chapter.*

PART A

Directions: Read the passages on the following pages (a poem and a short story) and answer the multiple-choice questions. Then write the essay described in **Your Task**. You may use the margins to take notes as you read and scrap paper to plan your response.

Your Task:

After you have read the passages and answered the multiple-choice questions, write a unified essay about the need for people to support and protect others, as revealed in the passages. In your essay, use ideas from **both** passages to establish a controlling idea about the need for people to support and protect others. Using evidence from **each** passage, develop your controlling idea and show how each author uses specific literary elements or techniques to convey that idea.

Guidelines:

Be sure to

- Use ideas from **both** passages to establish a controlling idea about the need for people to support and protect others
- Use specific and relevant evidence from **each** passage to develop your controlling idea
- Show how each author uses specific literary elements (for example: characterization, structure, point of view) or techniques (for example: imagery, symbolism, repetition, figurative language) to convey the controlling idea
- Organize your ideas in a logical and coherent manner
- Use language that communicates ideas effectively
- Follow the conventions of standard written English

Passage I

SHOULDERS

A man crosses the street in rain,
stepping gently, looking two times north and south,
because his son is asleep on his shoulder.

No car must splash him.
5   No car drive too near to his shadow.

This man carries the world's most sensitive cargo
but he's not marked.
Nowhere does his jacket say FRAGILE,
HANDLE WITH CARE.

10   His ear fills up with breathing.
He hears the hum of a boy's dream
deep inside him.

We're not going to be able
to live in this world
15   if we're not willing to do what he's doing
with one another.

The road will only be wide.
The rain will never stop falling.

—Naomi Shihab Nye

Passage II

BABY ON THE BEACH*

I heard a baby cry. Not sadly. Not in pain. But in a panic. It was screaming, and the cry was full of panic.

I put down my work and listened. There was something wild in that cry. Something awful and wild. The cry was loud. It sounded near, almost as if the
5   baby were there in the cabin with me. I stopped my work and walked out on the porch to listen. The sobs came louder, faster. I turned my head toward the sound. The screams hit me like blows.

From the top of the steps, at the edge of the porch, I saw him. Far below, on the beach, a small child stood alone. He seemed far away and tiny, down
10   there on the empty beach. But his cry was loud, like a gull's cry. His sobs came louder, faster. His face was turned up to the sky. He was screaming at the sky.

He was too small to be left alone. Where were his mother, his father? Down there on the empty beach, the child was far from the road, far from the
15   two small cabins full of summer people.

I took off, running toward the cry. I ran down the steps, my heart pounding all the way. From the bottom of the steps I couldn't see the beach or the child. But I heard him. I ran down the path from my cabin toward the beach, toward the cry.

20   When I got to the beach, I bent down and opened my arms. The child was still screaming. When I opened my arms, he came to me. I picked him up and held him. He was two, or maybe three. Still in Pampers. He looked at my face. Full of trust, he looked in my eyes. Then he let his head fall on my shoulder. He sobbed two or three more sobs. Then he closed his eyes, stopped crying,
25   and seemed to drop off to sleep.

He felt sweet in my arms. His eyes were red from crying. His hair was black. His face was red and wet and soft.

"Where's your mama?" I asked.

He opened his eyes and lifted his head. "Mama, there." He pointed to the
30   path that led up from the beach, away from the water. Toward the summer cabins behind the trees.

I looked. I saw no one. Only three gulls at the water's edge. You couldn't see the cabins from down there on the beach. You could see only the trees in front of the cabins. Again I asked, "Where's your mama?"

35   Again he pointed away from the water, toward the path. "Mama, there."

---

*For instructional purposes, the story "Baby on the Beach" is included here in its entirety. However, passages used in the actual Regents exam are usually shorter, and you're likely to encounter an excerpt from a longer work.

176

Still, I saw no one. I put the child down on the sand and took his hand. "Show me," I said. I wanted him to lead me to his mother. I was afraid to carry him. He felt so sweet in my arms. Like my own child. Maybe someone would think I stole him. "Show me where your mama is."

40 "Mama there," he said again. But he didn't go toward the path. Instead he lifted his arms. He wanted me to carry him.

"Show me," I pleaded. But he was too tired to walk. He had cried too long and too hard. He needed me to carry him.

The soft sand was hard to walk on. A wind was starting to blow. "Okay," I
45 said. I lifted him up.

It was a long walk across that windy beach with a child in my arms. What must it feel like to him? Nothing to see but sand and water. No cabins. No road. No people. Nothing to hear but wind and gulls. Nothing to feel but sun and sand. No wonder the child felt panic. What if I hadn't come?

50 I started off toward the path that led past the trees. I walked slowly, feeling the sweet cheek on my shoulder, the trusting hand in my hair. "Okay," I said. I kissed his head. "We'll find your mama."

At the edge of the water, two people were walking toward us. They had come from the path, way across the beach. A young woman and a little girl.

55 I pointed to them.

"Is that your mama?" I asked the boy.

He opened his eyes, then shook his head.

I put him down on the sand.

"Is that your mama?" I asked again, pointing.

60 "No," he said.

Then he looked at me pleadingly and held up his arms. Still too tired to walk. I lifted him again and carried him toward the people.

The woman had a pretty face. She had big soft eyes, a tiny nose, and smooth red hair that fell softly to her shoulders. She had long tan legs and arms. And
65 she was smiling.

"I'm not his mother," she said. The first thing that woman said to me was, "I'm not his mother." Smiling, she ran her hand across her long red hair.

"Do you like that baby?" asked the little girl. "His name is Tony."

The woman looked down at the girl and smiled. "Oh, are you giving Tony
70 away?"

Tony's arms held fast to my neck; his head still rested on my shoulder. I held on to him. "Where is his mother, then?" I asked. "He's pretty upset."

177

75 "Oh, it's not as bad as it looks," said the woman. "He's okay. His mother is my friend. They just came out to the beach for the day. It's okay."

It didn't look okay to me. The woman didn't hold out her arms to Tony. She didn't even look at him. She looked only at me.

80 "It was my idea," she said. "I told his mother to leave him there. He was acting awful. He didn't want to walk. He wanted to be carried. He was crying and screaming. He was so bad. He just wouldn't stop. So I said, Let's just keep walking and see how long he carries on like this. He can't keep it up all day. So we walked on home."

I stared at her. Crying was *bad?* "But he didn't know where you were," I said. "He couldn't see you."

85 "He couldn't see us, but we could see him from the cabin."

I looked at her, smoothing her hair with her hand, smiling. I shook my head. Who could leave a baby alone to panic on a strange beach? My heart was pounding again. I was getting more and more upset. But I didn't say any more. What could I say? Words would add nothing. The woman was upset.
90 What did she think? She never stopped smiling. She never looked at the child. She looked only at me.

I handed Tony to the woman. She took him without a word. He went smoothly into her arms. She didn't try to put him down. Full of trust, he didn't even look back.

95 "Take care of him," I said.

"Tony, say bye-bye," said the little girl. "Blow a kiss, Tony," she said. But Tony's head was on the woman's shoulder, and he didn't look back.

The wind had started up again. From my porch I looked down on the empty beach. Only the gulls over the water were crying now.

—Alix Kates Shulman

Q & A

**The Part A prompt calls for a "unified essay."
What exactly does that term mean?**

A *unified essay* is an extended written response that has two key characteristics: it conveys a clear central point (the controlling idea), and every paragraph in the essay relates to that point.

As in Session One, each element of the prompt has a specific purpose:

- **Directions** summarizes what you'll have to do for Part A.
- **Your Task** and **Guidelines** describe in detail the essay you will write.
- *The two reading selections* serve as your basis for answering the multiple-choice questions and for writing the essay.
- The *multiple-choice questions*, which appear later in the chapter, highlight key ideas and features in the selections.

Let's look more closely at these elements.

Directions tells you that you'll read two passages, answer questions, and then write your essay. The prompt also suggests that you take notes, which you can refer back to when you answer the multiple-choice questions and when you write your response.

> **Directions:** Read the passages on the following pages (a poem and a short story) and answer the multiple-choice questions. Then write the essay described in **Your Task**. You may use the margins to take notes as you read and scrap paper to plan your response.

The next part of the Part A prompt, **Your Task**, states exactly what your writing task involves. It's essential to read **Your Task** carefully to make sure you understand what's required.

Your Task:

After you have read the passages and answered the multiple-choice questions, write a unified essay about the need for people to support and protect others, as revealed in the passages. In your essay, use ideas from *both* passages to establish a controlling idea about the need for people to support and protect others. Using evidence from *each* passage, develop your controlling idea, and show how each author uses specific literary elements or techniques to convey that idea.

Notice that **Your Task** describes several different aspects of the writing task, which break down like this:

- "... write a unified essay about the need for people to support and protect others, as revealed in the passages."

  This part of **Your Task** identifies the common topic or theme that the two reading selections share. In this prompt, the common theme is "the need for people to support and protect others."

  Note especially the phrase, "as revealed in the passages." The phrase is important because it tells you that *the ideas and supporting details in your essay must be directly linked to the two passages.* While you can and should draw on your own knowledge and experience to support your analysis of the selections, the substance of your essay must be based on the selections themselves. This same phrase appears again in the **Guidelines.**

- "... use ideas from *both* passages to establish a controlling idea about the need for people to support and protect others."

  Note that the word *both* is in boldface type. This is a reminder that your controlling idea—the central point of your essay—must reflect key ideas from both reading selections, not just one.

- "Using evidence from *each* passage, develop your controlling idea ..."

  Here, *each* is in boldface type. The prompt is reminding you to use supporting details from both selections to develop your controlling idea.

180

". . . show how each author uses specific literary elements or techniques to convey that idea."

This part of the prompt tells you that as part of your analysis of the selections you need to discuss the authors' use of literary elements or techniques.

? *Answer in your own words:* The phrase "as revealed in the passages" appears in **Your Task** and again in the **Guidelines**. What does the phrase mean?

_____

_____

Q & A

The Part A prompt refers to establishing and developing a "controlling idea." Is a controlling idea the same as a "central point"? Is it also the same as a thesis?

Essentially, these terms are the same. As you read in Chapter 2 (page 30), "the central point . . . is the principal point, or main focus, that the writer wants to communicate." Various terms have basically the same meaning as *central point*, including *controlling idea* and *thesis*. Note, too, that the sentence that states the central point of an essay is commonly called the *thesis statement*. (You'll read more about thesis statements on page 217.)

The central point, or controlling idea, that you establish for your Part A essay should be the focus of your writing. In other words, to write the unified essay that Part A calls for, be sure all your paragraphs relate to your controlling idea.

The **Guidelines** that follow **Your Task** provide additional guidance and relate the writing task to the five scoring criteria. Note that the word *both* is again boldfaced for emphasis.

Guidelines:

Be sure to

- Use ideas from *both* passages to establish a controlling idea about the need for people to support and protect others
- Use specific and relevant evidence from *each* passage to develop your controlling idea
- Show how each author uses specific literary elements (for example: characterization, structure, point of view) or techniques (for example: imagery, symbolism, repetition, figurative language) to convey the controlling idea
- Organize your ideas in a logical and coherent manner
- Use language that communicates ideas effectively
- Follow the conventions of standard written English

The first three guidelines help clarify both your writing task and purpose. Notice that the second guideline refers to "specific and relevant evidence." Just as for other parts of the Regents exam, using supporting details that are too general or that do not relate to your task and purpose will lower your score.

Notice, too, that the third guideline mentions several examples of literary elements and techniques. Keep in mind that you're not limited to just these particular examples. You may discuss any of the various literary elements and techniques that you know. Look at the two *Basics* boxes on pages 189–191 for a description of common literary elements and techniques.

After the reading selections, the last section of Part A consists of ten multiple-choice questions. As in previous parts of the exam, this section has its own directions, reminding you that the multiple-choice questions may prove helpful when you write your response. These questions appear later in the chapter.

The Part A multiple-choice questions are divided into two groups, one group relating to "Passage I" and the other relating to "Passage II." Following the questions, the prompt advises you to review **Your Task** and the **Guidelines** and to use scrap paper to plan your essay.

Activity A: Examining a Part A Prompt

A portion of a Part A prompt appears below. Read the prompt, and answer the questions that follow.

Directions: Read the passages on the following pages (a novel excerpt and a memoir) and answer the multiple-choice questions. Then write the essay described in **Your Task**. You may use the margins to take notes as you read and scrap paper to plan your response.

Your Task:

> After you have read the passages and answered the multiple-choice questions, write a unified essay about the effects of discrimination on people as revealed in the passages. In your essay, use ideas from ***both*** passages to establish a controlling idea about the effects of discrimination. Using evidence from ***each*** passage, develop your controlling idea and show how each author uses specific literary elements or techniques to convey that idea.

Guidelines:

Be sure to

- Use ideas from ***both*** passages to establish a controlling idea about the effects of discrimination on the people who are discriminated against
- Use specific and relevant evidence from ***each*** passage to develop your controlling idea
- Show how each author uses specific literary elements (for example: setting, characterization, structure, point of view) or techniques (for example: symbolism, irony, figurative language) to convey the controlling idea

1. From where should your ideas and supporting details come for both the multiple-choice questions and the essay?

_____

_____

2. What is the common topic or theme that the two reading selections share?

_____

_____

3. In your own words, describe the specific writing task and purpose.

_____

_____

_____

4. Why is the phrase "as revealed in the passages" significant?

_____

_____

_____

5. Define the terms *unified essay* and *controlling idea,* and explain how the two terms are related.

_____

_____

_____

> **Distinguish Controlling Idea from Topic/Theme**   *TIP*
>
> The controlling idea that you establish for your Part A essay will relate directly to the topic or theme shared by the two selections. However, the controlling idea and the topic/theme are not exactly the same. Your controlling idea needs to be more specific and more sharply focused than the topic/theme.
>
> For example, two selections may both deal with this topic: "the conflicts that occur in the parent-child relationship during the teen years." The controlling idea for your essay, however, might be: "teenagers and parents can get along if they both make an effort" or "two-way communication is the key to a good parent-teen relationship."

2

EFFECTIVE READING AND NOTE-TAKING FOR PART A

In previous chapters, you learned various strategies for reading and taking notes. You can apply these same strategies to the Session Two, Part A selections. However, because Part A is based on literary rather than informational selections, and because the Part A writing task differs from preceding writing tasks, you'll need to approach the reading material with a somewhat different mind-set.

Strategies for Reading the Part A Literary Selections

There are many different kinds of literary works, ranging from poems and stories to novels and memoirs to plays and literary essays. Authors of these works sometimes express themselves clearly and directly. Other times, they communicate their meaning through subtle implication or through the use of various literary techniques. The following suggestions will help you read, interpret, and understand the literary selections that appear in Part A.

▶ **Before reading each selection, think about the topic or theme identified by the prompt.** What does the topic/theme mean? Restate it in your own words. Can you interpret the topic/theme in more than one way? As you read, begin to think about how you might translate the topic/theme into a controlling idea for your essay.

▶ **Skim the multiple-choice questions.** Before you read each selection, look over the multiple-choice questions. Looking at the questions in advance will alert you to important ideas and details to watch for as you read.

▶ **Relate the selections to the topic or theme.** Try to "see" the selections in terms of the topic/theme. Consider how they are linked. Remember that even though they have a topic/theme in common, the two selections are likely to reflect different or even opposing opinions.

? *Answer in a sentence or two:* Why is it a good idea to think about the topic or theme *before* reading the selections?

_____

_____

▶ **Consider how and why the writer uses specific literary elements and techniques.** Whether you're reading poetry or prose, watch for the literary elements and techniques that writers use to convey their ideas. Recognizing these elements and techniques will help you analyze the selections and prepare you for writing your essay.

▶ **Think about the author's purpose and point of view.** Why is the author writing this, and what is his or her attitude towards the subject?

▶ **When reading poetry, take your time.** It's possible that one of the selections you'll read in Part A of the Regents exam will be a poem. Analyzing poetry requires concentration. Here are some helpful tips:

◊ Always read a poem several times. Read slowly, pausing to think about words and images.

◊ Consider the kind of poem you're reading. Does it tell a story? Express an emotion? Describe a scene?

◊ Identify key ideas, stated and implied. Keep in mind that poetry is especially likely to call upon your ability to *infer* meaning.

◊ Don't limit your thinking to the literal. *Look for multiple levels of meaning,* especially the figurative and symbolic use of words. A poet may describe the hot summer sunshine as "nature's fiery fury" or use a baby to symbolize innocence.

◊ Reread difficult lines, and try to relate their meaning to lines of the poem you feel confident about. Use context clues to help you determine the meaning of unfamiliar words.

◊ Restate or summarize the poet's main idea(s) in your own words.

▶ **Read prose selections carefully.** Prose selections may be fiction or nonfiction. Examples of fiction include novels, short stories, and plays. Examples of nonfiction include memoirs, literary essays, and journals. Here are some tips for reading prose selections:

◊ Identify the genre (type of literature) you're reading.

◊ Think about the central point of the selection.

◊ Identify main ideas in the selection, both stated and implied.

◊ Reread all or parts of the selection as needed to fully grasp the author's meaning. Don't be tempted to skip sections that seem difficult. Instead, take the time to try to understand them.

◊ As with poetry, don't limit your thinking to the literal. Look for multiple levels of meaning. For example, authors typically use symbolism to convey meaning. Therefore, an eagle soaring across the sky may represent freedom.

Activity B: Relating a Poem to a Topic

This activity will give you practice in applying some of the strategies discussed above.

The topic identified by a Part A prompt is "how future expectations affect a person's life." Answer the following questions.

1. What do you think this topic means? Could you interpret it in more than one way? Explain.

   _____

   _____

   _____

   _____

2. Read the following poem. What does the poem seem to be saying? What words or images support your interpretation? Could the poem be suggesting something else? If so, what?

   _____

   _____

   _____

   _____

Dreams
　　Hold fast to dreams
　　For if dreams die
　　Life is a broken-winged bird
　　That cannot fly.

　　Hold fast to dreams
　　For when dreams go
　　Life is a barren field
　　Frozen with snow.

—Langston Hughes

TO UNDERSTAND A POEM...

→ Read it several times.

　→ Think about stated and implied ideas.

　　→ Look for multiple levels of meaning.

　　　→ Use context clues.

　　　　→ Restate ideas in your own words.

---

3. How does the poem relate to the Part A topic? Be specific.

_____

_____

_____

_____

4. How might you translate the topic into a controlling idea for an essay?

_____

_____

_____

_____

Reinforce Your Knowledge

TIP

Skill Builder 1, Recognizing Key Ideas and Information, pages 30–38, _Skill Builder 2, Making Inferences and Drawing Conclusions,_ pages 39–45, and _Skill Builder 3, Using Context Clues to Determine Meaning,_ pages 115–122, can help you identify and understand important ideas and details in the Part A reading selections.

The ◆ Basics

LITERARY ELEMENTS

Every work of literature is made up of a combination of elements. What makes each work unique is the creative way in which the author handles and blends these elements.

As part of the essay you write for Part A of the Regents exam, you will have to discuss the authors' use of specific literary elements, such as those described below.

◆ *Characterization* refers to the creation and development of *characters*, the people who carry on the action in a literary work.

◆ *Mood* refers to the atmosphere or feeling of a literary work. For example, the mood may be joyful, gloomy, or suspenseful.

◆ The *plot* of a short story, novel, or other narrative work is the sequence of events that take place.

◆ *Point of view* refers to the vantage point from which a story is told. For example, in *first-person* point of view, the narrator himself or herself tells the story and may participate in events. Works written in the first person use pronouns such as *I, me,* and *my.* In *omniscient,* point of view, the author is an all-knowing impersonal observer who does not take part in events but can describe the thoughts and actions of all characters. A *limited-omniscient* point of view limits the description to the thoughts and feelings of one character even though the actions of other characters may be described fully.

◆ *Setting* is the time and place in which events occur. For example, the setting of Shakespeare's play *Macbeth* is eleventh-century Scotland.

◆ *Structure* refers to how the parts of a literary work are organized and arranged. For example, the structure of a novel may be based on chronological order with occasional *flashbacks.* The structure of poetry includes the number, form, and pattern of lines and stanzas.

◆ The *theme* of a literary work is its central idea. For example, many authors have written on the theme that life is short, so everyone must make the most of each day.

◆ *Tone* is the attitude or viewpoint that an author shows toward his or her subject. For example, the tone may be serious, sympathetic, or angry.

The ◆ Basics

LITERARY TECHNIQUES

Authors and poets use many different techniques when they write. These techniques help to convey ideas and feelings and create memorable works of literature.

As part of the essay you write for Part A of the Regents exam, you will have to discuss the authors' use of specific literary techniques, such as those described below.

◆ *Allegory* is the representation of ideas or moral principles by means of symbolic characters, events, or objects. For example, Aesop's fables use allegory to teach lessons about life.

◆ *Alliteration* is the repetition of an initial (usually consonant) sound, as in "*s*wift, *s*ilent *s*erpent."

◆ *Figurative language* refers to the use of words in an imaginative, nonliteral sense. Similes and metaphors (see below) are examples of figurative language.

◆ *Figures of speech* are forms of expression in which the author uses language in an imaginative, nonliteral sense in order to make a comparison or produce a desired effect.

A *simile* is a comparison using *like* or *as*. Examples: Her eyes gleamed like stars. The house was as large as a castle.

A *metaphor* is a comparison between unlike objects that does not use *like* or *as*. Example: The girls were tigers on the playing field, ferociously mauling their opponents.

Personification is a figure of speech that applies human qualities to objects, ideas, or animals. Example: The sun smiled down on the village.

Hyperbole, or *exaggeration*, is overstatement for the purpose of emphasis. Example: His ears were so sharp he could hear dogs bark in the next county.

Onomatopoeia refers to the use of words that sound like the things they name. Examples: *bang, buzz, crackle, sizzle, hiss, murmur, roar.*

An *oxymoron* is a combination of two contradictory words. Examples: deafening silence, a definite possibility.

◆ *Flashback* refers to the insertion of a scene showing an earlier event, often one that took place before the opening scene of a literary work. For example, a novelist may include a flashback to reveal a childhood incident in the life of an adult character.

◆ *Foreshadowing* refers to the suggestion of events to come. For example, gray clouds at the beginning of a story may foreshadow a storm that occurs later.

◆ *Imagery* refers to the use of description of figurative language to create vivid images, or word pictures. These images may appeal to the sense of sight or to any of the other senses. Examples: Thick tree roots clutched the ground like gnarled fingers. The frightened screech of an unseen animal tore through the night.

◆ *Irony* refers to a situation or event that is the opposite of what is or might be expected. For example, it would be *ironic* if a lifeguard had to be saved from drowning.

Irony can also refer to the expression of an attitude or intention that is the opposite of what is actually meant, as when a latecomer is sarcastically told, "We're so glad you could join us!"

◆ *Repetition* is the repeating of a word or group of words for effect. For example, Archibald MacLeish's poem "The End of the World" concludes with these lines:

There in the sudden blackness the black pall
Of nothing, nothing, nothing—nothing at all.

◆ A *rhetorical question* is a question asked only for effect or to make a statement, not to get an answer. Example: How much longer will we put up with this injustice? Isn't it time that we took action?

◆ *Satire* refers to writing that uses humor, irony, or wit to attack or make fun of something, such as people's follies or vices.

◆ *Symbolism* is the representation of ideas or things by symbols. A *symbol* is something that stands for something else. For example, a writer may use a rose as a symbol of beauty or a snake as a symbol of evil.

Activity C: Understanding Literary Elements and Techniques

This activity will give you practice in exploring how authors use literary elements and techniques to convey their ideas. Draw on the information in the *Basics* boxes on pages 189–191 to carry out this activity, and use the strategies for reading poetry and prose discussed on pages 185–186.

Work with a small group of students. Each group member in turn should share with the group a brief, favorite selection (or excerpt), which may be poetry or prose. Then, as a group, discuss and analyze how the author of the selection used literary elements and techniques to communicate important ideas. Write your responses on a sheet of paper.

For each selection, answer the following questions:

Title of selection: _____

Author: _____

Genre: _____

1. What are the main ideas of the selection?

2. What literary elements did the author use to communicate these ideas?

3. What specific literary techniques did the author use to communicate the main ideas?

Taking Notes on Literary Selections

You've already learned various note-taking strategies and tips in previous chapters, so you can apply or adapt most of what you've learned when you read the Part A literary selections. In addition, here are some specific guidelines to help you get the most from the notes you take during Part A of the Regents exam:

▶ **Focus on what you'll need in order to write your essay.** When you take notes on the two selections, you should record three things:

◊ *Important ideas* in the selections, especially ideas that relate directly to the topic/theme

◊ *Literary elements and techniques* that the authors use to convey their ideas

◊ *Thematic similarities and differences* between the selections

Notice that these three items are interconnected. That is, authors use literary elements and techniques to communicate their ideas. Comparing these ideas will help you identify thematic similarities and differences between selections.

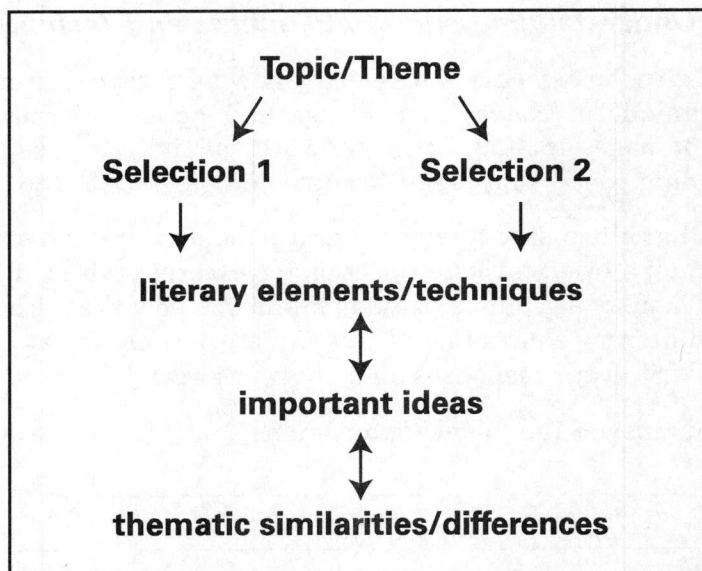

```
                        Topic/Theme
                     ↙              ↘
           Selection 1                Selection 2
                ↓                          ↓
              literary elements/techniques
                            ↕
                     important ideas
                            ↕
            thematic similarities/differences
```

▶ **Make your notes useful.** You'll certainly be referring back to the selections as you answer the multiple-choice questions and again when you write your essay. Your notes should help you identify key ideas and specific details and quickly find them in the text.

For example, if you notice that an author repeats a phrase in several places in a short story, make note of the phrase and where it appears so you won't have to go hunting through the story to find the phrase later.

Similarly, if you spot an important detail in the second selection that relates to something you remember from the first selection, make note of it.

▶ **Be brief.** There's no need to write elaborate notes of this sort:

In line 23, author uses simile to compare explosion to sound of thunder.

Instead, just write something simple like this:

L. 23—simile

Later, when you plan and write your essay, you can refer back to line 23 and further develop the idea as needed.

▶ **Draw tentative conclusions as you read.** Writing down preliminary conclusions as you read will help you think through and clarify for yourself how the selections connect with the topic or theme. Does the author of the first selection make a clear point related to the topic or theme? Does the author of the second selection seem to express a sharply different viewpoint? Jot down your thoughts and observations. You can always adjust or expand them later.

? *Answer in your own words:* How can jotting down your observations as you read a selection help you?

_____

_____

_____

Q & A

Should I take notes while I'm reading a selection or after I finish?

The answer to this question will vary. For short selections—especially poems—you're usually best off reading the whole selection at least once or twice before taking notes. For longer selections, you may feel comfortable jotting down some notes even during your first reading.

Some selections are easier to understand than others. The more challenging a selection is, the more time you should invest in reading and thinking before taking notes. Most important, you should develop a note-taking approach that works well for you. Practice your note-taking when you do school assignments and even when you read literature on your own.

Let's look at two examples of the kind of notes you might take when you read a pair of Part A selections. For the first selection, we'll use the poem that you read earlier:

Dreams
Hold fast to dreams
For if dreams die
Life is a broken-winged bird
That cannot fly.

5   Hold fast to dreams
For when dreams go
Life is a barren field
Frozen with snow.

—Langston Hughes

You'll recall that the topic identified by the Part A prompt was "how future expectations affect a person's life." Here are the notes that a student took on the poem, keeping that topic in mind:

"Dreams"

IMPORTANT IDEAS

   —*People shouldn't give up on their dreams*

   —*W/o dreams, life is empty, lacks inspiration (<u>ties in directly w/ topic of</u>*

      <u>prompt!!</u> → maybe something like, having a hope or dream gives you

      goal to shoot for in daily life)

LITERARY TECHNIQUES

   —*Bird <u>metaphor</u> in 1st stanza*

   —*Snowy field <u>metaphor</u> in 2nd stanza*

   —*Imagery/symbolism:*

     —*"broken-winged bird" (suggests being crippled)*

     —*"barren field frozen with snow" (suggests cold, emptiness)*

   —*<u>Repetition</u>: "hold fast to dreams"*

As you compare the notes with the poem, notice the following:

- The student focused on *important ideas* in the poem and the *literary techniques* used to convey them.

- The student used underlining and exclamation marks to highlight significant items.

- The student jotted down a tentative conclusion related to the topic: the idea that "having a hope or dream gives you a goal to shoot for in daily life."

- The student used quotation marks to identify direct quotations (the writer's exact words).

- The student kept notes brief, using phrases rather than whole sentences. The student also shortened or abbreviated several words.

? *Be specific in your answer.* Look back at *Activity B* on pages 186–188, questions 2 and 3. Did you focus on the same ideas that the student did in the notes above? Explain.

_____

_____

Now let's look at a second example. This selection is an excerpt from a literary essay. As you read the excerpt and the student's notes that follow, keep in mind that they are linked to the same topic that the poem was: "how future expectations affect a person's life."

HOOP DREAMS

Many of the dreams that I first dreamed while shooting baskets in Battle Ground, Indiana, I know I will never realize. For one thing, I never became a great ballplayer. And politics probably isn't in the cards for me either. I still like to shoot baskets, and I still daydream while doing so. But it's different now.
5   I miss the shapeliness and directedness of the basketball dreaming of my youth. All things converged on the court on those days, with reassuring swishes, thumps, and clangs serving as the aural signals of an orderly universe. All of my dreams were able to meet in this one place. I wasn't religious in those days (maybe a little), but I do see that period as a time of grace, a time of
10   instruction in possibilities.

Lyrical as some of those moments were, I don't long to relive the trials that accompanied my early adolescent dreaming. We seem to live our lives in stages (childhood, high school, college, etc.), and each stage has its own imaginative field and fruits thereof. Art, religion, and ambiguity were among the richest
15   findings of my young adulthood away from the the basketball court. Still, in my muscles and bones I can recall a rare unity that once was there when I had

a basketball in my hands. Body, spirit, and purpose were all held together in fine clarity.

20 That sense of completeness—or at least the possibility of completeness—has been replaced by an odd joy of dispersal, in which I now take pleasure and discomfort in not having all options before me, and often not knowing at all what the best option is. I guess this is what we call getting older and wiser. Sometimes it's hard, though, not to give in to the sentimentality of longing for 24 a time when a jump shot and a swish meant everything.

—Timothy P. Schilling

"Hoop Dreams"
_____

IMPORTANT IDEAS
_____

   —Writer has learned not all dreams come true (won't be "great
_____

     ballplayer" [2–3] or go into politics [3])
_____

   —As young person, dreams had "shapeliness" & "directedness" [5]
_____

   —Things seemed simpler when young— "orderly universe" [7]
_____

   —Writer misses "rare unity" [16] & "fine clarity" [18] of younger
_____

     days?
_____

   —Youth was "time of instruction in possibilities" [9–10]
_____

   —Each stage of life has "own imaginative field and fruits thereof"
_____

     [13–14]
_____

   —As get older, world opens up
_____

     —not just b'ball anymore
_____

     —"completeness" replaced by "dispersal" [19–20]
_____

     —causes feelings of both pleasure & discomfort (possible link to topic
_____

     of prompt: changing expectations as person gets "older and wiser"
_____

     [22])
_____

   —Many options as get older; often not clear which is best (uncertainty)
_____

LITERARY ELEMENTS & TECHNIQUES
_____

   —Use of 1st-person point of view to share personal feelings &
_____

     experiences w/ reader
_____

196

—*Tone* is reflective: writer looking back, comparing young person's outlook w/ "wiser" perspective now

—*Imagery/symbolism:*

    —b'ball as "orderly universe" [7]

    —"reassuring swishes, thumps, and clangs" [6–7]

    —"jump shot and a swish" [24] symbolic of simplicity, clarity, certainty

THEMATIC SIMILARITIES & DIFFERENCES

—Poem suggests your dreams should never die; essay suggests dreams have to change as you get older

—Poem too simplistic? Essay gives more realistic & balanced view?

—Possible link to topic. Hopes & expectations for future can color your life and add direction, but as adult you adjust your expectations.

Compare the student's notes with the excerpt from the literary essay, and notice the following:

- The student focused on *important ideas*—stated and implied—and the *literary elements and techniques* used to convey them. The student also included details that are likely to serve as "specific and relevant evidence" when he or she develops the controlling idea in the essay.

- The student quoted a number of words and phrases that seemed significant and included line numbers in parentheses for handy reference.

- Underlining serves to highlight important items. Question marks indicate points that the student isn't entirely sure about.

- Having read both of the selections, the student made additional notes about *thematic similarities and differences*.

- The student included two possible links to the topic. The second link relates to similarities/differences between the selections.

- The notes are concisely written, using phrases and shortened or abbreviated words.

Activity D: Taking Notes

Carefully review the prompt that appears on page 174. Then read and take notes on the two literary selections that appear on pages 175–178. You may write your notes in the margin or on a separate paper. Use the strategies you've learned for reading and taking notes on literary selections. You will refer back to your notes later in this chapter.

Activity E: Improving Note-Taking Skills

Pair up with another student. Exchange the notes you took for *Activity D*, and evaluate each other's work. Be *constructive* and specific in your comments and suggestions. Your goal is to help your partner improve his or her skills. Here are some guidelines:

- How well do the notes cover

  ♦ important ideas, especially those that relate to the topic/theme?

  ♦ literary elements and techniques used to convey ideas?

  ♦ thematic similarities and differences between selections?

- Has the student included enough details to serve as "specific and relevant evidence" when he or she develops the controlling idea in the essay?

- Are the notes as concise as they might be? How could they be made more concise?

- Are the notes well organized? How could the organization be improved?

- Are the notes clear and easy to understand? How could they be made clearer?

Prepare Yourself for Parts A and B

TIP

Literary elements and techniques (such as those in the *Basics* boxes on pages 189–191) play a significant role in Parts A and B of Session Two of the Regents exam. If there are any elements or techniques that you don't fully understand, learn about them before the exam. Ask your teacher for help, or consult a reference book.

Practice identifying elements and techniques in the literary works that you read. Think about how they shape the work and help to convey the author's meaning.

UNDERSTANDING AUTHOR'S PURPOSE AND POINT OF VIEW

SKILL FOCUS: To fully understand the literary selections of Session Two, Part A and the informational selections of Session One, it's important to recognize why the author is writing and how the author feels about his or her subject. This Skill Builder focuses on developing your ability to understand an author's purpose and point of view.

Authors have a purpose when they write. In achieving their purpose, they usually reveal their point of view. (This is different from point of view as explained on page 189.) Although an author's purpose and point of view are related, they are not the same. Understanding the difference will give you insight into the selections that you read.

CONCEPTS TO UNDERSTAND

- An author's writing **purpose** is his or her reason or goal for writing. For example, an author may want to tell about actual or imagined events (narrative writing), present information (informative writing), encourage readers to think or act in a certain way (persuasive writing), or depict people, places, or things (descriptive writing).

- Authors choose ideas and supporting information to suit their particular purpose. They decide how best to develop and organize their content to convey their meaning. They decide which details and what specific words to use to describe people, places, and events. These choices and decisions shape the written work.

- Authors often accomplish more than one purpose in their writing. For example, an author may write a short story about a young soldier's battle experiences. In addition to telling about the character and describing the events, the story may convey a persuasive message to readers about the horrors of war.

- In their writing, authors usually reveal their **point of view**. That is, they state or imply how they feel about their subject or theme.

Purpose	⟶	why an author writes
Point of view	⟶	how the author feels about the subject

● An author's purpose and point of view are always related, but the link between them varies with the written work. Look at the following chart.

EXAMPLES OF PURPOSE AND POINT OF VIEW

Written Work	Author's Purpose	Author's Point of View
poem	to describe the grace and beauty of cats	Thinks that cats are the most desirable pets.
essay	to persuade readers to help people in need	Believes that every person has a moral responsibility to help others.
article	to explain how the Internet works	Expects that soon everyone will have to be on-line.

? *Answer in your own words:* What is the difference between an author's purpose and an author's point of view?

_____

_____

_____

READING STRATEGIES

Use the strategies below to determine an author's purpose and point of view. These strategies can improve your reading and comprehension skills by helping you understand an author's attitude toward the subject and reason for writing.

Strategies for Determining an Author's Purpose and Point of View

▶ **Think about the selection as a whole**. Why did the author write it? To communicate a personal message or feeling? To describe a particular place or event? To explain a concept? To convince readers of something?

▶ **Think about structure.** An author's method of organization emphasizes certain ideas and details over others. This emphasis reveals what the author considers most important.

▶ **Pay close attention to the author's use of literary elements and techniques.** For example, an author's choice of imagery or use of exaggeration can tell you how the author feels. The characters an author creates and the words these characters speak may have symbolic meaning.

▶ **Notice an author's choice of words.** Language can cast people and events in a positive or negative light. *Slim, skinny,* and *scrawny* are all synonyms for *thin,* but each word has a different *connotation* (implied meaning).

▶ **Notice what information the author chooses to include and *not* include.** For example, an author sends a clear message by including only positive details about someone or something.

TRY THIS

Do activities *A* and *B* below. After you have finished, read the *Thinking It Through* that follows to see how one student responded.

A. An author wants to describe the town of Greendale. Here are some details that the author could use. Which of these details would the author use to show Greendale in a positive light? Which would show the town in a negative light? In the space next to each detail, write *P* for positive or *N* for negative.

_____ (1) Most residents of Greendale are well educated.

_____ (2) The town has a low crime rate.

_____ (3) Greendale's schools are overcrowded.

_____ (4) Newcomers to town are regarded with suspicion.

_____ (5) There are few employment opportunities in or near town.

_____ (6) Greendale is an attractive town, surrounded by woodlands.

_____ (7) There are few stores and no movie theaters within 20 miles of Greendale.

_____ (8) Greendale is located 3 miles from Crystal Lake, a popular lake for swimming, boating, and fishing.

B. In a descriptive paragraph, an author wants to portray a man named Jason Kobray in a favorable light. Underline the word or phrase in each pair that the author would probably choose to describe Jason.

(1) <u>daring</u>   reckless

(2) fearful   <u>cautious</u>

(3) smug   <u>self-confident</u>

(4) <u>determined</u>   stubborn as a two-year-old

(5) more muscle than brain   <u>brawny</u>

(6) childishness   <u>boyish playfulness</u>

Thinking It Through

A.

    __P__   *(1) Most residents of Greendale are well educated.*

    __P__   *(2) The town has a low crime rate.*

    __N__   *(3) Greendale's schools are overcrowded.*

    __N__   *(4) Newcomers to town are regarded with suspicion.*

    __N__   *(5) There are few employment opportunities in or near town.*

    __P__   *(6) Greendale is an attractive town, surrounded by woodlands.*

    __N__   *(7) There are few stores and no movie theaters within 20 miles of Greendale.*

    __P__   *(8) Greendale is located 3 miles from Crystal Lake, a popular lake for swimming, boating, and fishing.*

Including details 1, 2, 6, and 8 would show Greendale in a positive light.

These details all refer to positive aspects of the town or its people. The other details would give a negative impression. Detail 4, for example, implies that the people may be somewhat unfriendly, while detail 7 suggests that the town is isolated.

B.

(1) <u>*daring*</u>   *reckless*

Both words suggest a person who is ready to take action. However, <u>daring</u> describes someone who is brave, while <u>reckless</u> suggests someone who would take unnecessary risks.

(2)   *fearful*   *cautious*

The word *cautious* describes someone who is careful. *Fearful* goes beyond
that, describing a person who is afraid.

(3)   *smug*   *self-confident*

Self-confident is a positive term. *Smug* has a negative connotation.
Describing Jason as "smug" would suggest that he is too satisfied with
himself.

(4)   *determined*   *stubborn as a two-year-old*

A *determined* person has a definite purpose in mind and is intent upon
achieving that purpose. The simile *stubborn as a two-year-old,* however,
would suggest someone who's as unreasonable as a small child can be.

(5)   *more muscle than brain*   *brawny*

Brawny calls to mind someone who is big and muscular. *More muscle than
brain,* however, is clearly negative. The phrase suggests a person who may
be muscular but whose physical abilities are greater than his mental
abilities.

(6)   *childishness*   *boyish playfulness*

Childishness definitely has a negative meaning. The word suggests a
person who simply doesn't act his age. Describing Jason as having a *boyish
playfulness,* on the other hand, would suggest a positive quality—being as
playful as a boy.

Skills Practice

Read the following passage. Then choose the correct answer for each of the questions that follow.

Although they were twin sisters, their resemblance was purely physical. If I had a problem, I went to Lauren. She would listen patiently, then do whatever she could to help. If I was sad, Lauren could always raise my spirits. If I was happy, she'd share in my happiness. Cindy's main concern in life was, well, Cindy. "I have no time to listen to your little problems," she'd say. "I've got my own problems." If I was feeling low, Cindy usually wouldn't even notice. And when my spirits were high, Cindy would generally resent my happiness. When the two of them were old enough to head off for college, I had very mixed feelings. "Guess you're an only child now," Lauren said, as we walked to the car. "Don't get too spoiled, Princess Pea." That was her nickname for me, after some fairy tale character. I hugged her tightly, trying not to cry but blubbering all the same. When Cindy left the next week, the last thing she said to me was to keep out of her room. I told her that wouldn't be a problem.

1 The author's main purpose in this passage is to

   1 explain how Lauren got into college

   2 draw a comparison between two sisters

   3 express affection for Cindy

2 Based on the specific details included, the reader can conclude that the narrator

   1 likes both sisters equally

   2 cares more for Cindy than for Lauren

   3 cares more for Lauren than for Cindy

3 The quotations are included in the passage in order to

   1 contrast how the narrator related to each sister

   2 express the narrator's thoughts

   3 reveal important information about the narrator

4 The narrator's feelings about Cindy are

   1 implied

   2 directly stated

   3 not clear to the reader

3

ANSWERING THE MULTIPLE-CHOICE QUESTIONS FOR PART A

Session Two, Part A of the Regents exam includes eight to ten multiple-choice questions. The Part A questions focus on key ideas and features in two literary selections. To answer the questions, the strategies that you've learned for effective reading and note-taking will help. You'll also call on your skills at recognizing key ideas and making inferences (*Skill Builders 1* and *2* in Chapter 2), using context clues and distinguishing fact from opinion (*Skill Builders 3* and *4* in Chapter 3), and understanding author's purpose and point of view (*Skill Builder 5*).

Strategies for Answering the Part A Multiple-Choice Questions

In general, the guidelines that you learned for Session One will serve you equally well for Session Two multiple-choice questions. However, because you're focusing on literary passages rather than informational selections, you'll have to adjust your approach somewhat.

► **Refer to the reading selections in combination with your notes.** Some of the key ideas and details included in your notes are likely to appear in the questions. Nevertheless, you'll find it useful to refer to the selections themselves. For poetry, in particular, you may need to reread certain lines several times in order to answer a question.

► **Be sure you understand the question.** Know exactly what a question is asking before you start to consider possible answers. Watch for particular words or phrases in the question that offer clues to the correct answer. For questions pertaining to literary features, choose your answer with special care. Watch for questions that ask you to identify an element common to both selections. Be sure that the element you choose is indeed present in both passages, not just one.

► **Study the context to help you infer meaning.** Poetry and other literary selections typically require you to use your inferential skills to determine an author's meaning. Context clues can help, especially when you're trying to analyze imagery or interpret symbolism. Don't rush to answer: reread the relevant lines, and think about them before making an answer choice.

► **Pause to consider the question before looking at the answers.** Try to think what the answer *should* be.

► ***Reread* the question as needed.** Sometimes rereading the question with each possible answer is helpful, particularly with sentence-completion form questions.

▶ **Read, compare, and consider *all* the choices. Then pick the best and most complete answer.** This is especially important for literary selections because questions may deal with multiple levels of meaning, and the differences between answer choices may be subtle.

▶ **Narrow your search.** If you're not sure which answer is correct, cross out choices you know are incorrect. Then focus on the remaining choices.

▶ **Don't spend too much time on a troublesome question.** Make your best choice and move on. If you have time left, you can return to the question you were unsure about.

▶ **Answer every question.**

Let the Multiple-Choice Questions Help You

TIP

As you answer the multiple-choice questions, you're likely to gain additional insight into the two selections. You may, for example, recognize a literary technique that you hadn't noticed before, or you may come to understand a deeper level of meaning.

Be sure to add any significant new observations or conclusions to the notes that you took when you first read the selections. Your expanded insight will help you write your essay.

TRY THIS

Review the Part A prompt and the two reading selections on pages 174–178. Also review the notes you took for *Activity D* (page 198).

Next, answer the multiple-choice questions that follow. After you've answered the questions, read *Thinking It Through* to see how one student determined the correct answers.

Multiple-Choice Questions

Directions (1–10): Answer the following questions. Select the best suggested answer and circle the number. The questions may help you think about the ideas and information you might want to use in your essay. You may return to these questions anytime you wish.

Passage I (the poem) — Questions 1–5 refer to Passage I.

1 In lines 1 through 5, the attitude of the man is

  1 protective
  2 selfish
  3 indifferent
  4 carefree

2 "The world's most sensitive cargo" (line 6) refers to

  1 the man crossing the street
  2 a large package
  3 the boy
  4 a jacket

3 The dominant figure of speech in lines 6 through 9 is

1 oxymoron
2 personification
3 metaphor
4 alliteration

4 Lines 15 and 16 allude to the idea of

1 parenthood
2 mutual support
3 self-protection
4 independence

5 In lines 13 through 18, the image that was presented at the beginning of the poem is used to symbolize

1 father-and-son relationships in general
2 husband-and-wife relationships
3 the relationship between all adults and children
4 the relationship among the world's people

Passage II (the short story) — Questions 6–10 refer to Passage II.

6 The first several paragraphs of the story are meant to convey a feeling of

1 the beauty of the beach
2 how hard the narrator works
3 the child's isolation and fear
4 how loudly young children can cry

7 "The screams hit me like blows" (line 7) reveals the narrator's reaction through the use of

1 simile
2 metaphor
3 irony
4 allegory

8 The narrator's main concern is

1 not becoming involved in other people's business

2 the welfare of the child
3 the narrator's own well-being
4 getting back to work

9 The repetition of the phrase "full of trust" (lines 23 and 93) helps convey the child's

1 vulnerability
2 independence
3 honesty
4 loyalty

10 Lines 66–67 suggest that the woman

1 is probably very much like the narrator
2 wishes that the little boy were her own son
3 resents the narrator's interference
4 does not share the narrator's sense of responsibility

After you have finished these questions, review **Your Task** and the **Guidelines**. Use scrap paper to plan your response. Then write your response to Part A.

Thinking It Through

Passage I (the poem) — Questions 1–5 refer to Passage I.

1 *In lines 1 through 5, the attitude of the man is*

   1 protective

   2 selfish

   3 indifferent

   4 carefree

> After rereading and thinking about lines 1–5, I can infer that the correct choice is 1. Because the man is carrying his son, he is "stepping gently" and "looking two times north and south." He doesn't want cars to come too close. These details clearly suggest that the man feels protective, not selfish, indifferent, or carefree.

2 *"The world's most sensitive cargo" (line 6) refers to*

   1 the man crossing the street

   2 a large package

   3 the boy

   4 a jacket

> After rereading the first nine lines, I conclude that "the world's most sensitive cargo" refers to the boy, choice 3. Line 3 tells me that it's the boy the man is carrying. I also recognize that the word he's in line 7 and the word his in line 8 both refer to the boy. Still, I consider the other choices, just to be safe. In thinking about this question, I also realize that the poet is probably using the boy as a symbol of human beings in general—"the world's most sensitive cargo." I know that's an important observation and one I may want to use in my essay, so I add it to my notes.

3 *The dominant figure of speech in lines 6 through 9 is*

1 *oxymoron*

2 *personification*

3 *metaphor*

4 *alliteration*

> *In lines 6–9, the poet compares the boy to precious cargo, such as a package that would be marked "fragile, handle with care." I know that a metaphor is an implied comparison that does not use <u>like</u> or <u>as</u>. Therefore, the correct answer must be <u>3</u>. (Looking over the other choices, I also conclude that none of those techniques is used in the third stanza.)*

4 *Lines 15 and 16 allude to the idea of*

1 *parenthood*

2 *mutual support*

3 *self-protection*

4 *independence*

> *I have to think carefully about this question, because it relates to the levels of meaning of the poem. After rereading the poem once more, I ask myself, what exactly is it that "he's doing" (line 15)? He's carrying the boy, protecting him. Then I ask, what is it that the poet thinks we should be "willing to do . . . with one another." I infer that the poet believes people must be similarly willing to carry and protect one another, figuratively speaking. I don't think the poet is suggesting that people act as parents toward one another. Therefore, the best answer is choice <u>2</u>.*

5 *In lines 13 through 18, the image that was presented at the beginning of the poem is used to symbolize*

1 *father-and-son relationships in general*

2 *husband-and-wife relationships*

3 *the relationship between all adults and children*

4 *the relationship among the world's people*

> The image presented at the beginning is of a man carefully and protectively carrying his son on his shoulder as he crosses a street in the rain. That image takes on greater symbolic meaning by the end of the poem. I can eliminate choice 2 right away, because the poem doesn't focus on husbands and wives. Twice in the poem the writer uses the word world (lines 6 and 14). Also, it's clear that the "we" in the fifth stanza is meant to apply to everyone in the world. Therefore, choices 1 and 3 are too narrow. Choice 4 is the correct answer.

Passage II (the short story) — Questions 6–10 refer to Passage II.

6 *The first several paragraphs of the story are meant to convey a feeling of*

  1 *the beauty of the beach*

  2 *how hard the narrator works*

  3 *the child's isolation and fear*

  4 *how loudly young children can cry*

> *Reviewing the opening paragraphs of the story, I see that there is no description of either the beach's beauty or the narrator's work. Therefore, I can quickly eliminate choices 1 and 2. Although there is a suggestion of how loudly children can cry (choice 4), I know from the story that that's not really the point here. Instead, the opening of the story is meant to present a strong image of the child's isolation and fear. Details that support my conclusion include the author's repetition of words like "panic" and "empty beach" and the author's description of the child "screaming at the sky." Therefore, choice 3 is the correct answer.*

7 *"The screams hit me like blows" (line 7) reveals the narrator's reaction through the use of*

  1 *simile*

  2 *metaphor*

  3 *irony*

  4 *allegory*

> *I realize that the author is comparing the emotional impact of the screams to the physical impact of blows. I know that similes and metaphors are both forms of comparison. However, a simile uses like or as, while a metaphor does not. Since this figurative comparison uses like, I know that the correct choice is 1.*

8 *The narrator's main concern is*

   1 not becoming involved in other people's business

   2 the welfare of the child

   3 the narrator's own well-being

   4 getting back to work

> The narrator's actions, words, and thoughts all suggest a sincere concern for the child's welfare. The narrator certainly shows a willingness to get involved, so choice <u>1</u> is wrong. Choices <u>3</u> and <u>4</u> are not stated or implied in the story. Choice <u>2</u> is correct.

9 *The repetition of the phrase "full of trust" (lines 23 and 93) helps convey the child's*

   1 vulnerability

   2 independence

   3 honesty

   4 loyalty

> I think that vulnerable means capable of being hurt, so choice <u>1</u> seems reasonable: a two- or three-year-old is very trusting and very vulnerable. I want to consider the other choices, though, to be sure. Certainly, "full of trust" doesn't suggest independence or loyalty in the context of the story, so choices <u>2</u> and <u>4</u> are not correct. I can eliminate choice <u>3</u>, too, since honesty doesn't apply. Therefore, I'm sure that choice <u>1</u> is the correct answer.

10 Lines 66–67 suggest that the woman

   1 is probably very much like the narrator

   2 wishes that the little boy were her own son

   3 resents the narrator's interference

   4 does not share the narrator's sense of responsibility

> *When the woman says, "I'm not his mother," she's immediately avoiding*
>
> *responsibility. Her attitude is very different from that of the narrator. The*
>
> *narrator chose to accept responsibility for the boy, even without knowing*
>
> *him. Therefore, I can conclude that choice 4 is the correct answer. None of*
>
> *the other possible answers is supported by the story.*

Activity F: Evaluating Your Skills

Review the notes you took and the multiple-choice questions you answered. Then respond to the questions below. Be specific in your answers.

1. How helpful in answering the questions were the notes that you took? How could you have made your notes more useful?

   _____

   _____

   _____

2. Did you read the selections carefully enough? What could you have done to further improve your understanding of the selections?

   _____

   _____

   _____

3. Which multiple-choice questions did you find most challenging to answer? Why? What could you do to make answering such questions easier?

   _____

   _____

   _____

4. Share and compare your answers to the preceding questions with the answers of other students. What suggestions from other students did you find most useful?

_____

_____

_____

Build Your Vocabulary

TIP

The greater your vocabulary, the more words you will have at your command when you read, write, or speak. Here are some tips to help you build your vocabulary:

- Read! Spend time every day reading newspapers, magazines, and books.
- Whenever you read or hear a word that you don't understand, look it up in a dictionary. Don't just skip it.
- Keep a list of new words that you learn. Try to use them in your written and oral communication.

Look for ways to expand your vocabulary. For example, use a vocabulary-builder study book or a word-a-day desk calendar.

4

PLANNING AND WRITING YOUR PART A ESSAY

As discussed earlier, Session Two, Part A of the Regents exam asks you to write a unified essay in which you interpret and analyze two literary selections. The focus of your essay will be the central point, or controlling idea, that you establish based on the topic or theme shared by the selections.

Examining the Criteria as Applied to Part A

Readers will again evaluate your extended response holistically on the basis of meaning, development, organization, language use, and conventions.

SCORING CRITERIA

ORGANIZATION

DEVELOPMENT

MEANING

CONVENTIONS

LANGUAGE USE

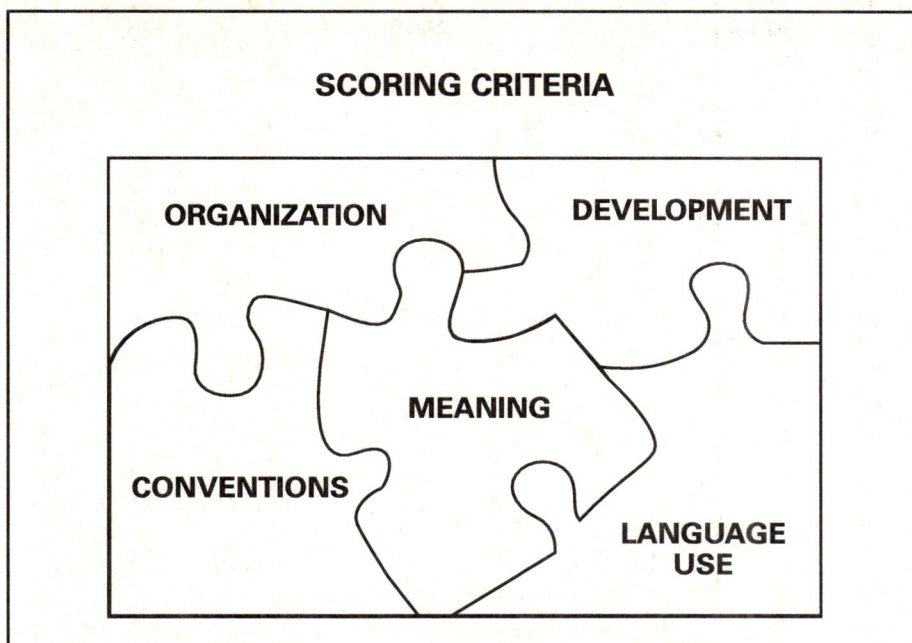

The following chart shows how the scoring criteria are applied to Session Two, Part A. You'll see that the evaluation for Session Two, Part A is very similar to that for Session One. However, Part A requires you to (1) establish and focus on a controlling idea, and (2) link that controlling idea with ideas in the selections and with the literary elements or techniques used to communicate those ideas.

SCORING THE PART A EXTENDED RESPONSE (ESSAY)

CRITERIA	WHAT YOUR PART A RESPONSE SHOULD SHOW
MEANING	• A controlling idea that demonstrates an in-depth understanding of both literary selections • Insightful connections between the controlling idea, the ideas in each selection, and the literary elements or techniques used to convey those ideas
DEVELOPMENT	• Clear development of ideas • Effective use of specific and relevant supporting details from both selections
ORGANIZATION	• Clear, consistent focus based on a controlling idea • Logical and coherent structure
LANGUAGE USE	• Effective and engaging language that is appropriate for the specific audience and purpose • Varied sentence structure and length
CONVENTIONS	• Strong control of grammar, punctuation, spelling, and other elements of writing, with few errors

In the following pages, you'll build on what you've learned in previous chapters as you see how to plan and write a Part A essay that meets these criteria.

Establishing Your Controlling Idea

Begin the writing process by first establishing the controlling idea that will serve as the focus of your essay. Remember that for an essay to be "unified," it must convey a clear central point—the controlling idea—and every paragraph in the essay must relate to that controlling idea.

The controlling idea of your essay must be more specific and more sharply focused than the general topic or theme described by the prompt. Most important, your controlling idea should reflect your understanding of the two reading selections.

Suppose, for instance, that the Part A prompt asks you to write a unified essay about "the importance of education to future success, as revealed in the passages." Passage I is a poem in which the author praises her college years as the turning point of her life. Passage II is a play excerpt in which a businessman explains how his "true" education came not from school, but from the hard lessons of life.

The controlling idea of your essay should reflect your understanding of *both* of these passages. For example, you might express your controlling idea this way: "Some people find that college opens the door to future success, while others discover that their most valuable lessons come from life." In your essay, you would then use specific ideas and details from passages I and II to develop this controlling idea. In addition, you would describe specific literary elements or techniques that the two authors used to convey their ideas.

General topic/theme:	*the importance of education to future success*
Specific controlling idea:	*Some people find that college opens the door to future success, while others discover that their most valuable lessons come from life.*

? *Fill in the blank:* Your controlling idea must be more _____ than the general topic or theme described by the prompt.

Here are some guidelines to help you establish your controlling idea and begin planning your Part A essay:

▶ **Think carefully about *Your Task* and *Guidelines*.** Be sure you understand what topic or theme you have to write about. Consider how the **Guidelines** relate to the various scoring criteria.

▶ **Consider how the two reading selections are related.** Ask yourself such questions as these: *Do the two passages express similar or different points of view? To what extent do the two authors agree or disagree?* Not only will the answers to such questions help you establish the controlling idea, but they can also help you organize your essay.

▶ **Think about literary elements and techniques in the selections.** By revealing an author's point of view, the particular elements or techniques used can help you formulate a controlling idea. For example, if an author uses striking imagery, ask yourself whether this imagery conveys a positive or negative impression of the subject.

▶ **Write a thesis statement.** As part of your planning, jot down your thoughts for a controlling idea. You can revise or further sharpen your idea as you go along.

Once you're satisfied with your controlling idea, express it in a sentence. This will be your *thesis statement*—a statement of the controlling idea, or central point, of your essay. *Your thesis statement should be clear and specific and should reflect your understanding of both reading selections.* You will later use your thesis statement in the first paragraph of your essay.

Earlier in this chapter (page 184), you saw two examples of thesis statements:

General topic/theme: *the conflicts that occur in the parent-child relationship during the teen years*

Specific controlling idea/   *Teenagers and parents can get*
thesis statement: *along if they both make an effort.*

    or

    Two-way communication is the key to a good parent-teen relationship.

Keep in mind that you can adjust or reword your thesis statement as needed once you begin writing your essay. However, expressing your controlling idea in a thesis statement as part of the planning process will help you establish and maintain your focus from the very start.

Activity G: Stating a Controlling Idea

Review the Part A prompt and the two reading selections on pages 174–178. Also review the notes you took for *Activity D* (page 198). Then write a thesis statement expressing a controlling idea for the essay.

_____

_____

_____

_____

PREWRITING
...thinking and planning
<u>before</u> writing

DRAFTING
...translating your plan
into a draft

THE WRITING PROCESS

REVISING
...changing and improving
your draft

EDITING/PROOFREADING
...making corrections and
polishing your work

Q&A

Are the "prewriting" techniques I've learned in school useful for helping me write the extended responses on the Regents exam?

Yes—but be careful to stay on track for your specific task. Brainstorming, clustering (also known as mapping or diagramming), and other prewriting techniques can be very useful, especially if you're having trouble getting started or you get stuck along the way. However, remember that the Regents responses you're asked to write are not open-ended like many of the writing assignments you do for school. For the Regents, you must tailor your response to the particular prompt, keeping in mind specific scoring criteria.

Developing and Organizing Your Essay

Previous chapters explained how to develop and organize ideas and supporting information for extended responses. Much of what you learned earlier applies to Session Two, Part A as well. In addition, follow the guidelines below to develop and organize your Session Two, Part A essay:

▶ **Think specifically in terms of essay structure.** Parts A and B of Session One may ask you to write in a variety of formats. The specified format for Part A of Session Two, however, is an essay. Therefore, you can plan on using this basic structure:

FIRST PARAGRAPH

This is the *introduction* to your essay. It should include your thesis statement. In this paragraph, you'll probably also briefly discuss thematic similarities/differences between selections with regard to the controlling idea.

↓

BODY PARAGRAPHS

In the *body* of your essay, you'll zero in on your main ideas, supporting details, and the literary elements and techniques used in the two selections. Use as many paragraphs as you need to carry out the task detailed in the prompt—there's no "correct" number. While high-scoring essays typically are at least four or five paragraphs long, you may choose to write a different number.

↓

LAST PARAGRAPH

This is the *conclusion* to your essay. In this paragraph, you'll summarize or reinforce your controlling idea and the key points you've made. You may also refer back to the thematic similarities/differences between selections.

To review the basics of essay structure, turn to *The Basics* box on pages 223–224.

? *Fill in the blank:* The first paragraph of your essay should include your _____.

▶ **Put together a rough outline.** Focus on one reading selection at a time as you outline your plan on paper. Consult your notes, the selection itself, and the multiple-choice questions. Identify important ideas and supporting details in the first selection that are directly linked to your controlling idea, along with relevant literary elements and techniques. Then do the same for the second selection.

Think about similarities and differences between selections with regard to your controlling idea. Chances are that you'll weave these into your discussion, especially in the first and last paragraphs.

As you proceed, your plan will take shape. Your rough outline might look something like the one below. Of course, the number of ideas, details, and elements/techniques will vary, as will the number of paragraphs and their organization.

FIRST PARAGRAPH
Introduction, including thesis statement

BODY PARAGRAPHS
Passage I:
IDEA
Supporting details and relevant literary elements/techniques
IDEA
Supporting details and relevant literary elements/techniques

Passage II:
IDEA
Supporting details and relevant literary elements/techniques
IDEA
Supporting details and relevant literary elements/techniques

LAST PARAGRAPH
Conclusion

When you're ready to start writing, you'll find that such a plan will effectively guide the structure of your essay. Of course, you may have to make adjustments as you go along. For example, you may decide to cover two ideas in the same paragraph. Or, you may need to use two paragraphs to fully develop one idea.

▶ **Work toward a *unified* essay.** Once you've determined your controlling idea, stay focused on it. Jot your thoughts, ideas, and supporting details down on paper, just as you did when planning your responses for Session One. Then review what you've written.

Keep those items that relate to your controlling idea, and eliminate those that don't. Don't be afraid to include more than you'll need. You can always eliminate some later.

▶ **Make appropriate comparisons.** Analyze the two selections specifically as they relate to the topic or theme. Don't write a so-called comparison-contrast essay. The emphasis is on writing about the topic/theme, not on comparing selections. This is an important distinction.

Nevertheless, you *should* make appropriate comparisons if they help you develop your controlling idea or show how the authors used literary elements or techniques with regard to the topic/theme.

Suppose, for example, that the prompt asks you to write about "how people are affected by their surroundings." As part of your essay, you want to explain how the two selections use setting and figurative language with regard to your controlling idea. To do this, you could:

◊ write a *single* paragraph discussing and comparing the use of setting and figurative language in both selections or

◊ break your analysis into *two* paragraphs, each paragraph focusing on one selection.

Examine these two approaches below. Which method of organization do you prefer? Why?

Example A: comparison in a single paragraph

> Both authors use setting and figurative language to show how people are affected by their surroundings. In Passage I, the poet first focuses on the "bleak, empty grayness" of the children's neighborhood. This description conveys a feeling of hopelessness. The author of Passage II starts by communicating the opposite feeling. This author describes in bright, colorful detail the small town's green trees and its "rainbow of flowers." Later in Passage I, the poet refers to "street noises echoing through sleepless nights." In Passage II, the author writes about "sweet, soothing hands of night." Such sharply contrasting images of nighttime help to show the ways in which . . .

Example B: comparison in separate paragraphs

> The setting of Passage I and the poet's use of figurative language work together to convey a feeling of hopelessness. For example, the poet begins by describing the "bleak, empty grayness" of the children's neighborhood. Next, the poet describes "street noises echoing through sleepless nights." This is a disturbing image that shows how . . .
>
> Passage II uses setting and figurative language, too, but to give a much more positive impression of the effects of a person's surroundings. For example, the author starts by painting a bright and colorful picture of the town's green trees and its "rainbow of flowers." Then the author writes about "sweet, soothing hands of night." This peaceful image suggests . . .

? *Be specific in your answer:* Explain how Examples A and B are different.

_____

_____

_____

One at a Time Is Usually (but Not Always) Best   *TIP*

Generally, it's easiest to write about one selection at a time, analyzing that selection in detail before moving on to the other selection.

Similarly, from an organizational standpoint, it's usually easiest to focus on one literary element or technique at a time—unless two elements or techniques are closely related. For example, an author's use of figurative language may help set the tone, in which case you may want to discuss figurative language and tone together.

These are just broad guidelines, however. Use your best judgment, and choose an organizational approach that you feel comfortable with.

► **Use direct quotations to develop your controlling idea.**
Quotations can be one of the most effective kinds of supporting
information to use to develop your controlling idea and discuss the
use of literary elements and techniques. For example, to make a
point, you can quote specific figures of speech, powerful images, or
significant words spoken by characters.

One important caution, however: do not quote *excessively*. That is,
don't just repeat line after line of text from the selections, or string
one quote after another after another. Use direct quotations as part
of the "specific and relevant evidence" called for in the *Guidelines,*
and use them to illustrate an author's literary methods. But don't
use them in place of your own writing!

Remember to enclose direct quotations in quotation marks. To
review the use of quotation marks, refer to *The Basics* box on
page 67.

Activity H: Making a Plan

Following the guidelines above, make a rough outline on scrap paper for
an essay responding to the Part A prompt and reading selections on pages
174–178. Use the notes you took for *Activity D* (page 198) and the thesis
statement you wrote for *Activity G* (page 218).

In the next section of this chapter, you'll compare your outline against a
sample plan.

The ◆ Basics

ESSAY STRUCTURE

*To be effective, an essay must be well structured. While no single approach
works for every essay, there are certain basics to keep in mind when organizing and presenting your ideas and supporting information. Remember, though,
that these are guidelines. Don't force a structure onto your writing. Don't feel
that you must write a specific number of paragraphs for the Regents exam.
Rather, write the number of paragraphs that will let you carry out your writing
task in the best way possible.*

◆ Essays usually have three parts: an introduction, a body, and a conclusion.
The *introduction* introduces readers to the topic and states the writer's
central point, or controlling idea, in a *thesis statement.* The *body* of the essay consists of the paragraphs that support and develop the controlling
idea. The *conclusion* summarizes or reinforces the writer's controlling idea
and other main ideas.

◆ Each paragraph in the body of an essay has its own main idea. The *main
idea* of a paragraph is the most important point the writer makes. It's what
the whole paragraph is about.

A typical five-paragraph essay might look like this. (Some essays have fewer than five paragraphs, while others have more.)

INTRODUCTION
Thesis statement ⟶ controlling idea

BODY PARAGRAPH
Main idea (topic sentence)
Supporting information

BODY PARAGRAPH
Main idea (topic sentence)
Supporting information

BODY PARAGRAPH
Main idea (topic sentence)
Supporting information

CONCLUSION

◆ You can add structure and clarity to your writing by stating the main idea of a paragraph in a *topic sentence.* Writers often make the topic sentence the first sentence of the paragraph.

◆ Always develop your main ideas/topic sentences with specific and relevant *supporting information,* such as details, examples, and quotations.

Looking at a Sample Plan

Having a well-thought-out plan will enable you to do your best on the Part A essay. Look at the sample plan below based on the prompt that you saw at the beginning of this chapter. Notice in particular—

● how the student has expressed the controlling idea in a thesis statement.

● how the outline includes ideas, details, and literary elements/techniques from both selections.

● how the outline reflects key points covered in the multiple-choice questions.

Later in this chapter you will read a Part A essay based on this plan.

Student's Plan for Session Two, Part A Essay

Note: For illustration purposes, this outline may be more detailed than yours needs to be. The plan you make for yourself need be only detailed enough for *you* to understand what you intend to write!

FIRST PARAGRAPH

Thesis statement: People have a responsibility to support and protect one another.

—Both passages make similar point, but in different ways

—Poem implies a more "global" view than short story does

BODY PARAGRAPHS

Passage I (cover in one or more paragraphs):

  —Poet's key point: "We're not going to be able to live in this world if we're not willing to do what he's doing with one another."

    —Metaphor used to compare boy to "sensitive cargo"

      —Boy is "world's most sensitive cargo"—maybe symbolic of human beings

    —Image of father carrying son across rainy street takes on deeper meaning in 5th stanza—becomes symbolic: one person supporting/protecting another

    —The word world repeated (line 14)—emphasizes global notion—world's people doing for "one another"

    —Image presented in last two lines suggests isolation, lack of harmony among world's people if we don't help one other

Passage II (cover in one or more paragraphs):

  —Child is all alone and very vulnerable

    —Setting: isolation of beach; child "screaming at the sky"

    —Repetition of certain words: cry, panic, wild, empty beach

    —Repetition of phrase "full of trust"

    —Narrator takes on protective responsibility for child that mother and/or mother's friend should have taken

—1st person point of view gives insight into narrator's feelings

—First thing woman says: "I'm not his mother"

—Simile: "screams hit me like blows"

—Narrator clearly disapproves

   —Repetition (line 78 and 92) "She looked only at me"

   —"Who could leave a baby alone to panic on a strange beach?"

    (line 88)

—Interesting similarity: both story and poem have adult carrying child

on shoulder

LAST PARAGRAPH

   —Both selections address notion of people taking on responsibility for

others (reinforce thesis statement)

   —Poem uses metaphor, imagery, symbolism, repetition

   —Story uses setting, repetition, point of view

Activity I: Evaluating a Plan

Answer the following questions about the student's plan. Before writing your answers, discuss your thoughts with a partner or a small group of students.

1. Overall, what are the strengths of the student's plan?

   _____

   _____

   _____

2. In what ways did the student make insightful connections between the controlling idea, the ideas in each selection, and the elements or techniques used to convey these ideas? Give specific examples to support your answer.

   _____

   _____

   _____

3. Give at least three examples of how the student developed ideas with specific and relevant supporting details.

_____

_____

_____

4. How do you think answering the multiple-choice questions helped the student focus on important points? Be specific in your answer.

_____

_____

_____

5. How will the student's plan make writing the response easier?

_____

_____

_____

Activity J: Comparing Plans

Carefully compare the student's plan above with the plan you made for *Activity H* (page 223). Then answer the following questions.

1. What are the main differences you see between the two plans?

_____

_____

_____

2. In what ways do you think your plan is better than the student's plan? Be specific.

_____

_____

_____

227

3. In what ways is the student's plan stronger than yours? Again, be specific.

_____

_____

_____

4. Do you think that either of the two plans could be used to write an effective Part A essay? Why or why not?

_____

_____

_____

Thoughtful Note-Taking Pays Off!

The better the notes you take when you read the selections, the more easily you'll be able to put together your essay plan. In fact, if you read carefully and take effective notes, you'll often be able to transfer much of what you've written directly into your rough outline.

TIP

Writing a Unified, Coherent Essay

To translate your Session Two, Part A plan into a unified essay, you can apply the same principles you used to write your responses for Session One. Here's a quick review of several key points covered in Chapters 2 and 3:

- **Connect your ideas and supporting information in a clear and logical way**. Your writing should flow in a way that makes sense and is easy to follow.

- **Maintain your focus.** For your essay to be "unified," it must clearly convey a controlling idea, and every paragraph in the essay must relate to that idea.

- **To make your writing coherent, use transitional words and phrases to connect ideas.** Take a moment to review the *Transitional Words and Phrases* chart on page 150.

- **Eliminate grammatical and mechanical errors.** Use the checklist on page 271 to help you avoid errors as you write and correct errors when you reread, edit, and proofread what you've written.

Using Language Effectively

If you look back at the **Guidelines** for the Part A prompt on page 174, you'll notice that the fifth one directs you to "use language that communicates ideas effectively."

Here are some tips to help you use language effectively:

Sentence Variety

● Vary your sentences in both structure and length.

● Don't begin several consecutive sentences in the same way.

Language

● Be precise. Example—

> Vague: *The author uses interesting imagery to make her point about the two cities.*

> Better: *The author uses startling images of fire and ice to contrast the two cities.*

● Avoid clichés. Examples—

last but not least	*it goes without saying*
to name but a few	*work like a dog*
worth its weight in gold	*sad but true*

Word Choice

● Avoid slang, except when you're quoting someone's words.

● Don't use several words when one word will do. Examples—

Wordy	*Better*
due to the fact that	*because*
at the present time	*at present* or *now*
during the time that	*while*
for the reason that	*because*

Other Elements

● Don't repeat the same wording or information unless you deliberately want to emphasize it.

● In general, use active, not passive, constructions. Example—

> Passive: *Dark clouds were used by the author to symbolize danger.*

> Active: *The author used dark clouds to symbolize danger.*

Activity K: Improving Writing Quality

The following excerpt comes from the first draft of a student's Part A essay. The excerpt contains a number of weaknesses that detract from overall quality, in addition to at least ten errors involving conventions of writing. Revise, edit, and proofread the excerpt using the checklist on page 271 and the tips for effective language use on page 229.

> Money has the power to bring happiness. Money also has the power to bring great unhappiness. In Passage I, for example, the author uses plot to show money's power to make people happy. The author also uses characterization to show money's power to make people happy. When Lisa and Michael inherits a large some of money from their aunt, they use it to start a school for people with disabilities. This school opens up new opportunities for the disabled people, in addition, Lisa learns how satisfying it can be to help others, while Michael discovers his preveously unknown abilities as a teacher.
>
> By contrast, Passage II shows moneys power to cause trouble. in this narrative poem, the author use many similes and metafors to describe how Lady Katherine, with all her wealth, does far more evil than good. Her money is used by her to drive away people she dislikes, "scattering them like a chill wind blowing autumn's leaves." one by one Lady Katherine's neighbors reject her due to the fact that they fear "her tiger's wrath and fox's cunning. It goes without saying that by the end of the poem. Lady Katherine is totally alone in her beautiful mansion, "a bitter queen in an empty castle."

Activity L: Making Additional Improvements

Work with two or three other students. Compare the editing and proofreading changes you made for *Activity K* with the changes that other students made. Discuss the similarities and differences. Then make any additional changes to the excerpt that you feel will further improve its writing quality.

Don't Omit the Last Step

TIP

The essential last step of the writing process is editing and proofreading. This is your opportunity to fix and polish your writing in any way that will enhance its overall quality. Remember that readers consider both conventions of writing and language use along with the other scoring criteria when they judge your Part A essay and your other Regents exam responses.

Of course, you do some editing and proofreading as you write, especially when you're rereading and revising your draft. You may, for example, correct some grammatical errors and tighten up a few wordy sentences. However, in the final step of the writing process, you approach your work with the specific goal of putting the finishing touches on your writing.

From Plan to Part A Essay: Taking a First Look

Let's see how the student's plan on pages 225–226 translates into a Part A essay.

Note: Paragraph numbers have been added for reference purposes. They are not part of the paper.

(1) People have a responsibility to support and protect one another. Passage I and Passage II both make this point, but in different ways. In Passage I, the poet focuses on one particular symbolic image to convey the poem's meaning. In Passage II, the writer uses a combination of elements to get the point across. These elements include setting, repetition, and point of view.

(2) The main image of Passage I is that of a father carrying his sleeping son across the street in the rain. The father is being extremely careful. He's trying his best to protect the sleeping boy. The poet refers to the boy as "the world's most sensitive cargo." This metaphor compares the child to a fragile package.

(3) In the next-to-last stanza, the poet states the poem's key point: "We're not going to be able to live in this world if we're not willing to do what he's doing with one another." In other words, for people to get along in the world, they must be willing to do what the father is doing. Of course, the poet doesn't mean that people should literally carry one another

around on their shoulders. The poet just means that people need to support and protect one another. The message here is a global one, which is why the poet repeats the word <u>world</u> twice. In the last two lines, the poet tells what will happen if people don't support and protect one another: "The road will only be wide. The rain will never stop falling." This image suggests that our burdens will be greater and that conditions will never improve.

(4) Both passages happen to use the image of a child on an adult's shoulders. However, Passage II approaches the idea of people's responsibility differently from Passage I. The author of the story uses a setting and a situation that emphasize the vulnerability of a child who is "full of trust." The little boy is alone on an empty beach, "screaming at the sky." The author repeats words like <u>cry</u> and <u>panic</u> to stress the feeling of isolation.

(5) The story is told from the first-person point of view. This approach lets the reader directly share the narrator's feelings and better understand the author's meaning. From the beginning, the narrator is upset. "The screams hit me like blows," the narrator says (using a simile), before running to help the boy. Meanwhile, while the narrator rushes to take responsibility for this child (whom the narrator doesn't even know), the boy's mother and her friend seem to take no responsibility at all. In fact, the first thing the mother's friend says is, "I'm not his mother." And, as the narrator notes more than once, "she looked only at me," not at the child.

(6) The writer is contrasting two attitudes: the person who willingly takes responsibility to protect another and the person who doesn't. The author clearly favors the narrator's protective attitude, as suggested in the line: "Who could leave a baby alone to panic on a strange beach?"

(7) People's responsibility to support and protect one another is an idea that both selections strongly communicate. Passage I relies mainly on a symbolic image to make its point, while Passage II blends various literary elements to convey its meaning.

Q & A

How much revising should I do? How do I know when I've done enough?

When rereading and revising your Part A essay—or any of your other Regents exam responses—pretend you've never seen the words before. Add, delete, clarify, or rearrange information to improve what you've written. Continue revising until you feel satisfied with your work, but leave yourself enough time to edit and proofread what you've written.

Here's an additional tip: When evaluating your work, use the same criteria that the readers will: meaning, development, organization, language use, and conventions.

From Plan to Part A Essay: Looking More Closely

Let's take a closer look at the student's essay. The student has organized the essay into seven paragraphs. The first paragraph is the introduction. The student begins this paragraph by presenting the controlling idea in a thesis statement. Then the student makes a comparison between the two selections.

Paragraphs 2 and 3 focus on the first selection, while paragraphs 4, 5, and 6 focus on the second selection. The final paragraph is the essay's conclusion, in which the student reinforces the controlling idea and summarizes the comparison of the selections.

The student develops the essay's points clearly, supporting them with specific details, carefully chosen quotations, and perceptive observations concerning the authors' use of literary elements and techniques. For example, the student doesn't just write that the story is told from the first-person point of view. The student also tells why: so that readers can "directly share the narrator's feelings and better understand the author's meaning." In fact, one of the strengths of this essay is how well the student explains the authors' use of literary elements to communicate ideas.

Note also the following:

- This essay follows the student's plan closely in both detail and basic structure. Such a close match is not always necessary, however. You may change or expand your plan as you're writing. Such adjustments are a normal part of the writing process.

● The student has organized the essay clearly, logically, and coherently. The student uses transitional words, phrases, and sentences to link ideas and guide readers. Note, for example, how the first sentence of paragraph 6 connects with paragraph 5.

● The student has used language effectively, expressing ideas clearly and precisely and varying sentence structure and length.

Activity M: Examining a Part A Essay

Answer the following questions about the student's essay.

1. What ideas, details, or literary elements/techniques would you have included that the student has not? Be specific in your answer.

   _____

   _____

   _____

2. What ideas, details, or literary elements/techniques has the student included that you would have omitted? Again, be specific.

   _____

   _____

   _____

3. Paragraph 3 begins with a topic sentence. What is the main idea that the sentence states? How does the rest of the paragraph develop that idea?

   _____

   _____

   _____

4. Has the student written a "unified" essay? Explain.

   _____

   _____

   _____

5. Could the student have organized this essay into a larger or smaller number of paragraphs? Do you think this would have been a good idea? Why or why not?

_____

_____

_____

6. Give at least three examples of transitional words or phrases. Explain what function each word or phrase serves. (You may include examples that do not appear in the chart on page 150.)

_____

_____

_____

Activity N: Writing a Part A Essay

Using the plan you created in *Activity H* along with the suggestions and student examples provided in this section, write your own extended response on a separate sheet of paper. Make revisions as needed and submit it to a classmate or teacher for evaluation based on the questions that follow. Then answer the questions about your own essay. Explain your answers, and give examples.

1. Does the essay have a controlling idea that demonstrates an in-depth understanding of both selections?

_____

_____

_____

2. Has the student made insightful connections between the controlling idea, the ideas in each selection, and the elements or techniques used to convey these ideas?

_____

_____

_____

3. Has the student developed ideas clearly, effectively supporting them with specific and relevant details?

_____

_____

_____

4. Does the essay have a clear, consistent focus on the controlling idea?

_____

_____

_____

5. Does the essay have a logical and coherent structure?

_____

_____

_____

6. Has the student used effective and engaging language appropriate for the audience and purpose?

_____

_____

_____

7. Has the student varied sentences in structure and length?

_____

_____

_____

8. Does the essay show a strong control of grammar, punctuation, spelling, and other elements of writing?

_____

_____

_____

5

CHAPTER REVIEW

Look back at the various lists, boldfaced items, boxes, and charts to quickly review many of the important ideas presented. Here are a few key points to get your review started:

- To write a unified essay, convey a clear central point—the controlling idea—and make sure that every paragraph in the essay relates to that point. Use specific and relevant details from *both* reading selections to develop your controlling idea.

- For Session Two, Part A, the ideas and supporting details in your essay must be directly linked to the two selections. Keep in mind that carefully selected quotations can effectively support and develop your controlling idea and illustrate the use of literary elements and techniques.

- The notes you take when you read the selections should focus on three things: (1) important ideas in the selections, especially ideas that relate directly to the topic/theme; (2) literary elements and techniques that the authors use to convey their ideas; and (3) thematic similarities and differences between the selections.

- Begin the writing process by establishing the controlling idea that will serve as the focus of your essay. Express this idea in a thesis statement that is clear and specific and reflects your understanding of both reading selections.

PRACTICE FOR SESSION TWO, PART A

The test and activities that follow will give you an opportunity to practice and develop the skills you'll need to do well on Part A of the Regents English exam. But don't limit yourself to just these activities. Practice on your own, or ask your teacher for help.

PRACTICE TEST (SESSION TWO, Part A)

Directions: Read the passages on the following pages (a poem and an essay) and answer the multiple-choice questions. Then write the essay described in **Your Task**. You may use the margins to take notes as you read and scrap paper to plan your response.

Your Task:

> After you have read the passages and answered the multiple-choice questions, write a unified essay about how memories of a parent continue to affect a person as an adult, as revealed in the passages. In your essay, use ideas from **both** passages to establish a controlling idea about how memories of a parent continue to affect a person as an adult. Using evidence from **each** passage, develop your controlling idea and show how each author uses specific literary elements or techniques to convey that idea.

Guidelines:

Be sure to

- Use ideas from **both** passages to establish a controlling idea about how memories of a parent continue to affect a person as an adult
- Use specific and relevant evidence from **each** passage to develop your controlling idea
- Show how each author uses specific literary elements (for example: tone, structure, setting, theme) or techniques (for example: imagery, symbolism, flashback) to convey the controlling idea
- Organize your ideas in a logical and coherent manner
- Use language that communicates ideas effectively
- Follow the conventions of standard written English

Passage I

The Courage That My Mother Had

The courage that my mother had
Went with her, and is with her still:
Rock from New England quarried;
Now granite in a granite hill.

5   The golden brooch my mother wore
She left behind for me to wear;
I have no thing I treasure more:
Yet, it is something I could spare.

Oh, if instead she'd left to me
10   The thing she took into the grave!—
That courage like a rock, which she
Has no more need of, and I have.

—Edna St. Vincent Millay

Passage II

Elegy*

Adapted by James D. Houston from his book The Men in My Life

At the county dump I am throwing away my father. His old paint rags, and stumps of brushes. Color charts. The spattered leather suitcase he used for so many years to carry the small tools and tiny jars of his trade, a suitcase so cracked and bent and buckle-ripped it's no good for anything now. I start to toss it on top 5 of the brushes and rags, but hold back.

I toss instead the five-gallon drums that once held primer. He stacked them against one wall of his shop, for no good reason, kept dozens more than he would ever use. Around these I toss the bottles and tubes from his medicine chest. And cracked boots, filled with dust, as if in his closet it has been raining dust for years. 10 And magazines. His fishing hat. Notes to himself:

Fix Window

Grease car

Call Harlow about job.

Bent nails in a jar, rolls of old wire, pipe sections, a fiddle he always intended 15 to mend, old paid bills, check stubs, pencils his teeth chewed. Ragtag bits of this and that he had touched, stacked, stored. Useless to anyone but him, and he's gone now.

So I toss it all out there among the refrigerators and lettuce leaves, truck tires, busted sofas, and flowerpots. Onto that heap I throw my father, saving for the last

---

For practice purposes, the essay "Elegy" is included here in its entirety. However, passages used in the actual Regents exam are usually shorter than this essay, and you're likely to encounter an excerpt from a longer work.

239

20 that suitcase of his I'd first seen twenty years back—and it was old then—that day he took me out on a job for the first time, wearing a pair of his spattered overalls, rolled thick at the cuff, and a Sherwin-Williams white billcap.

"What're ya gonna do, Dad?" I say that first morning.

25 He doesn't answer. He never answers, as if he prefers silence. And I always wait, as if each silence is an exception, and this time he will turn and speak. It's my big reason for coming along this morning, the chance that out here on the job something might pass between us. I would never have been able to describe it ahead of time, but . . . maybe . . . something.

30 I wait and watch. Two minutes of puckering lips and long, slow blinks while he studies the labels, then he selects one tube, unscrews its top, and squeezes out a little on his fingertips.

I follow him to the five-gallon drum he's mixing paint in. A short stick of plywood holds the color he's shooting for—pale, pale green. He's proud of his eye for color, his knack for figuring just how pale this green will be when it dries. I 35 watch and learn. Squeeze a green strip from the tube and stir it in, wide easy stirs while the green spirals out. Stir and stir. Then test: dip another stick in. Check the color. Stir.

"Okay, Jim. Take half this green paint and get that wall there covered."

He hands me a clean brush. Its black bristles shine with yesterday's thinner. 40 He pours a gallon bucket full of paint for me and cuts the fall off clean.

"I'll be back in a minute," he says.

It's the first time I've painted anything away from home. I do not yet know that before summer is out I will dread the look of any long unpainted wall and wince at the smell of paint and thinner. But now I want this one to be a good job. I want 45 to live up to the paint my dad has just mixed. I start by the living room door, taking my time, keeping the molding clear for a white trim later.

Ten minutes pass, and this first wall becomes my world. I am moving across the wide-open country—working my brush like Dad told me to, using the wrist, lapping strokes over—when I feel the need to turn around.

50 In the far doorway, the lady of the house stands glaring at me with a look of shock and anger. Next to the wall of her priceless living room she finds a kid dressed up in his father's overalls with the cuffs rolled thick. I realize how danger-ous I look to her. Under my new green freckles my face turns scarlet.

The woman is gone.

55 From the hallway I hear her loud whisper. "Mr. Houston! That boy painting my living room couldn't be over fifteen!"

"He's thirteen, Ma'am."

"He's what?"

240

"It's my boy, Jim. He's giving me a hand this summer."

60 "I just wonder if he knows what he's doing in there."

"I painted my first house when I was ten."

"Well . . . I . . . if . . . I'd certainly be keeping an eye on him if I were you."

"Don't worry, Ma'am, he knows what to do."

Behind me I hear her walking slowly across the room. I keep painting; I don't
65 look at her this time. Put plenty of paint on the brush. But don't let it run. Feather
it at the overlap. Cover. Cover.

Dad comes in and fills up another gallon bucket and helps me finish the wall.
He catches my eye once and winks. Then we are painting toward each other in a
silence broken only by the whish of bristles and the cluck of brush handle against
70 the can. Somewhere in the back of the house a radio is playing its faraway music.

We finish the room by quitting time. Dad looks over my work, finds a couple
of bald spots along the baseboard, and has me fill these in, saying only, "Keep an
eye out for them holidays." We clean the brushes. He drops the lid shut on his kit
of a suitcase, snaps the buckle to, straps it, and says, "Might as well take that on
75 out to the truck."

I had never paid much attention to his kit. Now I know just enough about
what's inside for it to be mysterious. A year from now I will know too much about
what's inside. By then I will be able to read his half smile, his apology for having
only this to offer me. But today carrying it is an honor. No one has ever carried
80 that kit but him. It has a manly weight, a fine weight for carrying from the house
to the curb, for hoisting onto the truck bed. It lands with a *thunk* and sits solid.

I wait for Dad to tie his ladder on the overhead rack, and we climb into
the cab. He winks once more as we prepare to leave Mrs. So-and-so behind.
Reeking of paint and turpentine, we are Sherwin and Williams calling it a day,
85 with no way to talk much over the rattle of his metal-floored Chevy, and no
need to talk. The clutch leaps. Wind rushes in, mixing paint and gasoline fumes,
and all you need to do is to stay loose for the jolts and the whole long rumble
ride home.

At the county dump, I am throwing away my father, lifting his old suitcase to
90 toss the last of him onto the smoking heap. It is crusted with splats of seventy
colors now, its lid corners split as if somebody sat on it. The ragged straps dangle.
One shred of leather holds the chromium buckle that still catches the sun where
the paint doesn't cover it. The shred of leather gives. The buckle breaks. The kit
flies open.

95 As if compressed inside, waiting to escape, the smell of oil and pigment cuts
through the smoke and rot that fills the air around me. My throwing arm stays. My
other hand reaches out. I'm holding the suitcase, inhaling the smell that always
clung to him, even after he had scrubbed. It rose from the creases in his hands, from
the white liners rimming his fingernails, from the paint specks he sometimes missed
100 with the thinner at the corners of his eyes. I breathe it in deep.

I close the suitcase slowly, prepare to heave it once and for all. This time with both hands, out and up. Out among all those things you find only by losing them.

105   One last glance. By five tonight this, too, will be gone for good, when the bulldozer comes to shove it over the side with the rest of today's collection—treasures of yesterday, old necessities, parts of the heart.

Multiple-Choice Questions

Directions (1–10): Answer the following questions. Select the best suggested answer and circle its number. The questions may help you think about the ideas you might use in your essay. You may return to these questions anytime you wish.

Passage I (the poem) — Questions 1–5 refer to Passage I.

1 The writer's tone in this poem is

    1 angry
    2 amused
    3 melancholy
    4 cheerful

2 The dominant figure of speech in the first stanza is

    1 metaphor
    2 hyperbole
    3 oxymoron
    4 personification

3 When the poet thinks of her mother, she feels

    1 bitterness
    2 admiration
    3 disappointment
    4 indifference

4 When the poet writes, "Yet, it is something I could spare" (line 8), she means that

    1 she has many other brooches
    2 some things are more important than material objects
    3 jewelry may be valuable, but it is not essential
    4 she and her mother had different values

5 The last stanza of the poem suggests that the poet

    1 faces difficulties in her present life
    2 believes that she and her mother had equal amounts of courage
    3 thinks that her mother was not so brave after all
    4 does not like the golden brooch

Passage II (the essay) — Questions 6–10 refer to Passage II.

6 The mood conveyed in this story is one of

  1 deep resentment
  2 tranquility
  3 mystery
  4 fond remembrance

7 The statement "At the county dump I am throwing away my father" is meant to suggest

  1 the narrator's rejection of his father's values
  2 how people forget loved ones after they are gone
  3 the symbolic meaning of people's possessions
  4 how short life is

8 The middle portion of this passage (lines 23–88) is an example of the use of

  1 allegory
  2 flashback
  3 oxymoron
  4 onomatopoeia

9 The statement "A year from now I will know too much about what's inside" (lines 77–78) suggests that

  1 the work of a painter became less appealing to the narrator
  2 the narrator learned all there was to know about painting
  3 the narrator discovered a secret about his father
  4 the narrator became a better painter than his father

10 The phrase "things you find only by losing them" (lines 102–103) refers to

  1 objects that were lost and never found
  2 unimportant things that should be discarded
  3 objects that are repeatedly lost and found again
  4 things whose value is appreciated after they are gone

After you have finished these questions, review **Your Task** and the **Guidelines**. Use scrap paper to plan your response. Then write your response to Part A.

Evaluating a Part A Essay

Exchange papers with a partner. (Choose a different partner from the one you paired up with previously.) Referring to the chart on page 215, *Scoring the Part A Extended Response*, evaluate your partner's written response on the basis of the five criteria.

Be as *positive, constructive, and specific* as you can in your comments and suggestions. Your goal is to help your partner improve his or her skills.

*MEANING:*_____

_____

_____

_____

*DEVELOPMENT:*_____

_____

_____

_____

*ORGANIZATION:*_____

_____

_____

_____

*LANGUAGE USE:*_____

_____

_____

_____

*CONVENTIONS:*_____

_____

_____

_____

Improving and Polishing Your Part A Essay

Use your partner's comments to help you revise, edit, and polish your essay. Make whatever changes you think are necessary to improve your work.

For additional practice, two actual Regents exams appear at the end of this book.

CHAPTER 5

Reading and Writing for Critical Analysis

⬛1

UNDERSTANDING THE SESSION TWO, PART B TASKS

Unlike the three previous parts of the Regents English exam, Session Two, Part B contains no reading or listening selections or multiple-choice questions. Instead, Part B asks you to write a critical essay based on your analysis of two works of literature that you have read. You may choose which works you will write about.

To provide a specific framework for your essay, the Part B prompt includes a feature referred to as the **Critical Lens**. This is a statement or quotation that you will use to analyze and evaluate the two literary works.

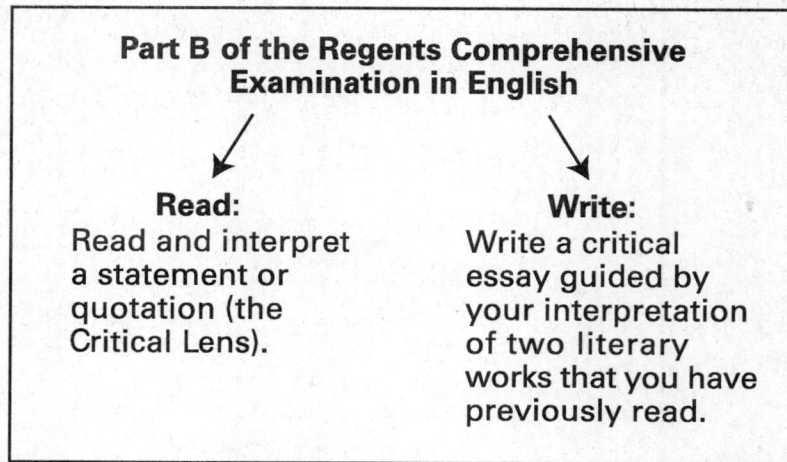

Part B of the Regents Comprehensive Examination in English

Read:
Read and interpret a statement or quotation (the Critical Lens).

Write:
Write a critical essay guided by your interpretation of two literary works that you have previously read.

✸ A QUICK LOOK ✸

What is Part B testing me on?

Part B tests your ability to analyze and evaluate two previously read literary works and write a critical essay about them. Part B also tests your understanding of literary elements.

How is Part B similar to other parts of the exam?

Part B is similar to Part A in that both parts require you to write about literary works rather than informational texts.

How does Part B differ from other parts of the exam?

Part B is the only part of the exam that does not include selections or multiple-choice questions. Instead, you're asked to write an essay about literary works that you've previously read.

Examining the Session Two, Part B Prompt

Look at the typical Part B prompt below. Note that the prompt consists of only three elements:

- **Your Task**
- **Critical Lens**
- **Guidelines**

PART B

Your Task:

Write a critical essay in which you discuss *two* works of literature you have read from the particular perspective of the statement that is provided for you in the **Critical Lens**. In your essay, provide a valid interpretation of the statement, agree *or* disagree with the statement as you have interpreted it, and support your opinion using specific references to appropriate literary elements from the two works. You may use scrap paper to plan your response.

Critical Lens:

> "Literature opens a dark window on the soul, revealing more about what is bad in human nature than what is good."

Guidelines:

Be sure to

- Provide a valid interpretation of the critical lens that clearly establishes the criteria for analysis
- Indicate whether you agree *or* disagree with the statement as you have interpreted it
- Choose *two* works you have read that you believe best support your opinion
- Use the criteria suggested by the critical lens to analyze the works you have chosen
- Avoid plot summary. Instead, use specific references to appropriate literary elements (for example: theme, characterization, structure, language, point of view) to develop your analysis
- Organize your ideas in a logical and coherent manner
- Specify the titles and authors of the literature you choose
- Follow the conventions of standard written English

Let's take a moment to look at each element of the Part B prompt. First, **Your Task** describes in detail the essay you'll have to write. Be sure to read **Your Task** carefully two or three times so that you'll know exactly what you have to do.

Here's the first sentence:

> Write a critical essay in which you discuss *two* works of literature you have read from the particular perspective of the statement that is provided for you in the **Critical Lens**.

Your Task starts by telling you to write a *critical* essay—that is, an essay based on thoughtful evaluation and analysis. Note that the word ***two*** is in boldface type to stress that you must discuss two works of literature, not just one. The first sentence goes on to explain that you are to use the critical lens statement as a framework for your essay.

? *Complete the sentence:* A *critical essay* is an essay based on _____ .

Q & A

The Part B prompt emphasizes the term "critical lens."
What is the significance of this term?

A lens is something you look through in order to see. The term *critical lens* is meant to suggest a way of "seeing" literature critically. In this sense, the statement or quotation provided in Part B is meant to guide your evaluation and analysis of the two works of literature.

Here's the rest of **Your Task**:

In your essay, provide a valid interpretation of the statement, agree *or* disagree with the statement as you have interpreted it, and support your opinion using specific references to appropriate literary elements from the two works. You may use scrap paper to plan your response.

This part of the prompt is important. It directs you to do three things in your essay:

● *interpret* the critical lens statement

● *agree or disagree* with the statement

● *support your opinion* using specific references to literary elements

In other words, you have to explain what you think the statement means, determine your opinion (and why), and then discuss specific literary elements in both works to support your opinion.

Critical Lens:

"Literature opens a dark window on the soul, revealing more about what is bad in human nature than what is good."

After **Your Task**, the prompt provides the **Critical Lens**. This statement or quotation is sometimes credited to a well-known author. It may relate specifically to literature, or it may be of a more general nature. *Think carefully about the critical lens statement before deciding whether you agree or disagree with it.*

After the **Critical Lens**, the **Guidelines** provide clarification and additional guidance. They also relate the writing task to the five scoring criteria.

Note that certain key words in the **Guidelines** appear in boldface type for emphasis.

Guidelines:

Be sure to

- Provide a valid interpretation of the critical lens that clearly establishes the criteria for analysis

Comment: You'll begin your essay by explaining your interpretation of the critical lens statement—what you think the statement means. Your interpretation will then serve as the basis for your analysis.

- Indicate whether you agree *or* disagree with the statement as you have interpreted it

Comment: You'll need to take a position—that is, state whether you agree or disagree with the statement, and why.

- Choose *two* works you have read that you believe best support your opinion
- Use the criteria suggested by the critical lens to analyze the works you have chosen

Comment: The choice of literature is up to you. Choose literary works that you can effectively connect with your interpretation of the critical lens statement.

- Avoid plot summary. Instead, use specific references to appropriate literary elements (for example: theme, characterization, structure, language, point of view) to develop your analysis

Comment: This guideline specifically tells you what *not* to do: don't just summarize the plot. Rather, develop your essay with specific references to literary elements in both works. The prompt mentions several examples of literary elements, but you're not limited to just these. You may discuss any literary elements that you know.

? *Complete the sentence:* Rather than summarize the plot, you should _____

_____.

- Organize your ideas in a logical and coherent manner

Comment: This same guideline appears in all four parts of the Regents exam, because no matter what you write, your ideas should be logically organized and clearly presented.

• Specify the titles and authors of the literature you choose

Comment: Be sure you know (and can spell) the titles and authors of literary works you've read in school. Remember that when you write the title of a long work, such as a novel or play, you need to underline it.

• Follow the conventions of standard written English

Comment: This guideline reminds you that your essay will also be judged for grammar, punctuation, and other writing conventions.

Write an Effective Position Paper

TIP

Although the prompt doesn't specifically say this, the kind of essay you're writing for Part B of the Regents exam is a *position paper.* Position papers are actually a kind of persuasive writing.

In a position paper, you state a position, or opinion, and then support your position or opinion with specific details, examples, reasons, or other information. *The goal of the position paper you're writing for Part B is to present a thoughtful and convincing critical analysis.*

Activity A: Examining a Session Two, Part B Prompt

A Session Two, Part B prompt appears below. Read the prompt, and answer the questions that follow.

Your Task:

Write a critical essay in which you discuss *two* works of literature you have read from the particular perspective of the statement that is provided for you in the **Critical Lens**. In your essay, provide a valid interpretation of the statement, agree *or* disagree with the statement as you have interpreted it, and support your opinion using specific references to appropriate literary elements from the two works. You may use scrap paper to plan your response.

Critical Lens:

> "A great book should leave you with many experiences, and slightly exhausted at the end."
>
> —William Styron

Guidelines:

Be sure to

- Provide a valid interpretation of the critical lens that clearly establishes the criteria for analysis
- Indicate whether you agree *or* disagree with the statement as you have interpreted it
- Choose *two* works you have read that you believe best support your opinion
- Use the criteria suggested by the critical lens to analyze the works you have chosen
- Avoid plot summary. Instead, use specific references to appropriate literary elements (for example: theme, characterization, structure, language, point of view) to develop your analysis
- Organize your ideas in a logical and coherent manner
- Specify the titles and authors of the literature you choose
- Follow the conventions of standard written English

---

1. In your own words, describe the specific writing task.

_____

_____

_____

2. Why is it important to think carefully about the critical lens?

_____

_____

_____

3. (a) How would you interpret the critical lens statement in this prompt? That is, what do you think the statement means?

_____

_____

_____

(b) Do you agree or disagree with the critical lens statement as you have interpreted it? Why?

_____

_____

_____

(c) What two works of literature that you have read would support your opinion? Write their titles and authors.

_____

_____

_____

4. Why would simply summarizing the plot of two works of literature not earn you a high score on Part B of the exam?

_____

_____

_____

5. Summarize how Part B of the Regents exam differs from other parts of the exam.

_____

_____

_____

6. Which two **Guidelines** appear in all four parts of the Regents exam? Why do you think they do?

_____

_____

_____

Preparing for Part B

To do well on Session Two, Part B of the Regents exam, you must be able to knowledgeably discuss two literary works. Here are several suggestions to help you get ready for this part of the exam:

▶ **Consider in advance which works you would feel most comfortable discussing.** Of course, you don't know ahead of time what the critical lens statement will be. However, most of the works of literature that you read for school will be suitable for a wide range of critical lens statements.

▶ **Be prepared to discuss several works.** The more works you've read and are ready to write about, the more you'll have to choose from for Part B. If you know only two books well, and one doesn't relate to the critical lens statement, you could be stuck for something to write about. Therefore, even though you have to write about only two, *try to be prepared with at least three* literary works that you would feel confident about using for the exam.

> **Watch Your Spelling**
> In addition to knowing how to spell the titles and authors of literary works, you should also be able to spell the names of important characters, places, and things that you may write about.
> Remember to capitalize proper nouns—specific persons, places, things, or ideas. Examples: Romeo, Alabama, Buddhism.
>
> *TIP*

▶ **Study and review.** Be sure you have a firm grasp of the content and meaning of literary works that you may want to discuss. *Take time to study and review the works' specific literary elements.* You may find it helpful to write additional notes while reviewing notes previously taken for school. Allow extra time for works that are no longer fresh in your mind.

▶ **Choose substantial works.** The richer the books you've read, the more substance you'll have to work with. These books lend themselves to various interpretations and, therefore, can be more useful for connecting with the critical lens.

Activity B: Choosing Literary Works

1. List the titles and authors of at least three works of literature you've read that you feel you could use for the Regents exam. *Be sure they are substantial works whose literary elements would lend themselves to critical analysis.*

   _____

   _____

   _____

2. Next to each work that you listed, indicate how much study and review you'll need to do before the Regents exam. Use the following system of one, two, or three stars to indicate the level of study and review needed:

   *I read this book very recently, and it's still fresh in my mind. I'll just need to look back over my notes.

   **It's been a while since I read this book. Although I remember it fairly well, I definitely need to set aside some time to refresh my memory before the test.

   ***This is a good book for the test, but it's been a long time since I read it. I need to review it in detail and maybe even reread parts.

NOTE: If you could not identify three suitable works of literature for Question 1 above, be sure to read such works before the exam. If you need help, speak with your teacher.

Don't Make a Poor Choice

TIP

Though you have complete freedom to choose the literature for this part of the exam, don't be tempted to take "shortcuts." Readers who score the Part B essay will not look favorably on essays that are written about movie or television versions of books. Obscure or unfamiliar books also may not work to your advantage, since the reader may not fully appreciate what you're saying. Instead, choose classic or contemporary titles that are widely recognized for their quality and richness. If in doubt about a suitable choice, ask your teacher.

---

2 PLANNING AND WRITING YOUR PART B ESSAY

The purpose of the essay that you write for Session Two, Part B of the Regents exam is critical analysis. From the perspective of the critical lens statement, you will analyze and evaluate two works of literature, using specific literary elements to support your opinion.

Examining the Criteria as Applied to Part B

As with other parts of the Regents exam, readers will score your Part B essay holistically on the basis of meaning, development, organization, language use, and conventions.

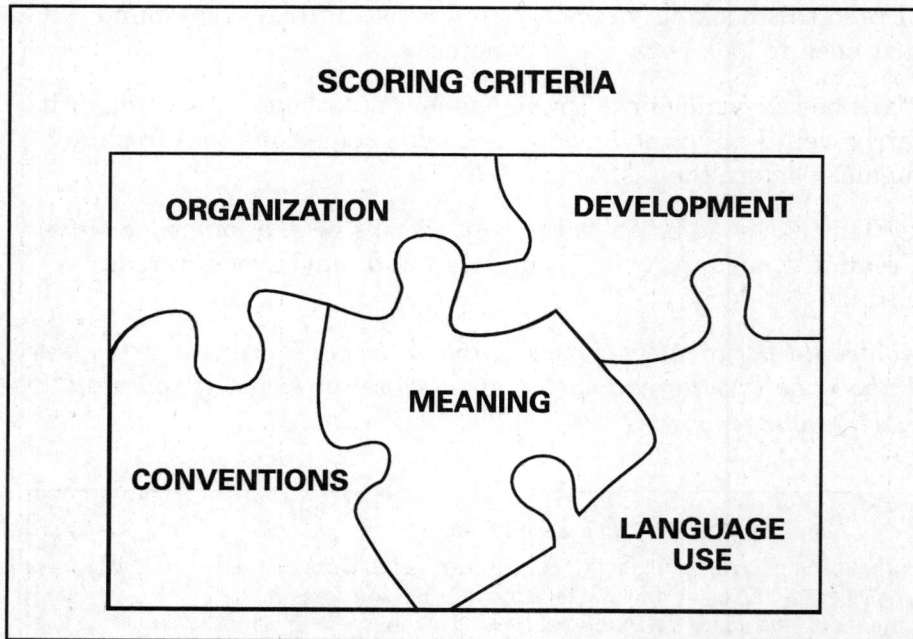

SCORING CRITERIA

ORGANIZATION

DEVELOPMENT

MEANING

CONVENTIONS

LANGUAGE USE

The following chart shows how the scoring criteria are applied specifically to Part B. Note that the evaluation for Part B is similar to that for previous parts, but the emphasis is clearly on critical analysis. Furthermore, *your essay must include an interpretation of the critical lens statement as the basis for, and focus of, your analysis.*

SCORING THE PART B EXTENDED RESPONSE (ESSAY)

CRITERIA	WHAT YOUR PART B RESPONSE SHOULD SHOW
MEANING	• Your interpretation of the critical lens statement, clearly establishing the criteria for your analysis • Insightful analysis of two chosen literary works, based on the criteria you've established
DEVELOPMENT	• Clear development of ideas • Effective use of specific and relevant supporting details from both works of literature, especially references to specific literary elements
ORGANIZATION	• Clear, consistent focus based on your interpretation of the critical lens statement • Logical and coherent structure
LANGUAGE USE	• Effective and engaging language that is appropriate for the specific audience and purpose • Varied sentence structure and length
CONVENTIONS	• Strong control of grammar, punctuation, spelling, and other elements of writing, with few errors

---

In the pages that follow, you'll build on what you've learned in previous chapters as you see how to plan and write a critical essay that meets these criteria.

Using the Critical Lens to Begin Planning

Before you can start work on your Part B essay, you first have to interpret the critical lens. Specifically, you have to:

● Read and think about the critical lens statement.

● Decide whether you agree or disagree with the statement, and why.

● Decide which works of literature to use in your essay.

One way to approach a critical lens statement is to think of it as a true-or-false question. That is, imagine that the phrase *True or false?* follows the statement. For example:

> "A great book should leave you with many experiences, and slightly exhausted at the end." *True or false?*

If you believe the statement is true, you agree with it. If you think the statement is *not* always true, you disagree. Either way, you should have specific reasons. Jot these reasons down on paper. You can refer to your notes when you plan and write your essay.

Here's an example of two opposing student reactions to the same critical lens statement. Imagine the phrase *True or false?* follows the statement. Which student's thoughts come closer to your own feelings?

Critical Lens:

"The only worthwhile literature is that which makes you think about your own life."

Student 1:

Absolutely true! Literature should make you think about such aspects of your life as your values, your accomplishments, and your goals. Thinking about a book's characters should help you gain insight into yourself.

Student 2:

Not true! All literature has some value, even the most mindless escapist books. For example, if I read an exciting novel whose plot keeps me hooked from start to finish, I'm enjoying myself. That alone makes the book worthwhile, whether or not it makes me think about my life.

? *Answer in your own words:* Which student do you agree with? Why?

_____

_____

_____

Once you've thought about the critical lens statement, you have to decide which works of literature you'll use to support your interpretation. *Try to base your decision on specific literary elements, since you'll need to discuss these elements in your essay.* Literary elements that you may want to write about include—but are not limited to—the following:

characters	setting
mood	structure
plot	theme
point of view	tone

Note that your particular interpretation of a critical lens statement may bring certain elements to mind at once. For example, Student 1 above thought immediately about characters, while Student 2 thought about plot.

Activity C: Interpreting Critical Lens Statements

Read and think about each critical lens statement below. Then answer the questions that follow.

> "To be truly memorable, a book must have at its core one of life's great quests: the quest for love, truth, or power."

1. Briefly explain your interpretation of this statement.

   _____

   _____

   _____

   _____

2. Do you agree or disagree with the statement as you have interpreted it? Explain why.

   _____

   _____

   _____

3. Write the title and author of a book that would support your opinion.

   _____

   _____

4. For the book you have chosen, what literary elements would best serve to support your interpretation? Why?

_____

_____

"Courage is measured by an individual's willingness to continue fighting even when the likelihood of victory is small."

5. Briefly explain your interpretation of this statement.

_____

_____

_____

_____

6. Do you agree or disagree with the statement as you have interpreted it? Why?

_____

_____

_____

7. Write the title and author of a book that would support your opinion. (Choose a different book from the one you chose for Question 3 above.)

_____

_____

8. For the book you have chosen, what literary elements would best serve to support your interpretation? Why?

_____

_____

Developing and Organizing Your Critical Essay

In Chapters 2–4, you learned how to develop and organize ideas and supporting information to write extended responses. The main points you've learned will also apply to Part B.

As in Part A, the specified format for Part B is an essay—in this case a *critical essay*. Before reading on, take a moment to review the basics of essay structure in *The Basics* box on pages 223–224.

You can plan on organizing your Part B critical essay this way:

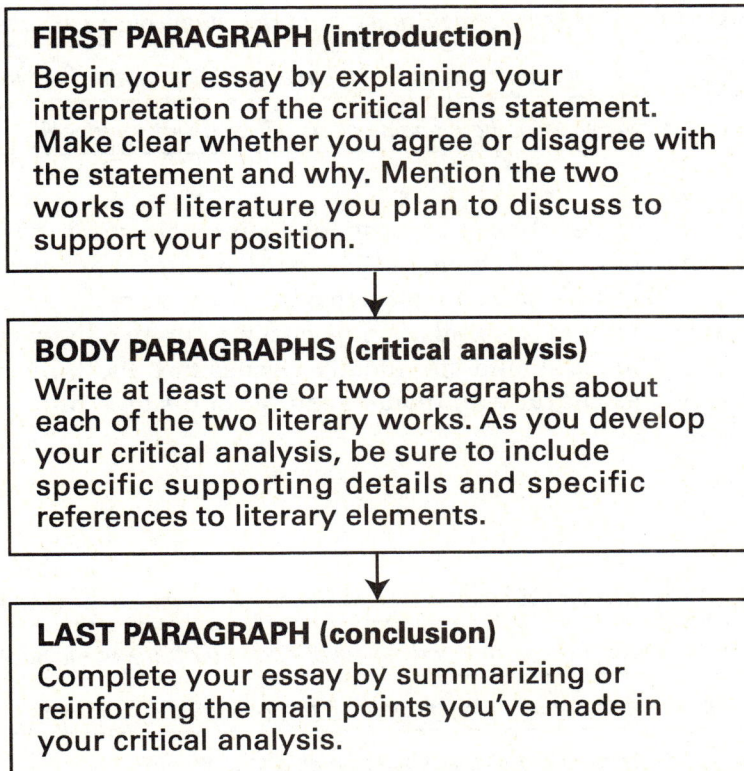

FIRST PARAGRAPH (introduction)

Begin your essay by explaining your interpretation of the critical lens statement. Make clear whether you agree or disagree with the statement and why. Mention the two works of literature you plan to discuss to support your position.

BODY PARAGRAPHS (critical analysis)

Write at least one or two paragraphs about each of the two literary works. As you develop your critical analysis, be sure to include specific supporting details and specific references to literary elements.

LAST PARAGRAPH (conclusion)

Complete your essay by summarizing or reinforcing the main points you've made in your critical analysis.

? *Fill in the blank:* In your Part B essay, you should write at least _____ paragraphs about each literary work.

To develop your essay, follow these guidelines:

▶ **Clearly establish the criteria for your analysis.** In other words, use your interpretation to create a guiding framework for your essay.

To better understand what this means, study the two examples below. They are based on the opposing student reactions to a critical lens statement that you saw on page 260.

Critical Lens:

"The only worthwhile literature is that which makes you think about your own life."

Student 1:

Absolutely true! Literature should make you think about such aspects of your life as your values, your accomplishments, and your goals. Thinking about a book's characters should help you gain insight into yourself.

Criteria for analysis: Based on Student 1's interpretation, the analysis should support the idea that "worthwhile" literature makes you "think about such aspects of your life as your values . . . accomplishments . . . goals." In discussing the two literary works, this student should specifically discuss how by thinking about particular characters, readers can "gain insight" into themselves.

Student 2:

Not true! All literature has some value, even the most mindless escapist books. For example, if I read an exciting novel whose plot keeps me hooked from start to finish, I'm enjoying myself. That alone makes the book worthwhile, whether or not it makes me think about my life.

Criteria for analysis: Based on Student 2's interpretation, the analysis should support the idea that literature can be "worthwhile" without making readers think about their own lives. In discussing the two literary works, this student should specifically discuss how, for example, an exciting plot can provide great enjoyment, which in itself makes reading worthwhile.

Keep in mind that the criteria described for the above examples represent starting points. Both students may further develop, expand, or refine their criteria as they carry out the writing process.

Note, too, that you don't necessarily have to refer to the same literary elements for both works of literature. You might want to focus on characters for one book but setting and structure for the other. That's fine—*as long the particular literary elements you discuss support your interpretation of the critical lens statement.*

Q&A

How many literary elements should I discuss in my essay?

The answer to this question will vary, depending on the critical lens statement and on the specific literary works discussed. Keep in mind that it's better to cover a small number of literary elements in detail than to mention numerous elements without discussing any in depth.

Note, too, that you don't have to discuss the same number of literary elements for both literary works. You might, for example, discuss two elements for one work and three for the other.

► **Prepare a rough outline.** As you outline your plan on paper, focus on one work of literature at a time. Use the criteria you've established to develop an insightful analysis of the first literary work. Jot down your main ideas, along with specific and relevant supporting details, especially references to specific literary elements. Then do the same for the second literary work.

You'll generally find it easiest to deal with just one literary element per paragraph, *unless* two elements are closely linked. For example, depending on the literary work, you may want to discuss mood and setting together, or structure and plot, or theme and characterization. Choose whatever method of organization lets you communicate your ideas most clearly. Use as many paragraphs as you need to make your points effectively.

The structure of your rough outline will look something like this:

FIRST PARAGRAPH
   Introduction, including your interpretation of the critical lens statement and whether you agree or disagree with it; criteria for analysis

BODY PARAGRAPHS
   Critical analysis of first literary work
      —Supporting details and literary elements

   Critical analysis of second literary work
      —Supporting details and literary elements

LAST PARAGRAPH
Conclusion

Don't worry about including more information in your outline than you may need. Instead, when your outline is finished, carefully review it. Zero in on the most important items, and eliminate any items that are unimportant or irrelevant to your criteria for analysis.

Q&A

I notice that the scoring criteria for Part B do not refer to "a controlling idea," as the criteria for Part A did. Does this mean I should forget about controlling ideas and thesis statements?

No. It's true that for scoring purposes the Part B criteria emphasize the critical lens, while the Part A criteria emphasized the controlling idea. Nevertheless, *the basic characteristics of a well-written essay remain the same.*

In Chapter 4 you learned that for an essay to be *unified,* it must convey a clear central point—the controlling idea—and every paragraph in the essay must relate to that point. You also learned that expressing controlling idea in a thesis statement helps you establish and maintain your focus.

For Part B, your interpretation of the critical lens statement in effect becomes your controlling idea. Furthermore, just as for Part A, expressing this idea in a thesis statement in your first paragraph will help you establish and maintain your focus.

Activity D: Establishing Criteria for Analysis

To respond to the following questions, refer back to your answers for *Activity C* on pages 261–262.

1. Based on your interpretation of the first critical lens statement (Question 1), describe the criteria you would use to write your analysis.

_____

_____

_____

_____

_____

2. Based on your interpretation of the second critical lens statement (Question 5), describe the criteria you would use to write your analysis.

_____

_____

_____

_____

_____

Looking at a Sample Plan

Let's see how a plan can help you write an effective critical essay for Part B. Look at the student's plan below, based on the prompt that you saw at the beginning of this chapter. The critical lens for the prompt was:

> "Literature opens a dark window on the soul, revealing more about what is bad in human nature than what is good."

As you look at the plan, notice how the student has included enough specific ideas and supporting information to shape an essay. Of course, the student will make changes and adjustments in the process of writing. But having a basic plan to work from will help ensure a well thought out and logically organized essay. Later, you'll read the essay that the student wrote based on this outline.

Student's Plan for Session Two, Part B Critical Essay

Note: For illustration purposes, this outline may be more detailed than yours needs to be. The plan you make for yourself need be only detailed enough for _you_ to understand what you intend to write!

FIRST PARAGRAPH

My interpretation of critical lens:

Literature shows more about the bad aspects of people than about the good.

My position:

Disagree. Literature shows the good and bad more or less equally, both in terms of people's personal qualities and their actions.

(→ Convert my position to a thesis statement.)

Literary works to support my position:

    <u>To Kill a Mockingbird</u> *by Harper Lee*

    (→ elements to discuss: characterization, plot)

    <u>Of Mice and Men</u> *by John Steinbeck*

    (→ elements to discuss: characterization, plot)

BODY PARAGRAPHS

<u>*To Kill a Mockingbird*</u>

    Characterization shows good and bad—people's qualities

        —Atticus Finch: good qualities (courage, integrity, willingness to take a stand)

        —Bob Ewell: Bad qualities

        —People's bigotry and prejudice

    —Plot shows good and bad—people's actions

        —People cruelly and unjustly accuse Tom Robinson because he is black

        —Atticus confronts lynch mob outside jail

        —Boo Radley saves the kids

<u>*Of Mice and Men*</u>

    Characterization—people's good and bad qualities

        —Relationship between George and Lennie: friendship, loyalty

        —Curley: troublemaker

    Plot—people's good and bad actions

        —George protects Lennie, takes care of him

        —Curley bullies Lennie

        —Ending: Curley wants to shoot Lennie down; George kills Lennie to save him from worse fate

LAST PARAGRAPH

    Summarize/reinforce: Through characterization and plot, the two books reveal both good and bad aspects of human nature.

Before continuing, consider these observations about the student's essay outline:

- For the first paragraph, this student has made clear and specific notes regarding interpretation and position. The student has also included a personal reminder: *Convert my position to a thesis statement.*

  Although it is not always possible (or necessary) to "convert" a position neatly into a one-sentence thesis statement, your first paragraph should explain your interpretation of the critical lens, state your position, and establish the criteria for your subsequent analysis.

- The student has also made specific notes about the literary elements to be discussed—characterization and plot. In this case, it's the same two elements for both books, since both work well with the critical lens and with the student's criteria for analysis. In other instances, the literary elements discussed for one book might be different from those discussed for the other.

Activity E: Evaluating a Plan

Answer the following questions about the student's plan. Before writing your answers, discuss your thoughts with a partner or a small group of students.

1. What criteria for analysis does the student establish in the first paragraph?

   _____

   _____

   _____

   _____

2. How does the student plan to use the established criteria in the body paragraphs? Be specific.

   _____

   _____

   _____

   _____

3. Overall, what are the strengths of the student's plan?

_____

_____

_____

_____

4. For each of the literary works, give examples of supporting details that the student plans to include as part of the critical analysis.

_____

_____

_____

_____

5. How will this outline help the student to write the essay?

_____

_____

_____

_____

Activity F: Making a Plan

1. Review the prompt that appears in *Activity A* on pages 254–255. On a sheet of paper, use what you've learned to make a rough outline for a critical essay responding to that prompt.

2. Exchange papers with a partner. Evaluate each other's plans. Offer your partner specific and constructive comments and suggestions.

Using Language Effectively and Correctly

As you apply the writing process to your critical essay for Part B, do your best to use language both effectively and correctly. And be sure to allow time for revising, proofreading, and polishing what you've written.

Review the expanded checklist below. You can use it to help you improve the quality of your writing.

CHECKLIST FOR EDITING AND PROOFREADING

Using Language Effectively

Sentence Variety

✔ Have I varied my sentences in structure and length?

✔ Have I avoided beginning consecutive sentences in the same way?

Language

✔ Have I used precise language?

✔ Have I avoided clichés?

Word Choice

✔ Have I avoided using slang, except when quoting someone's words?

✔ Have I avoided unnecessary wordiness?

Other Elements

✔ Have I avoided repeating the same wording or information unnecessarily?

✔ Have I used active, not passive, constructions?

Using Language Correctly

Punctuation

✔ Have I used commas, apostrophes, and periods where needed?

✔ Have I used quotation marks appropriately and correctly?

✔ Have I underlined the titles of long works?

Capitalization

✔ Have I capitalized the first word of every sentence?

✔ Have I capitalized all proper nouns?

Grammar

✔ Have I written complete sentences?

✔ Have I avoided run-on sentences?

✔ Do my subjects and verbs agree?

Spelling

✔ Have I spelled words correctly?

✔ Have I used the words that I meant to use (for example, *your / you're, there / their, to / too, affect / effect*)?

271

> **How to Improve Your Spelling** **TIP**
>
> Many books contain lists of frequently misspelled words. You can improve your spelling by studying a few of these words at a time.
>
> If you write on a computer, pay close attention when you run the spell-check utility. Don't just accept the software-suggested corrections. *Look* at them closely, and try to fix them in your memory.
>
> Learn the basic rules of spelling. If you're not sure what they are, consult a spelling book or check with your teacher.
>
> Beware of words that aren't really words. For example, there's no such word as *irregardless* (the word is *regardless*) or *tonite* (the word is *tonight*).

Activity G: Improving Writing Quality

The following excerpt comes from the first draft of a student's Part B critical essay. The excerpt contains a number of weaknesses that detract from overall quality, in addition to at least nine errors involving conventions of writing. Use the *Checklist for Editing and Proofreading* on page 271 to help you revise, edit, and proofread the excerpt.

> Literature can provide insight into family relationships. Through a variety of literary elements, Shakespeare's <u>King Lear</u> does just that. For , example shakespeare structures the play in such a way that the main plot and and the subplot is smoothly blended and complement each other. Together, the main plot and and subplot highlight various emotional aspects of family relationships, such as love, loyalty, jealously, and selfishness to name but a few. As the play progresses, the reader gains insight into the important role these aspects play in relationships between parent and child The render also gains insight into the important role these aspects play in relationships between siblings.
>
> In addition, the characters in King Lear illustrates how the actions and feelings of one family member directly effect other members of a family for example, the stubbornness of Cordelia, Lears youngest daughter, at the beginning of the play triggers the king's rash and angry response.

Similarly, Edmund's scheme to elimenate his brother Edgar leads to tragic

consequences for their father, Gloucester.

Activity H: Making Additional Improvements

Work with two or three other students. Compare the editing and proofreading changes you made for *Activity G* above with the changes that other students made. Discuss how your changes were alike and different, and why. Then make any additional changes to the excerpt that you feel will further improve its writing quality.

Reinforce Your Knowledge

For Part B, as for all parts of the Regents exam, you can make your writing coherent by using transitional words and phrases to connect ideas. Pause here to review the *Transitional Words and Phrases* chart on page 150. What transitional words and phrases can you find in the *Activity G* essay excerpt on pages 272–273?

TIP

From Plan to Part B Essay: Taking a First Look

Let's take a look at how the student's plan from pages 267–268 translates into a Part B critical essay.

Note: Paragraph numbers have been added for reference purposes. They are not part of the paper.

> <u>(1)</u> *"Literature opens a dark window on the soul, revealing more about*
> *what is bad in human nature than what is good." This statement suggests*
> *that literature shows more about the bad aspects of people than about*
> *the good. I disagree. I think that literature shows good and bad sides of*
> *human nature about equally, both in terms of people's personal qualities*
> *and in terms of their actions. To Kill a Mockingbird, by Harper Lee, and*
> *Of Mice and Men, by John Steinbeck, are two books that illustrate this*
> *balance of good and bad.*
>
> > <u>(2)</u> *The characters of To Kill a Mockingbird represent a wide range of*
> *human nature. For example, Atticus Finch is a character with very positive*
> *qualities. He is a model of courage and integrity, someone willing to take a*

stand for what he believes in. By contrast, Bob Ewell is evil and violent. He has many of the worst qualities of human nature. Furthermore, most of the other people of Maycomb, Alabama, where the story takes place, show attitudes of bigotry, prejudice, and racism.

(3) The plot of To Kill a Mockingbird similarly shows both good and bad through people's actions. On the negative side, people cruelly and unjustly accuse Tom Robinson of rape because he is black. Bob Ewell curses Atticus and spits in his face. However, many positive events occur, too. For instance, Atticus risks his own safety to confront a lynch mob outside the jail. And the neighbor, Boo Radley, comes out of hiding to save Atticus's children when Bob Ewell attacks them. Such heroic actions suggest the basic decency of human nature.

(4) The characters of Of Mice and Men also show people's good traits as well as their bad. In the relationship between George and Lennie, we see such positive qualities of human nature as friendship, loyalty, and trust. But Curley, a mean troublemaker, shows just how unpleasant people can be.

(5) The plot of Of Mice and Men shows how good or bad people can be in their actions. George protects Lennie and takes care of him. At the end, George has to shoot his friend to save him from a worse fate. Meanwhile, Curley is a bully. It's he who wants to shoot Lennie down after Lennie accidentally kills Curley's wife. It's interesting that George shoots Lennie out of friendship, while Curley wanted to shoot him for revenge. These two motives in themselves suggest the range of human nature.

(6) Books such as To Kill a Mockingbird and Of Mice and Men show the interaction between positive and negative aspects of human nature. Rather than emphasize the bad, they present a more or less balanced view of people's good and bad qualities and actions.

Activity I: Using the Scoring Criteria to Evaluate a Part B Essay

Work with a partner as you answer the following questions about the student's essay. Explain each of your answers, giving specific reasons or examples as appropriate.

1. Has the student made an effective interpretation of the critical lens statement, clearly establishing the criteria for analysis?

   _____

   _____

   _____

2. Has the student made an insightful analysis of the two chosen literary works based on the criteria established?

   _____

   _____

   _____

3. Has the student developed ideas clearly, supporting them with details from both works of literature, especially references to specific literary elements?

   _____

   _____

   _____

4. Does the essay have a clear, consistent focus based on the student's interpretation of the critical lens statement?

   _____

   _____

   _____

5. Does the essay have a logical and coherent structure?

   _____

   _____

   _____

6. Has the student used effective and engaging language appropriate for the audience and purpose?

_____

_____

_____

7. Has the student varied sentences in structure and length?

_____

_____

_____

8. Does the essay show a strong control of grammar, punctuation, spelling, and other elements of writing?

_____

_____

_____

Use All the Time You Have

When revising, editing, and proofreading your Part B essay, take your time. Review your work with a critical eye. Look for ways to make it better. Remember, there's no extra credit for finishing early. Use all the time you have available to do the best job you can.

TIP

From Plan to Part B Essay: Looking More Closely

Let's take a detailed look at the student's critical essay. The student has written a well-organized six-paragraph essay, which closely follows the structure mapped out in the plan:

1 FIRST PARAGRAPH
    interpretation; criteria for analysis: " . . . people's personal qualities and . . . their actions"

BODY PARAGRAPHS
To Kill a Mockingbird:
2   characterization (*qualities*)
3   plot (*actions*)

Of Mice and Men:
4   characterization (*qualities*)
5   plot (*actions*)

6 LAST PARAGRAPH
      summary/conclusion

The student begins the essay by first quoting the critical lens statement and then interpreting it. Next, the student states a position and establishes criteria for analysis. Notice how the sentence in italic type expresses the controlling idea of the essay:

(1) *"Literature opens a dark window on the soul, revealing more about what is bad in human nature than what is good." This statement suggests that literature shows more about the bad aspects of people than about the good. I disagree. I think that literature shows good and bad sides of human nature about equally, both in terms of people's personal qualities and in terms of their actions. To Kill a Mockingbird, by Harper Lee, and Of Mice and Men, by John Steinbeck, are two books that illustrate this balance of good and bad.*

The boldfaced sentence is a thesis statement, which establishes the focus of the essay. The last sentence of the paragraph then serves as a transition to the body of the essay. The student also uses the final sentence to specify the titles and authors of the works to be discussed.

Paragraphs 2 and 3 discuss the first book, focusing on two literary elements: characterization and plot. Paragraphs 4 and 5 discuss the second book, similarly focusing on characterization and plot.

Notice how the student develops the body of the essay step by step, using specific ideas and information. Notice, too, how the last two sentences of paragraph 5 add an extra dimension to the student's critical analysis.

The final paragraph concludes the essay by summarizing and reinforcing the controlling idea.

Several other points are worth noting:

● The student has included in the essay all the ideas and details that appeared in the plan. However, in the process of writing and revising, the student has also added supporting information that was *not* in the plan.

277

For example, in paragraphs 2 and 3, the student refers to Maycomb, Alabama and tells how Bob Ewell cursed and spat at Atticus. In paragraph 5, the student mentions that Curley is motivated by revenge. Expanding or changing a plan in the course of writing is a normal part of the process.

● Paragraphs 2, 3, 4, and 5 all begin with topic sentences, effectively guiding the reader through the student's critical analysis. The student also used various transitional words and phrases to link ideas and guide the reader.

● The student makes effective use of language, expressing ideas clearly and precisely and varying sentence structure and length.

Activity J: Examining a Part B Essay

Answer the following questions about the student's essay.

1. Paragraph 2 begins with a topic sentence. What is the main idea that the sentence states? How does the rest of the paragraph develop that idea?

   _____

   _____

   _____

   _____

2. Has the student written a "unified" essay? Explain.

   _____

   _____

   _____

   _____

3. Do you think the student could have organized this essay into a larger or smaller number of paragraphs? Do you think this would have been a good idea? Why or why not?

   _____

   _____

   _____

   _____

4. Give at least three examples of transitional words or phrases. Explain what function each word or phrase serves. (You may include examples that do not appear in the *Transitional Words and Phrases* chart on page 150).

_____

_____

_____

_____

Neatness Counts!

TIP

Even the most brilliant writing won't receive a high score if readers have trouble reading the words. Do your best to keep your handwriting neat and legible *throughout* the Regents exam. Hard-to-read handwriting can bring down your score because readers may find it hard to follow your ideas. Illegible papers will not be scored.

Here are two additional tips for making your papers easy to read:

- Indent the first line of each paragraph.
- Leave adequate margins.

3

CHAPTER REVIEW

Look back at the various lists, boldfaced items, boxes, and charts to quickly review many of the important ideas presented. You may also find it helpful to review Chapters 1–4. Here are a few key points to get your review started:

- Session Two, Part B of the Regents exam includes a "critical lens"—a statement or quotation that you will use to analyze and evaluate two previously read works of literature. The critical lens statement gives you a specific framework for your essay.

- After reflecting on the critical lens statement, decide which literary works to use to support your interpretation. Try to base your decision on specific literary elements, because you'll have to discuss literary elements in your essay.

- Even though Part B requires you to write about only two literary works, it's wise to be well prepared to discuss at least three. The more works you can knowledgeably discuss, the more you'll have to choose from.

● Begin your essay by interpreting the critical lens statement and explaining whether you agree or disagree with it, and why. Then write at least one or two paragraphs about each of the literary works. Include specific supporting details and specific references to literary elements. Conclude your essay by summarizing or reinforcing the main points you've made.

PRACTICE FOR SESSION TWO, PART B

The test and activities that follow will give you an opportunity to practice and develop the skills you'll need to do well on Part B of the Regents English exam. But don't limit yourself to just these activities. Practice on your own, or ask your teacher for help.

PRACTICE TEST (SESSION TWO, Part B)

Your Task:

Write a critical essay in which you discuss *two* works of literature you have read from the particular perspective of the statement that is provided for you in the **Critical Lens.** In your essay, provide a valid interpretation of the statement, agree *or* disagree with the statement as you have interpreted it, and support your opinion using specific references to appropriate literary elements from the two works. You may use scrap paper to plan your response.

Critical Lens:

> "Readers can learn as much about life from the villains of literature as from the heroes."

Guidelines:

Be sure to

- Provide a valid interpretation of the critical lens that clearly establishes the criteria for analysis
- Indicate whether you agree *or* disagree with the statement as you have interpreted it
- Choose *two* works you have read that you believe best support your opinion
- Use the criteria suggested by the critical lens to analyze the works you have chosen
- Avoid plot summary. Instead, use specific references to appropriate literary elements (for example: theme, characterization, structure, language, point of view) to develop your analysis
- Organize your ideas in a logical and coherent manner
- Specify the titles and authors of the literature you choose
- Follow the conventions of standard written English

Evaluating a Part B Essay

Exchange papers with a partner. (Choose a different partner from the one you paired up with previously.) Referring to the chart on page 259, *Scoring the Part B Extended Response,* evaluate your partner's written response on the basis of the five criteria.

Be as *positive, constructive, and specific* as you can in your comments and suggestions. Your goal is to help your partner improve his or her skills.

*MEANING:*_____

_____

*DEVELOPMENT:*_____

_____

*ORGANIZATION:*_____

_____

*LANGUAGE USE:*_____

_____

*CONVENTIONS:*_____

_____

Improving and Polishing Your Part B Essay

Use your partner's comments to help you revise, edit, and polish your essay. Make whatever changes you think are necessary to improve your work.

For additional practice, two actual Regents exams appear at the end of this book.

REGENTS EXAMS
(Listening passages are in Answer Key.)

SESSION ONE

Part A

Overview: For this part of the test, you will listen to an account about yellow rice, answer some multiple-choice questions, and write a response based on the situation described below. You will hear the account twice. You may take notes on a separate piece of paper anytime you wish during the readings.

> **The Situation:** Your communications class is studying propaganda. You have been asked to write an essay on one industry's use of propaganda. You have chosen the biotechnology industry. In preparation for writing your essay, listen to an account by Michael Pollan about yellow rice. Then use relevant information from the account to write your essay.

Your Task: Write an essay for your communications class explaining the use of propaganda by the biotechnology industry.

Guidelines:

Be sure to

- Tell your audience what they need to know about the use of propaganda by the biotechnology industry as described by Pollan
- Use specific, accurate, and relevant information from Pollan's account to support your explanation
- Use a tone and level of language appropriate for an essay for a communications class
- Organize your ideas in a logical and coherent manner
- Indicate any words taken directly from the account by using quotation marks or referring to the speaker
- Follow the conventions of standard written English

Multiple-Choice Questions

Directions (1–6): Use your notes to answer the following questions about the passage read to you. Select the best suggested answer and write its number on a separate answer sheet. The questions may help you think about ideas and information you might use in your writing. You may return to these questions anytime you wish.

1 According to the speaker, blindness in Asian children is caused by a lack of vitamin

   (1) A   (3) C
   (2) B   (4) D

2 The new strain of rice gets its ability to produce beta-carotene from a gene originally found in

   (1) lilacs   (3) daffodils
   (2) dandelions   (4) roses

3 According to the speaker, Asians prefer to eat rice that is

   (1) wild   (3) brown
   (2) sweet   (4) white

4 The speaker mentions Gordon Conway, president of the Rockefeller Foundation, in order to

   (1) propose a solution
   (2) support an argument
   (3) support a change
   (4) appeal to self-interest

5 The speaker asserts that the public relations campaign attempts to persuade based on

   (1) facts   (3) morals
   (2) logic   (4) emotion

6 The speaker accuses the biotechnology industry of attempting to save itself by using

   (1) suffering children
   (2) generous foundations
   (3) well-off first worlders
   (4) poor farmers

After you have finished these questions, review **The Situation** and read **Your Task** and the **Guidelines.** Use scrap paper to plan your response. Then write your response to Part A on a separate piece of paper. After you finish your response for Part A, complete Part B.

Part B

Directions: Read the text and study the time line on the following pages, answer the multiple-choice questions, and write a response based on the situation described below. You may use the margins to take notes as you read and scrap paper to plan your response.

> **The Situation:** Your economics class is studying the effects of consumerism. For a class debate, your teacher has asked you to write a position paper discussing whether consumer culture has had a positive *or* negative impact on society.

Your Task: Using relevant information from *both* documents, write a position paper for your economics class in which you discuss whether consumer culture has had a positive *or* negative impact on society.

Guidelines:

Be sure to

- Tell your audience what they need to know about the impacts of consumer culture
- Discuss whether consumer culture has had a positive *or* negative impact on society
- Use specific, accurate, and relevant information from the text *and* the time line to support your position
- Use a tone and level of language appropriate for a position paper for an economics class
- Organize your ideas in a logical and coherent manner
- Indicate any words taken directly from the text by using quotation marks or referring to the author
- Follow the conventions of standard written English

The Consumer Culture

Steve Brigance joined the throngs of shoppers at the vast Potomac Mills mall in Woodbridge, Va., for one reason: to pick up a pair of shoes for his wife. His mission accomplished, he pushes his young son and daughter in their stroller from store window to store window, checking out the season's offerings. But he's
5   done his shopping for the day....

And Potomac Mills — with its 230 stores and 1.7 million square feet of space — is the place to go. Indeed, Brigance says, malls like the mammoth emporium literally feed our nation's obsession with acquiring things....

But while the unbridled consumerism symbolized by Potomac Mills worries
10   Brigance, other shoppers at the bustling mall are untroubled by Americans' embrace of shopping as recreation.

"I don't see anything wrong with it," says Rebecca Michalski, a sixth-grade teacher from Fairfax, Va. "I come to Potomac Mills sometimes with my family, and we find that it's a good way to spend time together." Moreover, she dismisses
15   the criticism of people like herself who enjoy shopping. "Look, people spend their time the way they want to," she says, "and that's no one else's business."

That may be true, says Michael Jacobson, executive director of the Center for Science in the Public Interest, a consumer advocacy group. But advertising and marketing have become such strong forces in our society, he says, that
20   consumption for many people has become less a question of personal choice and more a compulsion....

According to Jacobson, [author Mark] Buchanan and other critics of consumerism, the need to buy is literally programmed into us by the media, through advertising and the glorification of material wealth.
25   "The idea that you can buy fulfillment is repeated constantly in the media, like background noise," says Betsy Taylor, executive director of the Center for a New American Dream, a think tank in Takoma Park, Md., that focuses on "quality of life" issues.

In addition, critics say, consumerism has displaced other, more important
30   yearnings, such as spending time with our families and in our communities. "Even among religious people I see it," Buchanan says. "They rush out of church on Sunday so that they can go to the mall and shop."

But other observers, economists among them, see the criticism of consumerism as misdirected. They argue that consumers are not brainwashed
35   slaves to shopping but intelligent people who know what they want and usually purchase things they genuinely feel that they need....

In the final analysis, [economists Diane] Furchtgott-Roth, [Martin] Regalia and others say, consumer spending drives the economy, creating jobs and bringing material prosperity to many millions of Americans.
40   "The people who make all of these goods use the money they're paid to do things like buy a house, send their kids to school and build their churches," Regalia says.

Still, the critics contend, society needs to impose some limits on what they see as rampant and harmful consumerism, especially when it's directed at children.
45   Many critics of consumerism even say that television advertising aimed at children should be severely limited at the very least, or banned....

"Kids are very susceptible to advertising, and advertisers know it," says Kathryn C. Montgomery, president of the Center for Media Education, a children's advocacy group.
50   In addition, Montgomery and others argue, the constant barrage of advertising prods children to frequently ask for things that their parents either can't afford or don't want them to have....

But others argue that it is for parents, not government regulators, to decide what their children watch. "Parents have certain standards, and they impose those standards on their kids," says Jeff Bobeck, a spokesman for the National Association of Broadcasters (NAB).

Opponents of putting limits on advertising also argue that commercials do not send children pernicious[1] messages or turn them into bad citizens. Indeed, Bobeck and others point out, most of today's adults grew up on television and are now productive and law-abiding citizens....

Taylor and others argue that the desire to reduce or even replace important needs in our lives with consumption is prompted to a large extent by the media, with their almost relentless barrage of advertisements. Indeed, according to a recent article in *Business Week*, the average American is exposed to 3,000 commercial messages per day, from television and newspaper advertisements to billboards, signs and logos on clothing....

"The message is that you are the center of the universe, that you have needs and that you won't be fulfilled until you buy the right product to fill those needs," Taylor says....

The problem with this message, Jacobson and others say, is that it's misleading, because happiness and fulfillment are not the natural byproducts of consumption. "It's a quick fix, at best, because while you feel better for a little while, it doesn't last and then you have to go buy something else," says Taylor.

Ironically, Taylor and others say, excessive shopping is not only unsatisfying but highly impractical.

"One of the things that consumerism has done is to teach us to value things too little," Buchanan says. "We always want the newest or the best version of a computer or car or whatever even when we really have no need to replace what we have."

We need to recapture the "sacredness" of things, Buchanan continues, "to appreciate the things we already have and not constantly be lusting after something more."

But others dispute this vision of addicted, unhappy consumers who buy simply to satisfy other needs, arguing that people generally purchase goods and services because they think they need them....

For Furchtgott-Roth and others, the beauty of the American consumer economy is that it gives people an array of choices. "On balance, more and better choices make people much happier," says CATO's [Stephen] Moore. "The proof is in the pudding," he adds, referring to the simple economic reality that if Americans didn't want more choice, the market wouldn't respond by creating more. "And besides," he says, "you always have the choice not to buy."

Indeed, Furchtgott-Roth and Moore argue that, contrary to what the critics of consumerism say, people are not entirely in the thrall of advertisers and marketers. "I don't believe in the idea that the supply is creating the demand," Moore says, "because a lot of products fail even though they've been introduced with sophisticated promotional and advertising campaigns." For example, he points to failed promotional campaigns for new products, such as the infamously unsuccessful effort to introduce New Coke in the mid-1980's....

Finally, the supporters say, even habitual shoppers who spend most of their time in malls shouldn't be criticized or looked down upon. "Shopping is a leisure activity for some people," Furchtgott-Roth says. "If it's something that they want to do, something they get value from, there's nothing wrong with it."

---

[1]pernicious — highly destructive

But opponents of consumerism say that rampant buying is inherently wrong and that society has a responsibility to find ways to discourage it. One way,
105   according to Robert Frank, professor at Cornell University in Ithaca, N.Y., would be to make it more expensive for people to spend their money, especially on luxury goods. "We need to tax savings less and consumption more, to encourage people to spend less and save more," Frank says....

But CATO's Moore warns the critics to be careful about what they wish for.
110   "Our whole economy is based on consumers buying things," he says, "and if we stopped buying as much as we now do, the whole economy would naturally slow down" and the results would be devastating. "For starters, many people would lose their jobs."

A cutback on consuming would cause other, equally devastating results,
115   Moore and others say. "Consumerism tends to speed the pace of innovation," says Debbie van Opstal, senior vice president at the Council on Competitiveness, a nonprofit membership group that seeks to increase public awareness of the value of economic competition. According to van Opstal, highly selective consumers impel companies to constantly work at building better mousetraps for less.
120   "There's nothing that forces companies to do things better, cheaper and faster than demanding customers," she says....

— David Masci
excerpted from "The Consumer Culture"
CQ Researcher, November 19, 1999

TIME LINE

1900–Present

The rise of radio and TV, then the Internet, spurs consumerism.

1900
Businesses are spending $500 million annually on advertising.

1920
First radio station broadcasts in Pittsburgh.

1948
Commercial television begins broadcasts to larger audiences.

1950
Diners Club issues the first credit card.

1955
First shopping malls appear.

1960
Some 90 percent of American homes have a television.

1978
Federal Trade Commission attempts, unsuccessfully, to ban TV advertising aimed at children.

1990
Average credit card debt for U.S. household is $2,250 (adjusted for inflation).

1991
FCC [Federal Communications Commission] sets some limits on children's advertising on television.

1996
Consumer debt grows 20 percent. Average credit card debt per U.S. household reaches $4,250 (adjusted for inflation).

1998
Individual bankruptcy filings reach a record high.

1999
Average credit card debt for U.S. household is $4,500 (adjusted for inflation).
Credit card debt exceeds $500 billion. Internet sales are expected to total $20 billion.

2004
Sales of products on-line are expected to reach $185 billion.

Sources: (excerpted and adapted) "The Consumer Culture"
CQ Researcher, November 19, 1999 and
Federal Reserve Bank of Cleveland
Economic Trends, May 2000

Multiple-Choice Questions

Directions (7–16): Select the best suggested answer to each question and write its number on a separate sheet of paper. The questions may help you think about ideas and information you might want to use in your writing. You may return to these questions anytime you wish.

7 Consumer critic Michael Jacobson believes that shopping has become
(1) a primary goal
(2) a harmless pastime
(3) an extension of work
(4) an Internet activity

8 According to lines 29 and 30, our consumer culture has the effect of
(1) hampering financial planning
(2) replacing family activities
(3) inspiring worthless products
(4) causing traffic congestion

9 "Critics of consumerism" believe there should be limits placed on
(1) spending in malls
(2) prices for entertainment
(3) repackaging of products
(4) marketing to children

10 An example of the "barrage of advertisements" (line 63) includes endorsements on
(1) furniture   (3) clothing
(2) food   (4) appliances

11 According to Stephen Moore (lines 109 through 113), slowing consumerism would result in
(1) increased inflation   (3) new taxes
(2) rising unemployment   (4) more innovation

12 According to Debbie van Opstal (lines 115 through 121), as consumers become more selective, industry is pushed to
(1) generate new products
(2) promote workers faster
(3) offer fewer choices
(4) build customer loyalty

13 The time line indicates that the first attempt to respond to the harmful effects of television commercials took place in
(1) 1948   (3) 1978
(2) 1960   (4) 1991

14 According to the time line, the most recent contributor to consumerism is the
(1) credit card   (3) television
(2) Internet   (4) shopping mall

15 The time line implies that consumerism is a product of
(1) advertising use   (3) population growth
(2) government control   (4) increased wealth

16 A valid conclusion that can be drawn from the time line is that since 1950 consumers have increased their
(1) purchases of expensive goods
(2) number of credit cards
(3) money in savings
(4) buying on credit

After you have finished these questions, review **The Situation** and read **Your Task** and the **Guidelines.** Use scrap paper to plan your response. Then write your response to Part B on a separate piece of paper.

SESSION TWO

Part A

Directions: Read the passages on the following pages (a short story and a poem). Write the number of the answer to each multiple-choice question on your answer sheet. Then write the essay as described in **Your Task.** You may use the margins to take notes as you read and scrap paper to plan your response.

Your Task:

> After you have read the passages and answered the multiple-choice questions, write a unified essay about the natural world as revealed in the passages. In your essay, use ideas from **both** passages to establish a controlling idea about the natural world. Using evidence from **each** passage, develop your controlling idea and show how the author uses specific literary elements or techniques to convey that idea.

Guidelines:

Be sure to

- Use ideas from **both** passages to establish a controlling idea about the natural world
- Use specific and relevant evidence from **each** passage to develop your controlling idea
- Show how each author uses specific literary elements (for example: theme, characterization, structure, point of view) or techniques (for example: symbolism, irony, figurative language) to convey the controlling idea
- Organize your ideas in a logical and coherent manner
- Use language that communicates ideas effectively
- Follow the conventions of standard written English

Passage I

It was evening in late March. The sun was nearing its setting, its soft rays gilding[1] the western limestone headland of Rathlin Island and washing its green hills with wet gold light. A small boy walked jauntily along a hoof-printed path that wriggled between the folds of these hills and opened out into a crater-like

5 valley on the cliff-top. Presently he stopped as if remembering something, then suddenly he left the path, and began running up one of the hills. When he reached the top he was out of breath and stood watching fan-shaped streaks of light radiating from golden-edged clouds, the scene reminding him of a picture he had seen of the Transfiguration.[2] A short distance below him was the cow

10 munching at the edge of a reedy lake. Colm ran down to meet her waving his stick in the air, and the wind rumbling in his ears made him give an exultant whoop which splashed upon the hills in a shower of echoed sound. A flock of gulls lying on the short green grass near the lake rose up languidly, drifting lazily like blown snowflakes over the rim of the cliff.

15 The lake faced west and was fed by a stream, the drainings of the semicircling hills. One side was open to the winds from the sea, and in winter a little outlet trickled over the cliffs making a black vein in their grey sides. The boy lifted stones and began throwing them into the lake, weaving web after web on its calm surface. Then he skimmed the water with flat stones, some of them jumping the

20 surface and coming to rest on the other side. He was delighted with himself, and after listening to his echoing shouts of delight he ran to fetch his cow. Gently he tapped her on the side and reluctantly she went towards the brown-mudded path that led out of the valley. The boy was about to throw a final stone into the lake when a bird flew low over his head, its neck astrain, and its orange-coloured legs

25 clear in the saffron[3] light. It was a wild duck. It circled the lake twice, thrice, coming lower each time and then with a nervous flapping of wings it skidded along the surface, its legs breaking the water into a series of glittering arcs. Its wings closed, it lit silently, gave a slight shiver, and began pecking indifferently at the water. The boy with dilated eyes watched it eagerly as he turned back and

30 moved slowly along the edge of the lake. The duck was going to the farther end where bulrushes, wild irises and sedge[4] grew around sods of islands and bearded tussocks. Colm stood to watch the bird meandering between tall bulrushes, its body, black and solid as stone against the greying water. Then as if it had sunk it was gone. The boy ran stealthily along the bank looking away from the lake,

35 pretending indifference to the wild duck's movements. When he came opposite to where he had last seen the bird he stopped and peered closely through the gently-sighing reeds whose shadows streaked the water in a maze of black strokes. In front of him was a soddy islet guarded by the spears of sedge and separated from the bank by a narrow channel of water. The water wasn't too

40 deep—he could wade across with care.

Rolling up his short trousers he began to wade, his arms outstretched, and his legs brown and stunted in the mountain water. As he drew near the islet, his feet sank in the mud and bubbles winked up at him. He went more carefully and nervously, peeping through the avenues of reeds and watching each tussock

45 closely. Then one trouser fell, and dipped into the water; the boy dropped his hands to roll it up, he unbalanced, made a splashing sound, and the bird arose

---

[1]gilding — covering with gold
[2]Transfiguration — a famous religious painting
[3]saffron — yellow
[4]sedge — a marsh plant

with a squawk and whirred away over the cliffs. Colm clambered on to the wet-soaked sod of land, which was spattered with seagulls' feathers and bits of wind-blown rushes. Into each hummock[5] he looked, pulling back the long grass,
50 running hither and thither as if engaged in some queer game. At last he came on the nest facing seawards. Two flat rocks dimpled the face of the water and between them was a neck of land matted with coarse grass containing the nest. It was untidily built of dried rushes, straw and feathers, and in it lay one solitary egg. Colm was delighted. He looked around and saw no one. The nest was his. He
55 lifted the egg, smooth and green as the sky, with a faint tinge of yellow like the reflected light from a buttercup; and then he felt he had done wrong. He left it back quickly. He knew he shouldn't have touched it and he wondered would the bird forsake it. A vague sadness stole over him and he felt in his heart he had sinned. Carefully smoothing out his footprints he hurriedly left the islet and ran
60 after his cow. The sun had now set and the cold shiver of evening enveloped him, chilling his body and saddening his mind.

In the morning he was up and away to school. He took the grass rut that edged the road, for it was softer on the bare feet. His house was the last on the western headland, and after a mile or so he was joined by Peadar Ruadh; both
65 boys, dressed in similar hand-knitted blue jerseys and grey trousers, carried home-made school bags. Colm was full of the nest and as soon as he joined his companion he said eagerly: "Peadar, I've a nest—a wild duck's with one egg."

"And how do you know it's a wild duck's?" asked Peadar, slightly jealous.

"Sure I saw her with my own two eyes, her brown speckled back with a
70 crow's patch on it, and her little yellow legs and——"

"Where is it?" interrupted Peadar in a challenging tone.

"I'm not going to tell you, for you'd rob it," retorted Colm sensing unfriendliness.

"Aach! I suppose it's a tame duck's you have or maybe an old gull's," replied
75 Peadar with sarcasm.

Colm made a puss at his companion. "A lot you know!" he said, "for a gull's egg has spots and this one is greenish-white, for I had it in my hand."

And then the words he didn't want to hear rushed from Peadar in a mocking chant: "You had it in your hand! She'll forsake it! She'll forsake! She'll forsake!"
80 Colm felt as if he would choke or cry with vexation.[6] His mind told him that Peadar was right, but somehow he couldn't give into it and he replied: "She'll not forsake! She'll not! I know she'll not!"

But in school his faith wavered. Through the windows he could see moving sheets of rain—rain that dribbled down the panes filling his mind with thoughts
85 of the lake creased and chilled by the wind; the nest sodden and black with wetness; and the egg cold as a cave stone. He shivered from the thoughts and fidgeted with the ink-well cover, sliding it backwards and forwards mechanically. The mischievous look had gone from his eyes and the school-day dragged on interminably.[7] But at last they were out in the rain, Colm rushing home as fast as
90 he could.

He spent little time at his dinner of potatoes and salted fish and played none with his baby brothers and sisters, but hurried out to the valley, now smoky with drifts of slanting rain, its soaked grass yielding to the bare feet. Before long he was at the lake-side where the rain lisped ceaselessly in the water and wavelets
95 licked the seeping sides leaving an irregular line of froth like frost on a grey slate.

[5]hummock — small hill
[6]vexation — annoyance
[7]interminably — endlessly

Opposite the islet the boy entered the water. The wind was blowing into his face rustling noisily the rushes, heavy with the dust of rain. A moss-cheeper, swaying on a reed like a mouse, filled the air with light cries of loneliness. The boy reached the islet, his heart thumping with excitement, wondering did the bird forsake. He
100 went slowly, quietly, on to the strip of land that led to the nest. He rose on his toes, looking over the sedge to see if he could see her. And then every muscle tautened. She was on, her shoulders hunched up, and her bill lying on her breast as if she were asleep. Colm's heart thumped wildly in his ears. She hadn't forsaken. He was about to turn stealthily away. Something happened. The bird moved, her neck
105 straightened, twitching nervously from side to side. The boy's head swam with lightness. He stood transfixed. The wild duck, with a panicky flapping, rose heavily, squawking as she did so, a piece of straw and a white object momentarily entwined in her legs. The egg fell on the flat wet rock beside the nest, besmearing it with yellow slime. A sense of tremendous guilt seized Colm, a throbbing silence
110 enveloped him as if everything had gone from the earth leaving him alone. Stupefied, numbed to every physical sense, he floundered across the black water, running wildly from the scene of the disaster.

—Michael McLaverty
"The Wild Duck's Nest"
from *The Irish Monthly*, April 1934

Passage II

In Time of Silver Rain

In time of silver rain
The earth
Puts forth new life again,
Green grasses grow
5 And flowers lift their heads,
And over all the plain
The wonder spreads
    Of life,
    Of life,
10   Of life!

In time of silver rain
The butterflies
Lift silken wings
To catch a rainbow cry,
15 And trees put forth
New leaves to sing
In joy beneath the sky
As down the roadway
Passing boys and girls
20 Go singing, too,
In time of silver rain
    When spring
    And life
    Are new.

—Langston Hughes
from *Selected Poems of Langston Hughes*, 1959
Alfred A. Knopf

Multiple-Choice Questions

Directions (1–10): Select the best suggested answer to each question and write its number on a separate sheet of paper. The questions may help you think about the ideas and information you might want to use in your essay. You may return to these questions anytime you wish.

Passage I (the short story) — Questions 1–5 refer to Passage I.

1 The development of the opening paragraph relies on the use of

   (1) cause and effect
   (2) comparison and contrast
   (3) appeal to the senses
   (4) accumulation of generalizations

2 The boy's mood as he walks to get his cow can best be described as

   (1) carefree   (3) unhappy
   (2) confused   (4) cautious

3 In line 32, the word "meandering" most nearly means

   (1) pausing   (3) falling
   (2) wandering   (4) dancing

4 Colm's initial delight at finding the wild duck's egg is followed quickly by

   (1) amusement   (3) anger
   (2) relief   (4) guilt

5 The author uses the dialogue between the two boys to

   (1) intensify Colm's feeling
   (2) provide essential information
   (3) lessen Peadar's hostility
   (4) inject comic relief

Passage II (the poem) — Questions 6–10 refer to Passage II.

6 The narrator's use of the word "silver" (line 1) suggests that the rain is

   (1) warm   (3) valuable
   (2) hard   (4) safe

7 According to the poem, "wonder" (line 7) is inspired by the

   (1) discovery of truth
   (2) renewal of nature
   (3) flight from reality
   (4) freedom from stress

8 The narrator describes the actions of both the flowers (line 5) and the leaves (lines 16 and 17) by using

   (1) alliteration   (3) metaphor
   (2) hyperbole   (4) personification

9 The actions of the "Passing boys and girls" (line 19) suggest

   (1) celebration   (3) escape
   (2) discovery   (4) denial

10 The overall attitude of the narrator toward nature is one of

   (1) disappointment (3) uncertainty
   (2) appreciation   (4) curiosity

After you have finished these questions, review **Your Task** and the **Guidelines**. Use scrap paper to plan your response. Then write your response to Part A on a separate piece of paper. After you finish your response for Part A, complete Part B.

Part B

Your Task:

Write a critical essay in which you discuss *two* works of literature you have read from the particular perspective of the statement that is provided for you in the **Critical Lens.** In your essay, provide a valid interpretation of the statement, agree *or* disagree with the statement as you have interpreted it, and support your opinion using specific references to appropriate literary elements from the two works. You may use scrap paper to plan your response. Write your essay for Part B on a separate sheet of paper.

Critical Lens:

> "To gain that which is worth having, it may be necessary to lose everything else."
>
> —Bernadette Devlin
> *The Price of My Soul,* 1969

Guidelines:

Be sure to

- Provide a valid interpretation of the critical lens that clearly establishes the criteria for analysis
- Indicate whether you agree *or* disagree with the statement as you have interpreted it
- Choose *two* works you have read that you believe best support your opinion
- Use the criteria suggested by the critical lens to analyze the works you have chosen
- Avoid plot summary. Instead, use specific references to appropriate literary elements (for example: theme, characterization, setting, point of view) to develop your analysis
- Organize your ideas in a unified and coherent manner
- Specify the titles and authors of the literature you choose
- Follow the conventions of standard written English

SESSION ONE

Part A

Overview: For this part of the test, you will listen to an account about saving the ocean environment, answer some multiple-choice questions, and write a response based on the situation described below. You will hear the account twice. You may take notes on a separate piece of paper anytime you wish during the readings.

> **The Situation:** In order to increase membership in the environmental club at your school, you have decided to give a presentation to students in your school on saving the ocean environment. In preparation for writing your presentation, listen to an account about the ocean environment by Peter Benchley, author of the novel *Jaws*. Then use relevant information from the account to write your presentation.

Your Task: Write a presentation for students in your school on saving the ocean environment as a way of persuading students to join the environmental club.

Guidelines:

Be sure to

- Tell your audience what they need to know about saving the ocean environment
- Use specific, accurate, and relevant information from the account to support your discussion
- Use a tone and level of language appropriate for a presentation to students in your school
- Organize your ideas in a logical and coherent manner
- Indicate any words taken directly from the account by using quotation marks or referring to the speaker
- Follow the conventions of standard written English

Multiple-Choice Questions

Directions (1–6): Use your notes to answer the following questions about the passage read to you. Select the best suggested answer and write its number on a separate answer sheet. The questions may help you think about ideas and information you might use in your writing. You may return to these questions anytime you wish.

1 The bodies of sharks whose fins were used for soup were found near

    (1) Newfoundland   (3) Long Island
    (2) Costa Rica   (4) Cape Cod

2 The harvesting of shrimp is used as an example of

    (1) wasteful practices
    (2) growing conservation
    (3) useful technology
    (4) increasing harvests

3 In addition to the shark, sea life noted in the account as being seriously harmed includes

    (1) lobster   (3) scallops
    (2) whales   (4) salmon

4 The greatest source of oil pollution in oceans comes from

    (1) fishing vessels
    (2) oil tankers
    (3) passenger cars
    (4) underwater pipelines

5 As used in the text, the phrase "fouling the breeding grounds" means

    (1) draining them   (3) flooding them
    (2) cultivating them   (4) dirtying them

6 The speaker labels mankind's pollution of the sea as "suicidal folly" because the pollution

    (1) destroys beaches
    (2) endangers humankind
    (3) fosters environmental legislation
    (4) scatters in ocean water

After you have finished these questions, review **The Situation** and read **Your Task** and the **Guidelines.** Use scrap paper to plan your response. Then write your response to Part A on a separate piece of paper. After you finish your response for Part A, complete Part B.

Part B

Directions: Read the text and study the chart on the following pages, answer the multiple-choice questions, and write a response based on the situation described below. You may use the margins to take notes as you read and scrap paper to plan your response.

> **The Situation:** Your state senator is preparing to vote on a bill that would ban the use of vending machines in all New York State schools. Write a letter to your state senator recommending whether he/she should vote for *or* against the bill and explaining the reasons for your position.

Your Task: Using relevant information from *both* documents, write a letter to your state senator in which you recommend whether he/she should vote for *or* against the bill banning the use of vending machines in New York State schools and explain the reasons for your position. *Write only the body of the letter.*

Guidelines:

Be sure to

- Tell your audience what they need to know about the use of vending machines in schools
- Recommend whether your state senator should vote for *or* against the bill banning the use of vending machines in New York State schools
- Explain the reasons for your position
- Use specific, accurate, and relevant information from the text *and* the chart to support your position
- Use a tone and level of language appropriate for a letter to a state senator
- Organize your ideas in a logical and coherent manner
- Indicate any words taken directly from the text by using quotation marks or referring to the author
- Follow the conventions of standard written English

Text

For countless American children, breakfast or lunch drops out of a vending machine at school: a can of soda, perhaps, washing down a chocolate bar or a bag of potato chips.

5   Now, a growing number of states are striking back, trying to curb the rise in childhood obesity by placing strict limits on the sale of candy, soft drinks and fatty snacks in schools. Nearly a dozen states are considering legislation to turn off school vending machines during class time, strip them of sweets or impose new taxes on soft drinks to pay for teacher salaries and breakfast programs.

In California, legislators appear close to passing a law that would prohibit any
10   drinks but milk, water or juice from being sold in elementary schools, and curtail the hours older students can fuel up at vending machines. In Hawaii, legislators are pushing to oust sodas from school machines altogether.

The wave of legislation, unusual both for its breadth and its assertiveness, grew out of the newest statistics on child obesity from the Centers for Disease
15   Control and Prevention. Teenagers today are almost three times as likely to be overweight as they were 20 years ago, the agency announced this year, prompting many lawmakers to take aim at the junk food they believe is to blame.

"It can't help when a child is eating chips and soda at 8 in the morning," said Martha Escutia, a state senator who backed California's bill.

20   The food industry says children need more exercise, not fewer choices. The bills have also angered school administrators nationwide, intensifying an already heated debate over the prevalence of commercialism in the education system.

Once little more than a novelty in schools, vending machines have become a principal source of extra money for districts across the nation, bringing in
25   hundreds of millions of dollars for extracurricular activities each year. With dozens of machines lining their hallways, some schools annually earn $50,000 or more in commissions, then use the money for marching bands, computer centers and field trips that might otherwise fall by the wayside.

To keep such programs going, schools are emerging as the staunchest
30   opponents of the proposed restrictions, invoking the same principles of local control that the states themselves use to fight federal standards for academic testing. In many cases, the resistance from schools has been vociferous[1] enough to water down or defeat measures, or at least stall them until the next legislative session rolls around.

35   "Let the parents, the students and the school community sit down and decide how to handle this," said Robert E. Meeks, legislative director for the Minnesota School Boards Association, which has organized against legislation to curtail soda sales. Mr. Meeks added that Minnesota schools earn roughly $40 million a year from vending machines. "The states only seem to be interested in local control
40   when it suits them," he said.

Many lawmakers say they find it odd that educators are their biggest foes, considering that the schools are supposed to look after the welfare of their students.

Half the students in some Texas and California districts are overweight,
45   officials say.

"I can understand why school districts go in search of extra resources," said Jaime L. Capelo Jr., a state representative in Texas who introduced a measure to pare down the amount of junk food in schools. "But it's shameful when they obtain additional resources through contracts with soda companies with little or
50   no regard to the health of their students."

----

[1]vociferous — characterized by an insistent outcry

Even some students express concern over the abundance of snack foods in their schools. Nell S. Geiser, a 17-year-old senior at New Vista High School in Boulder, Colo., says the vending machines in the building never shut down. At 7:30 a.m., outside classrooms with corporate symbols like I.B.M. painted on the

55 walls, she says her fellow students gather in front of the humming machines, comparing schedules on daily planners with logos of the WB network, courtesy of a local television station.

"Plenty of kids make their breakfast from a Mountain Dew and a bag of Doritos," said Nell, who organizes fellow students to oppose soda contracts in

60 schools. "You're brought up thinking it's all right to be constantly bombarded with ads and junk food because they're in your school."

Educators, in turn, say that it is the lawmakers who are hypocritical, because as tax revenues sag in tandem with the economy, state legislatures are cutting school budgets, leaving districts with few choices but to search for substitute

65 funds.

"Maybe it's not the best way of making money," said Paul D. Houston, executive director of the American Association of School Administrators. "But who is responsible for providing funding for schools? The very people who are now saying that we can't engage in creative ways of raising money."

70 Though they are often sympathetic to the economic woes of school districts, many lawmakers argue that encouraging children to indulge at an early age is ultimately fiscally irresponsible. As students become heavier and their health deteriorates, more serious ailments like diabetes can arise, leading to higher health care costs over time....

75 The Department of Agriculture tried to ban soda and candy sales in schools more than two decades ago, but was thwarted by a federal appeals court in 1983. Now, federal regulations simply require schools to turn off soda and candy machines in the cafeteria during meal times. Those that sit outside in the hallways can stay on all day.

80 Several states go further. New York, which, like a handful of other states, is considering ways to increase exercise in schools, already prohibits food of "minimal nutritional value" from being sold until after lunch. New Jersey and Maryland have similar policies. But lawmakers say that such rules often make little difference.

85 "They're totally ignored," said Paul G. Pinsky, a state senator in Maryland and former high school teacher who introduced a bill this year to switch off vending machines during the school day. "After the sugar high wore off and they were finished bouncing off the walls, my students' heads would fall on the desk," he said. "It made it really difficult to teach."

90 Part of the problem, legislators say, is that the agreements between schools and soda companies sometimes deter principals from following state policy, especially since how much schools make is often tied to how much they sell.

One contract between the Pepsi-Cola Company and the Montgomery Blair High School in Silver Spring, Md., stated that "if the Board of Education actively

95 enforces the policy in which vending machines are turned off during the school day," the school will not get its guaranteed commission. But the company is now taking a more conciliatory stand. Officials of Pepsi, a unit of PepsiCo, say they have redrawn the contract and others like it over the last year, so that they reflect what the company calls the "spirit and the letter" of state policies.

100 In other states, legislators question whether schools have disregarded state guidelines simply by allowing soda machines on campus. In recent years, North

Carolina schools have signed vending contracts with soft drink companies, even though the state's official policy allows only sales that "contribute to the nutritional well-being of the child and aid in establishing good food habits."

105   "It's a bit of a conflict, isn't it?" said Ellie G. Kinnaird, a state senator in North Carolina who is seeking a moratorium on soft drink contracts in schools.

    Six months ago, the Coca-Cola Company said that it would scale back on binding contracts with schools. But the new guidelines do not pertain to existing contracts, and may not affect future ones either.

110   On average, Americans drink nearly 60 gallons of soda each year, almost 8 gallons more than they did just 10 years ago. For many lawmakers, it is a given that the increase has worsened childhood obesity. To the food industry, assigning the blame to any one type of food is simplistic.

    "There are no such things as good foods and bad foods," said Chip Kunde, a

115 legislative director for the Grocery Manufacturers of America, a food industry trade group. "There are just good diets and bad diets."

    Researchers vacillate[2], pointing out that children are eating more of almost everything, not just sweets, while exercising less. In fact, only 29 percent of students attended daily physical education classes in 1999, compared with 42

120 percent in 1991, according to the Centers for Disease Control and Prevention, making it harder for them to burn off the extra calories they have put on.

---

[2]vacillate — change point of view

— Greg Winter
excerpted from "States Try to Limit
Sales of Junk Food in School Buildings"
The New York Times, September 9, 2001

Chart

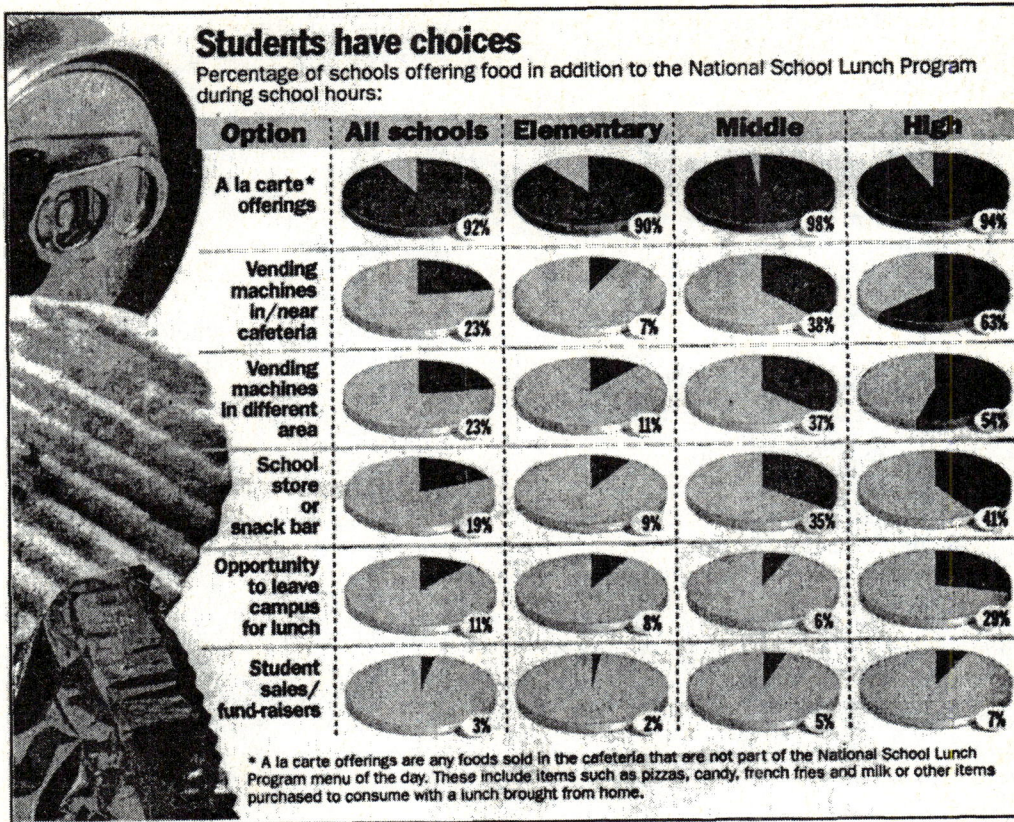

Students have choices

Percentage of schools offering food in addition to the National School Lunch Program during school hours:

Option	All schools	Elementary	Middle	High
A la carte* offerings	92%	90%	98%	94%
Vending machines in/near cafeteria	23%	7%	38%	63%
Vending machines in different area	23%	11%	37%	54%
School store or snack bar	19%	9%	35%	41%
Opportunity to leave campus for lunch	11%	8%	6%	29%
Student sales/ fund-raisers	3%	2%	5%	7%

* A la carte offerings are any foods sold in the cafeteria that are not part of the National School Lunch Program menu of the day. These include items such as pizzas, candy, french fries and milk or other items purchased to consume with a lunch brought from home.

Source: USDA Food and Nutrition Service, "School Nutrition Dietary Assessment Study II", April 2001 and Jeff Boyer/*Times Union*

Multiple-Choice Questions

Directions (7–16): Select the best suggested answer to each question and write its number on your answer sheet. The questions may help you think about ideas and information you might want to use in your writing. You may return to these questions anytime you wish.

7 The text indicates that the move to ban vending machines in schools came about as a reaction to

(1) parental pressure
(2) health concerns
(3) legal opinions
(4) funding uncertainty

8 According to the text, the proposed California law (lines 9 through 11) would prohibit the sale of

(1) junk food in elementary schools
(2) milk or juice in elementary schools
(3) soft drinks in high schools
(4) soft drinks in elementary schools

9 According to the text, food industry representatives argue that schools are failing to provide students with adequate

(1) counseling sessions
(2) economic awareness
(3) physical education
(4) legislative protection

10 According to lines 29 through 40, schools often view "junk food" legislation as conflicting with their right to

(1) make decisions
(2) teach nutrition
(3) enforce standards
(4) monitor student health

11 According to the text, vending machines in schools send students a conflicting message about

(1) educational opportunity
(2) user convenience
(3) physical activity
(4) good nutrition

12 The text implies that lawmakers feel the availability of "junk foods" in schools is

(1) shortsighted
(2) essential
(3) acceptable
(4) declining

13 Paul G. Pinsky's opinion (lines 85 through 89) is most probably cited because of his experience as a

(1) food distributor
(2) high school teacher
(3) cafeteria worker
(4) school board member

14 According to the text, contracts between schools and soda companies may pressure schools to

(1) ignore existing legislation
(2) become creative fund-raisers
(3) reduce variety in cafeterias
(4) raise beverage prices

15 The chart indicates that the availability of food choices in addition to foods which are part of the National School Lunch Program generally increases with the

(1) number of lunches sold
(2) location of vending machines
(3) age of students
(4) length of school day

16 According to the chart, more elementary schools than middle schools allow their students to

(1) hold fund-raisers
(2) use vending machines
(3) visit snack bars
(4) leave for lunch

After you have finished these questions, review **The Situation** and read **Your Task** and the **Guidelines.** Use scrap paper to plan your response. Then write your response to Part B on a separate piece of paper.

SESSION TWO

Part A

Directions: Read the passages on the following pages (a poem and an excerpt from a memoir). Write the number of the answer to each multiple-choice question on your answer sheet. Then write the essay as described in **Your Task.** You may use the margins to take notes as you read and scrap paper to plan your response.

Your Task:

> After you have read the passages and answered the multiple-choice questions, write a unified essay about the influence of grandmothers as revealed in the passages. In your essay, use ideas from **both** passages to establish a controlling idea about the influence of grandmothers. Using evidence from **each** passage, develop your controlling idea and show how the author uses specific literary elements or techniques to convey that idea.

Guidelines:

Be sure to

- Use ideas from **both** passages to establish a controlling idea about the influence of grandmothers
- Use specific and relevant evidence from **each** passage to develop your controlling idea
- Show how each author uses specific literary elements (for example: theme, characterization, structure, point of view) or techniques (for example: symbolism, irony, figurative language) to convey the controlling idea
- Organize your ideas in a logical and coherent manner
- Use language that communicates ideas effectively
- Follow the conventions of standard written English

Passage I

Lineage

My grandmothers were strong.
They followed plows and bent to toil.
They moved through fields sowing seed.
They touched earth and grain grew.
5 They were full of sturdiness and singing.
My grandmothers were strong.

My grandmothers are full of memories
Smelling of soap and onions and wet clay
With veins rolling roughly over quick hands
10 They have many clean words to say.
My grandmothers were strong.
Why am I not as they?

—Margaret Walker
from *For My People*, 1942
Yale University Press

Passage II

...With my grandmother there was a brief ritual phrase in her dialect mouthed by us children when we went to the old Queen Anne style house in Utica where my mother and all her brothers and sisters grew up. My grandmother was always in the kitchen, dressed in black, standing at a large black coal range stirring soup or something. My brothers and I, awkward in the presence of her foreignness, would be pushed in her direction by our mother during those holiday visits, and told "Go say hello to Gramma."

We'd go to the strange old woman who didn't look like any of the grandmothers of our friends or like any of those on the covers of the *Saturday Evening Post* around Thanksgiving time. Gramma didn't stuff a turkey or make candied sweet potatoes and pumpkin pies. She made chicken soup filled with tiny pale meatballs and a bitter green she grew in her backyard along with broad beans and basil, things that were definitely un-American in those days. Her smell was like that of the cedar closet in our attic. She spoke strange words with a raspy sound.

When we stepped into her kitchen to greet her she smiled broadly and tweaked our cheeks. We said in a rush the phrase our mother taught us. We didn't know what it meant. I think we never asked. And if we were to know it meant "how are you?" what difference would it have made? What further knowledge would we have had of the old woman in the shapeless black garment, with her wisps of gray hair falling out of the thick knob crammed with large old-fashioned tortoise-shell hairpins? None. We were strangers.

When on a visit upstate I had occasion to drive through Cazenovia, a village on the shores of Lake Cazenovia, it appeared to me as if in a dream. I saw again the lakeshore meadow that has always remained indelibly imprinted on my mind from childhood, but that I had thought must, by now, have vanished from the real world. That meadow, now called Gypsy Bay Park, was the site of family picnics to which we and Aunt Mary's family proceeded from Syracuse, while the other contingent (which was by far the greater number—my mother's three brothers, two other sisters and all their families plus our grandmother) came from Utica. Cazenovia was the approximate half-way point, and there in the meadow on the lake the cars would all pull up and baskets of food would be unloaded for the great summer reunion....

It was Gramma who had decreed this annual outing. When two of her daughters married and moved from Utica, she had made known her wish: that the family should meet each summer when travel was easier and eat together *al fresco.*[1] It was her pleasure to have all her children, and their children, convene in the meadow, and spend the day eating, singing, playing cards, gossiping, throwing ball, making jokes and toasts. It was a celebration of her progeny[2] of which she, long widowed, was the visible head, the venerable ancestor, the symbol of the strong-willed adventurer who had come from the old world to make a new life and to prosper.

She was monumental. I can see her still, an imposing figure, still dressed in black although it was summer, seated on a folding camp chair (just for her) under the shade of a large, leafy elm tree. She sat there as silently as a Sioux chief and was served food, given babies to kiss, and paid homage to all day. The others

[1]al fresco — in the open air

[2]progeny — offspring

spread around her, sitting on blankets on the grass, or on the running boards of their Oldsmobiles and Buicks. What made my grandmother so intriguing was the mystery of her. For, despite its gaiety, the family picnic was also a time of
50 puzzlement for me. Who was this stranger in black with whom I could not speak? What was her story? What did she know?

What I knew of my grandmother, I heard from my mother: she believed in good food on the table and good linen on the bed. Everything else was fripperies³ and she had the greatest scorn for those who dieted or got their nourishment
55 through pills and potions. She knew you are what you eat and she loved America for the great range of foods that it provided to people like her, used to so little, used to making do. She could not tolerate stinginess; she lived with her eldest son and his family of eleven and did all the gardening and cooking, providing a generous table....

60 We were about fifty kin gathered in that meadow, living proof of the family progress. Gramma's sons and daughters vied to offer her their services, goods, and offspring—all that food, those cars, the well-dressed young men who would go to college. And Butch, an older cousin, would take me by the hand to the water's edge and I'd be allowed to wade in Cazenovia's waters, which were always
65 tingling cold and made me squeal with delicious shock.

And yet with all that, for all the good times and good food and the happy chattering people who fussed over me and my brothers, I still felt a sense of strangeness, a sense of my parents' tolerating with an edge of disdain this old world *festa* only for the sake of the old lady. When I asked my mother why
70 Gramma looked so strange and never spoke to us, I was told, she came from the old country ... she doesn't speak our language. She might as well have been from Mars.

I never remember hearing our own mother speak to her mother, although she must have, however briefly. I only recall my astonishment at mother's grief when
75 Gramma died and we went to Utica for the funeral. How could mother really feel so bad about someone she had never really talked to? Was it just because she was expected to cry? Or was she crying for the silence that had lain like a chasm between them?...

---

³fripperies — nonessentials

—Helen Barolini
excerpted from "How I Learned to Speak Italian"
Southwest Review, Winter 1997

Multiple-Choice Questions

Directions (1–10): Select the best suggested answer to each question and write its number on your answer sheet. The questions may help you think about the ideas and information you might want to use in your essay. You may return to these questions anytime you wish.

Passage I (the poem) — Questions 1–5 refer to Passage I.

1 The narrator implies that the strength of grandmothers results from their
  (1) cheery songs   (3) large bodies
  (2) long lives   (4) hard work

2 "They touched earth and grain grew" (line 4) suggests the grandmothers' role of
  (1) protector   (3) teacher
  (2) provider   (4) entertainer

3 In order to emphasize her feelings about her grandmothers, the narrator uses
  (1) repetition   (3) simile
  (2) onomatopoeia   (4) symbolism

4 The narrator's feeling toward her grandmothers is best described as
  (1) resentment   (3) admiration
  (2) embarrassment   (4) concern

5 In comparison to the grandmothers, the narrator is seen as
  (1) more nurturing   (3) less intelligent
  (2) more religious   (4) less capable

Passage II (the excerpt from a memoir) — Questions 6–8 refer to Passage II.

6 According to the narrator, the "annual outing" celebrated the importance of
  (1) solitude   (3) family
  (2) responsibility   (4) travel

7 The comparison between the Native American chief and the grandmother (line 45) characterizes her as
  (1) courageous   (3) intelligent
  (2) respected   (4) kind

8 The narrator's description of her mother's reaction to the death of "Gramma" is an example of
  (1) irony   (3) alliteration
  (2) personification   (4) humor

Questions 9 and 10 refer to both passages.

9 Both passages reveal the theme of
  (1) grandparents' trust
  (2) generational difference
  (3) social conflict
  (4) family rivalry

10 The grandmothers of Passage I differ from the grandmother in Passage II in the ability to
  (1) discipline   (3) survive
  (2) heal   (4) communicate

After you have finished these questions, review **Your Task** and the **Guidelines.** Use scrap paper to plan your response. Then write your response to Part A on a separate piece of paper. After you finish your response for Part A, complete Part B.

Part B

Your Task:

Write a critical essay in which you discuss *two* works of literature you have read from the particular perspective of the statement that is provided for you in the **Critical Lens.** In your essay, provide a valid interpretation of the statement, agree *or* disagree with the statement as you have interpreted it, and support your opinion using specific references to appropriate literary elements from the two works. You may use scrap paper to plan your response. Write your essay for Part B on a separate sheet of paper.

Critical Lens:

> "The human heart has ever dreamed of a fairer world than the one it knows."
>
> —Carleton Noyes
> "Poetry: General Introduction"
> from *Lectures on the Harvard Classics*, 1914

Guidelines:

Be sure to

- Provide a valid interpretation of the critical lens that clearly establishes the criteria for analysis
- Indicate whether you agree *or* disagree with the statement as you have interpreted it
- Choose *two* works you have read that you believe best support your opinion
- Use the criteria suggested by the critical lens to analyze the works you have chosen
- Avoid plot summary. Instead, use specific references to appropriate literary elements (for example: theme, characterization, setting, point of view) to develop your analysis
- Organize your ideas in a unified and coherent manner
- Specify the titles and authors of the literature you choose
- Follow the conventions of standard written English